HE SHALL GO OUT FREE

AMERICAN PROFILES

Norman K. Risjord
SERIES EDITOR

Thomas Jefferson
Norman K. Risjord

Mary Boykin Chesnut
Mary A. DeCredico

John Quincy Adams
Lynn Hudson Parson

ALSO BY DOUGLAS R. EGERTON

*Charles Fenton Mercer and the
Trial of National Conservatism*

*Gabriel's Rebellion: The Virginia Slave
Conspiracies of 1800 and 1802*

American Profiles

HE SHALL GO OUT FREE

The Lives of Denmark Vesey

Douglas R. Egerton

MADISON HOUSE

Madison 1999

Egerton, Douglas R.
He Shall Go Out Free: The Lives of Denmark Vesey

LIBRARY OF CONGRESS CATALOGING-IN-PUBLICATION DATA

Egerton, Douglas R.
   He shall go out free : the lives of Denmark Vesey / Douglas R. Egerton.
— 1st ed.
      p. cm. — (American profiles)
   Includes bibliographical references (p.) and index.
   ISBN 0-945612-67-2 (cloth : alk. paper)
   ISBN 0-945612-68-0 (pbk. : alk. paper)
      1. Vesey, Denmark, ca. 1767–1822.   2. Charleston (S.C.)—History—
Slave Insurrection, 1822.   3. Slave insurrections—South Carolina—
Charleston.   4. Afro-Americans—South Carolina—Charleston—
Biography.   5. Slaves—South Carolina—Charleston—History.   I. Title.
F279.C49 N423 1999
975.7′91503′092—dc21
[B]
                                                                99-043648

Typeset in Fairfield, Berthold Walbaum, and ITC Fenice
Designed by William Kasdorf

Printed in the United States of America
on acid-free paper

Published by Madison House Publishers, Inc.
P.O. Box 3100, Madison, Wisconsin 53704
www.madisonhousebooks.com

FIRST EDITION

For Kearney and Hannah

Contents

Illustrations

Editor's Foreword

THE COMPLAINT OF MANY PEOPLE who dislike history is that it is full of obscure names, arcane dates, and big words that always seem to end in "ism." The problem is that history, in some ways, is like a foreign language. The grammar has to be mastered before thought, discussion, and interpretation is possible. The task confronting the teacher of history is how to sugarcoat the pill.

For some years I have given a talk to educators at meetings and seminars around the country entitled "Making History Human." It is essentially a pitch for a biographical approach as a pedagogical device. I am not advocating the reduction of history to a series of human-interest stories. My thesis, instead, is that complex and often dry subjects (when presented in general terms) can be enlivened and given meaning through a focus on one of the individual stories. For example, P. T. Barnum's impact on popular amusements can add a new dimension to the concept of democracy in nineteenth-century America. The story of Jackie Robinson can add poignancy to the often legalistic (because of its emphasis on statutes and court decisions) story of civil rights in the middle decades of the twentieth century.

That is the basic purpose of Madison House's *American Profiles* series—to add a human dimension to the study of history. *American Profiles* offers relatively concise and swiftly-paced sketches that contribute significantly to the discourse on the American past. Each narrative takes advantage of the explosion of recent historiography while the author's interpretive insights serve as a basis for organizing that mass of complex and often disparate information.

What we hope to do with the books in the *American Profiles* series is to tell the American story—to tell the multitude of our national stories. Our goal is to arouse interest and provoke thought. Once that is accomplished, we can truly begin to teach our history.

NORMAN K. RISJORD
Series Editor

Acknowledgments

THE MOST ENJOYABLE PART of writing a book is thanking those friends and colleagues who helped make the long, solitary journey a pleasure. Kimberly Hanger, Peter P. Hinks, Norrece T. Jones, Mitchell Snay, Margaret Washington, and Donald R. Wright all read parts of the manuscript and made invaluable suggestions— which is not to say I always had the wit to follow their sage advice. Edward Pearson graciously allowed me an advance look at the lengthy introduction to his forthcoming collection of Vesey trial documents, and I have enjoyed our ongoing conversations about which actor should best play the role of Vesey in the big-budget film we both fantasize about.

At the South Carolina Department of Archives and History, Columbia, Charles Lesser kindly pointed me in the direction of several important collections I would otherwise have missed, and Wylma Wates shared with me her research on what is generally, but evidently wrongly, believed to be Vesey's Bull Street house. Stephen C. Crane corrected some of my errors regarding Vesey family genealogy. Robert Paquette shared the fruits of his Cuban research with me, and Svend Holsoe provided me with several Haitian newspapers pertinent to Vesey's youth. Daniel L. Schafer furnished me with dates critical in piecing together Jack Pritchard's arrival in Charleston. Special thanks also to Connie and Carl Schultz, whose kind hospitality made my time spent in Columbia a pleasure.

Most of this project was funded by a generous grant from Le Moyne College's Committee on Research and Development, for which I am extremely grateful. Chapter 5, in a somewhat different form, appeared in the *South Carolina Historical Magazine,* and is republished here with the permission of editor W. Eric Emerson. At Madison House, series editor Norman K. Risjord did a superb job editing the manuscript, and Gregory M. Britton proved unusually patient with my many whims and chronic lateness. John P. Kaminski and Kevin Morrissey also deserve thanks for their support and kind attention to detail. As always, John Langdon cheerfully read the galleys with unusual speed and skill.

I am especially grateful to Alan Gallay and Graham Russell Hodges, who read and reread every page; their advice, support, and friendship is worth more than I can say. Marcus Rediker weighed in at a critical moment with good words of advice and encouragement. My best and toughest critic, Linda Egerton, read the entire manuscript and bluntly told me what chapters worked and what chapters needed to be tossed out and redone. Her love and patience, however, far more than her editorial ability, made this study possible.

This book is dedicated to my daughters Kearney and Hannah, who slowed its completion down by a good year, at the very least, and in the process made every moment of my life an absolute joy.

D. R. E.
Fayetteville, New York
October, 1998

Introduction

THE ART OF BIOGRAPHY is deceptively simple. Even when the subject proves a willing participant by leaving behind diaries and letters and autobiographies, there is little guarantee that the biographer can accurately recover the past. (Some people deceive themselves and their diaries as easily as they deceive others.) The biographer has to explain not just the what and the when of history, but also the why; the practitioner of this art must spend years of reading and research learning not just to walk in the subject's shoes, but to creep into the subject's consciousness as well.

The long, obscure life of Denmark Vesey has intimidated more than one biographer into giving up the task. Although a resident of Charleston for nearly four decades, the proud freedman made it his life's work to avoid tax collectors, census takers, and city directories. He left behind no letters or diaries. Although literate in several languages, his teachings come to us second-hand, repeated by his disciples before a vengeful tribunal and hastily scribbled onto a page by a harried court clerk. Restoring to life any distant figure is difficult enough, but the prospect of completing a biography of an anti-slavery activist who dwelled in the hidden alleys of Charleston's slave community should dissuade any rational scholar. That this book exists at all is perhaps more of a testimony to the author's foolishness than to his determination.

Certainly Vesey is as well-known today as he was in his own century, thanks in large part to popular culture. The drama of his

xiii

story has proven especially attractive to artists. Numerous plays and musicals depict his struggle. George Gershwin and Charleston native DuBose Heyward, following their critical (if not financial) success in transforming Heyward's novella *Porgy* into the operatic *Porgy and Bess,* considered Vesey's saga as a "more explicitly political" sequel. Gershwin's death two years later stalled the project, but Heyward searched for a new musical collaborator until his own death in 1940. (In 1948 DuBose's wife, playwright Dorothy Heyward, finally completed the project as a nonmusical play entitled *Set My People Free.*) Walter Robinson of Harvard's W. E. B. DuBois Institute for Afro-American Research returned Vesey to the stage in his 1988 "folk opera," *Look What Jesus Has Done,* and Vincent Plush scored a beautiful, searing oratorio, *Denmark Vesey Takes the Stand.* John O. Killens' 1972 novella, *Great Gittin' Up Morning,* echoes Robinson's opera in depicting Vesey as an inspirational Christian leader. In 1982, PBS produced a moving television docudrama, *Denmark Vesey's Rebellion,* featuring the charismatic—if then too youthful—Caribbean-born actor Yaphet Kotto as the aged revolutionary. A painting of Vesey preaching in the African Church today graces Charleston's Gaillard Auditorium. (The painting, stolen by critics of the tribute, is now firmly bolted to the wall.)

Vesey's life may be easier for artists to fictionalize than it is for historians to faithfully recover. Despite numerous cameo appearances in studies on nullification, black resistance, slave culture, and African American religion, Denmark Vesey has long defied both historians and biographers. The only modern account of Vesey's plot is the late journalist John Lofton's pioneering 1964 narrative, *Insurrection in South Carolina,* in which the focus understandably remains on Vesey's conspiracy rather than on his extraordinary life. Edward Pearson's forthcoming collection of trial documents, *Designs Against Charleston,* however, contains a lengthy and insightful introduction.

The Denmark Vesey who stalks these pages only occasionally resembles the abolitionist of film and stage. I make no claims of producing the definitive life, of course. Each generation writes, or perhaps rewrites, its own history, and a personality as elusive as Vesey's will always be subject to numerous interpretations. But data enough exists to correct or at least qualify much that has been written about Vesey. Far from being a wealthy, tyrannical mulatto who practiced polygamy and ruled his seven wives and numerous children with an iron hand, the public record reveals only a domineering but devoted father who labored long hours, six or seven days a week in hopes of avoiding an impoverished dotage. Although deeply religious and, for a time at least, a practicing Presbyterian, Vesey turned his back on the Christian passivity commonly taught by white ministers and free black preachers in favor of an Old Testament activism forged of wrath and justice.

Playwrights and novelists were right in believing this story to be an important one. But Thomas Carlyle was wrong: The history of the world is *not* but the biography of great men. Vesey did not make history, at least not the history that he hoped to make. The old carpenter was as much shaped by events as he shaped them. Yet it is certainly true that his failed exodus altered the course of Southern history, and although biographies traditionally end with the death of one's subject, the concluding chapter of this work instead examines Vesey's influence on white Carolinians and shows how black Americans and Northern abolitionists employed his name as a battle cry through the end of the Civil War.

That battle cry, of course, was the outgrowth of Vesey's extraordinary life. One man, however determined and charismatic, cannot create a revolution, yet every popular revolt requires a leader, a Georges Danton or Boukman Dutty or Sam Adams to give shape and form to widespread anger and discontent. Vesey's plot was unique in the annals of slave rebellions in North America because he was unique; his goals, as well as the methods he chose to achieve them, were the product of a long, hard life's experience. His greatest act may have been his dream of a black exodus to liberty in Haiti, but perhaps the best way to understand that dream is through biography.

Textbook writers, who admittedly lack the space for detailed biographical digressions, tend to construct generic slave rebels, who usually grace a single paragraph in a chapter on the cotton kingdom. (Imagine drafting a single paragraph that could say anything intelligible about George Washington, Andrew Jackson, and Abraham Lincoln!) Vesey's plan to lead his disciples out of the United States set him apart from earlier black insurgents. Whereas most of those who rose for their freedom during the 1790s, such as Toussaint Louverture in Haiti or Gabriel in Virginia, fought to join political society on equal terms, Vesey simply sought to escape it. Unlike Nat Turner's chaotic revolt, Vesey's plan was hardly doomed to failure; his precise design, months if not years in conception, struck his contemporaries as eminently feasible. Far from quixotically expecting to bring slavery crashing down in South Carolina, the old carpenter simply intended to liberate as many of his followers as possible before sailing to freedom in Haiti. Vesey's exceptional fifty-five year journey to his 1822 conspiracy is the subject of this book.

Chronology

1740   South Carolina Assembly passes the comprehensive slave code, commonly known an the Negro Act.

1747   Joseph Vesey born in Warwick, Bermuda.

1767?   Birth of Telemaque (Denmark Vesey), most likely on the Danish sugar island of St. Thomas.

1781   *Fall:* Captain Joseph Vesey purchases 390 slaves, including Telemaque, at the port city of Charlotte Amalie for resale in the French colony of Saint Domingue.

1782   *April 23:* Captain Vesey returns to Cap François and is forced to repurchase Telemaque, who becomes his cabin boy.
December 14: British evacuate Charles Town; Joseph Vesey and his family arrive shortly thereafter.

1783   *July 16:* Joseph Vesey rents house at 281 King Street and opens business as ship chandler on East Bay Street.

1790   *November 1:* Charleston mulattoes organize exclusive Brown Fellowship Society.

1791   *August 22:* Slaves led by Boukman Dutty set fire to cane fields in northern Saint Domingue.
November: Boukman killed in skirmish near Cap François. Toussaint Breda (later Louverture) joins the rebels at Grande Riviere.

1793   *May:* Cotton gin invented.

1793   *August:* Secret Keeper slave plot uncovered in Williamsburg, Virginia; slave patrols are enlarged around Charleston.

1794   *February 4:* French National Convention abolishes slavery in its Caribbean empire.

1797   *May:* Toussaint Louverture is officially named Commander in Chief of all French forces in Saint Domingue.

1799   *November 9:* Denmark wins East-Bay Lottery.
         December 31: Denmark purchases his freedom.

1800   *January 1:* Denmark's first day as a free man. He subsequently adopts surname of Vesey.

1803   *April 7:* Toussaint Louverture dies of starvation in Bonaparte's prison at Fort Joux near the Swiss border.
         November: South Carolina legislature reopens Atlantic slave trade effective January 1, 1804.
         December 31: Jean-Jacques Desselines declares Haitian Independence.

1806   *April:* Gullah Jack Pritchard purchased in Charleston by ship carpenter Paul Pritchard.

1807   *March 2:* Congress passes law prohibiting importation of slaves from Africa, effective January 1, 1808.

1816   *April 9:* Representatives of five mid-Atlantic black churches meet in Philadelphia to form confederated African Methodist Episcopal Church under the leadership of the Reverend Richard Allen.

1817   *April:* Vesey "admitted to communion" at Second Presbyterian Church. During same month, 4,376 blacks quit Bethel Methodist Church in protest over destruction of black cemetery.
         April: David Walker moves to Charleston from his native North Carolina.

1818   *March:* Jean-Pierre Boyer elected president of Haiti. Two years later, Boyer places advertisements in American newspapers inviting free African Americans to relocate to the black republic.

1818   *Spring:* Charleston's African Methodist Episcopal Church erected in predominantly black Hampstead neighborhood. *June 7:* City guard arrests 140 "free Negroes and Slaves" for worshipping in violation of city ordinances of 1800 and 1803; Vesey is perhaps among them.

1820   Several black congregants arrested for holding late night service at the African Church. *December 20:* State Assembly forbids private manumissions by deed or self-purchase.

1821   *January 15:* Charleston City Council warns the Reverend Moses Brown not to allow African Church classes to become "schools for slaves." *December:* Vesey begins to plan mass exodus out of Charleston.

1822   *May 22:* William Paul reveals plot to Peter Prioleau. *May 30:* Peter Prioleau betrays plot to master John Prioleau, who rushes news to Intendant James Hamilton. *May 31:* Intendant Hamilton orders the arrest of Peter Poyas and Mingo Harth; both men are released after questioning. *June 14:* George Wilson warns Major John Wilson of conspiracy. *June 15:* Governor Bennett orders the arrest of Peter Poyas, Mingo Harth, and his own domestic household, including Rolla Bennett. *June 16:* Vesey's second date for the proposed slave uprising. *June 22:* Vesey arrested. *June 26:* Vesey's two-day trial begins. *June 27:* Monday Gell arrested. *July 2:* Vesey, Peter Poyas, Rolla Bennett, Ned Bennett, Batteau Bennett, and Jesse Blackwood are hanged. *July 5:* Gullah Jack Pritchard arrested. *July 12:* John Horry and Gullah Jack Pritchard are executed. *July 14:* Original date set for Vesey's revolt; Celebrated in French-speaking world as Bastille Day, and by Massachusetts blacks as day of liberation.

1822   *July* 26: Twenty-two slaves, including Bacchus Hammet and Polydore Faber, are hanged.

1825   Conspiracy of slaves in Spanish Cuba involves bond rebels sold away from Charleston; Sandy Vesey may have been involved.

1829   David Walker, a former member of Charleston's African Church, publishes his incendiary *Appeal to the Coloured Citizens of the World.*

1835   *May* 20: Joseph Vesey dies of natural causes at the age of eighty-eight.

List of Abbreviations

CLS	Charleston Library Society
DUL	Duke University Library
GM	Governor's Messages
JSH	*Journal of Southern History*
RGA	Records of the General Assembly
SCDAH	South Carolina Department of Archives and History
SCHM	*South Carolina Historical Magazine*
SCHS	South Carolina Historical Society
SCL	South Caroliniana Library, Columbia
SHC, UNC	Southern Historical Collection, University of North Carolina
UNC	University of North Carolina
USC	University of South Carolina

Prologue: 1865

HISTORY DOES NOT FOLLOW a simple path. It is rarely clear when one chapter is finished and another begins; sometimes forty-three years may pass before the narrative is concluded. Stepping ashore onto the smoking heap of rubble that was once Fort Sumter, Robert Vesey, an aged black carpenter and builder, may well have savored that bittersweet irony. The date was April 14, 1865, four years to the day after the federal surrender in Charleston harbor, and Union soldiers under the command of Major General Robert Anderson prepared to raise the very flag they had withdrawn from the beleaguered fort. Several thousand Union officers, antislavery politicians, and Northern abolitionists gathered at the fort to celebrate the end of the war and the death of slavery. Henry Ward Beecher, the fiery abolitionist minister and the brother of novelist Harriet Beecher Stowe, delivered the keynote address. Gesturing toward Charleston, Beecher thundered at the "unprincipled ruling aristocracy" who had started the conflict. Vesey sat in a place of honor, next to war hero Robert Smalls, Major Martin Delany, and William Lloyd Garrison, who would soon print the last issue of the *Liberator*.[1]

But for Charleston's black community, the real celebration came the following fall, when 3,000 freedmen and women cheered

---

1. Bernard E. Powers, *Black Charlestonians: A Social History, 1822–1885* (Fayetteville, 1994), 70; Walter J. Fraser, Jr., *Charleston! Charleston! The History of a Southern City* (Columbia, 1989), 273.

as the cornerstone was laid for the new African Methodist Episcopal Church. The Reverend Randolph, a Union chaplain, read the opening prayer, while the African "choir rendered an appropriate chant." The church's new minister, the Reverend E. J. Adams, "looking truly like an African Prince," promised his brethren that the promise of the Old Testament had at long last been fulfilled: "If thou wilt walk in my statutes and execute my judgements, then I will perform my word with thee." The modest structure of yellow pine stood on Calhoun Street between Meeting and Elizabeth Streets, not far from the location of the earlier African Methodist Episcopal Church, which had been razed by city authorities in late 1822. Every man "who is working on it is a colored man," bragged a black Carolinian. "Robert Vesey, son of Denmark Vesey, is the architect."[2]

2. Philadelphia *Christian Recorder,* October 14, 1865.

HE SHALL GO OUT FREE

═══════════════○═══════════════

Chapter One

The Book of Telemaque
1767–1782

AT LENGTH, he would be known as Denmark Vesey; but that was far into the future. In 1822, Captain Joseph Vesey, who was the boy's second and fourth owner, recalled that when he first purchased the child in 1781 he appeared to be "about 14 years" old. But the boy, evidently of Ashanti descent, grew into a giant of a man, and so he may simply have been unusually large for his age. If so, he could have been born one or two years after the old captain's rough guess of 1767. And if Joseph Vesey ever bothered to inquire by what name the boy's parents called him, he neglected to pass that information on to the magistrates who proved so incurious about the grown man's past. They failed even to inquire where he was born. Perhaps nothing speaks more eloquently about the dehumanizing nature of Atlantic slavery than the fact that one of the most influential abolitionists in antebellum America lacks a known birthplace and birthdate and, for approximately the first fourteen years of his life, even a name.[1]

1. Archibald H. Grimké, *Right on the Scaffold, or, The Martyrs of 1822* (Washington, D.C., 1901), 3; James Hamilton, *An Account of the Late Intended Insurrec-*

Most likely, the boy was born on the Caribbean sugar island of St. Thomas, one of three islands claimed by the kingdom of Denmark. Several scholars, however, have theorized that he was born in Africa, and certainly that is possible. Danish slave ships based at the Gold Coast (present-day Ghana) fort at Christiansborg routinely shipped Africans to their colony for resale to other Caribbean islands. With its deep and magnificent harbor, the port city of Charlotte Amalie functioned more as a transit slave station than an entrepôt to the island's sugar plantations. On at least two occasions Joseph Vesey purchased recently imported Africans in St. Thomas for shipment to Saint Domingue. But during the eighteenth century, no more than ten percent of all Africans carried to the Americas were children. Although mortality rates on the middle passage were no higher for children than for adults, they took up almost as much room on the slave ships but brought a far smaller price in Caribbean markets. Moreover, later in life the boy told acquaintances that as a young seaman he "had travelled through almost every part of the world," including Africa; had he been born there as well he would surely have said so. Perhaps it is simply that the boy reached an age and height that would fetch a goodly sum and so was placed in the coastal baracoons—seaboard fortresses where captives were held while awaiting shipment—with newly arrived Africans, where he was purchased by Joseph Vesey.[2]

---

tion Among a Portion of the Blacks of the City (Charleston, 1822), 17. Both Grimké and Hamilton based their discussions of Vesey's youth on oral sources. Grimké, born a slave in Charleston in 1849 to slaveholder Henry Grimké and Nancy Weston, a mulatto nurse, received some of his information from black Carolinians and from his white aunt, abolitionist Angelina Grimké, who was seventeen at the time of the conspiracy. See Dickson D. Bruce, Jr., *Archibald H. Grimké: Portrait of a Black Independent* (Baton Rouge, 1993), 89. Intendant Hamilton, writing in the year of the conspiracy, obviously interviewed Captain Joseph Vesey, who lived in Charleston until his death in 1835. Neither, however, noted where Denmark was born. Herbert Aptheker, *American Negro Slave Revolts* (New York, 1943), 268, flatly states that Vesey was born in Africa, although the source he cites, Lionel Kennedy and Thomas Parker, eds., *An Official Report of the Trials of Sundry Negroes* (Charleston, 1822), makes no mention of Vesey's birth.

2. Herbert S. Klein, *African Slavery in Latin America and the Caribbean* (New

Founded a century before in 1671, well after English cannon and French buccaneers had broken Spain's monopoly on the Caribbean, the tiny colony of St. Thomas, like its Danish neighbors St. John and St. Croix, never achieved the spectacular profits for European investors derived from Spanish Cuba or French Saint Domingue. Floating in the shadow of the lucrative Spanish colony of Puerto Rico, St. Thomas' small population and even smaller revenue betrayed Denmark's belated entrance into the great game of empire; by the time Danish warships arrived in the Caribbean, little was left to seize. When the boy entered the world in the late 1760s, St. Thomas was well past whatever golden age it once enjoyed. Anxious absentee planters, most of them bourgeois residents of Copenhagen, bought out neighboring plantations and relied ever more heavily on white managers and *bombas*—black drivers—in hopes of realizing a return on their considerable investment.[3]

According to colonial records dated 1770, when the boy was roughly three years of age, St. Thomas was home to only 4,833 souls. Nestled atop the Lesser Antilles, St. Thomas, like the other islands of the eastern Caribbean, was of volcanic origin. Rugged peaks towered 1,600 feet above sea level, giving the island a deceptively large appearance that belied its size of only thirty-two square miles. Just more than 4,000 African slaves worked on eighty plantations, under the watchful eye of 428 white overseers and colonial administrators. Sixty-seven free people of color—most of them of mixed ancestry—completed the population.[4]

York, 1986), 148; Hugh Thomas, *The Slave Trade: The Story of the Atlantic Slave Trade, 1440–1870* (New York, 1997), 256; Second confession of Monday Gell, July 23, 1822, Records of the General Assembly, Governor's Messages, South Carolina Department of Archives and History (hereafter RGA, GM, SCDAH).

3. Neville A. T. Hall, *Slave Society in the Danish West Indies: St. Thomas, St. John, and St. Croix*, ed. B. W. Higman (Baltimore, 1992), 1–2; Eugene D. Genovese, *The World the Slaveholders Made: Two Essays in Interpretation* (New York, 1969), 38. In 1917 Denmark sold the three islands to the United States; they are today collectively known as the Virgin Islands of the United States.

4. Gudrun Meier, "Preliminary Remarks on the Oldendorp Manuscripts," in Stephanie Palmie, ed., *Slave Cultures and the Cultures of Slavery* (Knoxville, 1995), 69; Hall, *Slave Society*, 3–5.

Despite its Danish ownership, St. Thomas boasted a population that reflected its geographic location in the commercial heart of the Atlantic basin. The colonial officials who governed the island —civil servants, clerks, soldiers, and clergymen—were overwhelmingly Danish. But Jewish tradesmen and French shopkeepers peddled their wares to Spanish adventurers and Dutch sailors. Scots-Irish overseers marketed their services to German landowners, who were in fact the majority of resident planters. According to Christian G. A. Oldendorp, a German missionary in the Moravian Church who arrived on St. Thomas in 1767, the island was Babel reborn. Residents both white and black spoke a creole idiom called Cariolisch or Negerhollands—black Dutch—a rough mixture of African, Dutch, English, and German. Despite his keen interest in the African labor force, Oldendorp thought the language sounded more European than African. "Since the number of masters who speak Low German was greatest," he observed, "the majority of their words were adopted into the Creole with some modification." But the modification, that is, the grammar and syntax, was African. The African majority in St. Thomas did not simply assimilate into European culture; rather through the process of transculturation both cultures fused to produce a hybrid that was as much African as it was European. Despite later claims to the contrary, black Dutch, and not pure Danish, was the boy's first language.[5]

Somewhat harder for the missionaries to grasp was the nature of marriage on the island. In theory, Danish slave marriage was a solemn affair protected by law. The slave code of 1733, drafted by Governor Philip Gardelin, explicitly protected husband and wife from separation by sale or auction, even in the common event of debt. Children could not be sold away from their parents. But laws were crafted by men to serve their needs, and need on St. Thomas was defined as the right of Europeans to steal the bodies of African men and women and appropriate their labor. To this end, Gardelin

---

5. Meier, "Oldendorp Manuscripts," 69; Hall, *Slave Society,* 6–7, 110–11; C. G. A. Oldendorp, *History of the Mission of the Evangelical Brethren on the Caribbean Islands of St. Thomas, St. Croix, and St. John,* ed. Johann Bossard (Ann Arbor, 1987), 156.

and the flower of the Danish bar provided the Copenhagen investors with a legal loophole: before slaves could marry they first had to obtain their master's permission. Not willing to be constrained by the rule of law, few landlords gave it. In the eyes of the pious Oldendorp, the slaves' informal living arrangement constituted a "moral wreckage."[6]

For the slaves on St. Thomas, however, their extra-legal families were hardly superficial marriages of convenience. Although slaves undoubtedly preferred the legal protection that state-approved marriage allowed them, Africans on the island recreated kinship groups in the name of human survival. In the absence of true kin, who might have been left behind in Africa or sold to a distant plantation upon arrival, blacks in the Caribbean forged fictive families. Older slaves, who had lost their children to death or sale, adopted young Africans in need of a parent in highly ritualized ceremonies. Newly arrived adolescents attached themselves to these recently-constructed clans and called those who took them in their tribesmen and their godparents. Despite the cultural dislocation produced by the endless cycle of importation and resale, newcomers were quickly integrated into the St. Thomas slave community. Because of their cultural biases and their lack of familiarity with West African traditions, missionaries like Oldendorp failed to understand the nature of these substitute families or appreciate how they resembled the extended kinship networks the slaves had left behind on the African coast.[7]

Just as the boy's name is lost to history, so too is the identity of his parents. By the 1760s, the slave population on St. Thomas was divided into two interrelated groups. Danish settlers called those slaves born in Africa the *bussalen,* while blacks and mixed-race mulattoes born on the island were dubbed Creoles. The boy who would come to be known as Denmark Vesey was almost certainly a Creole, but there is no evidence to suggest that his father was also his master. Despite persistent attempts on the part of modern historians to portray him as a mulatto, no contemporaneous document does so.

6. Meier, "Oldendorp Manuscripts," 69; Hall, *Slave Society,* 61.

7. Barbara Bush, *Slave Women in Caribbean Society, 1650–1838* (Bloomington, Ind., 1990), 105; Oldendorp, *History of the Mission,* 214; Hall, *Slave Society,* 83–85.

The Charleston authorities who would much later charge him with a capital crime failed to do so, although they felt confident in describing some of the men who associated with him as mixed-race. South Carolina's planter elite, and not without good reason, typically exhibited an unusually sophisticated knowledge of African ethnicity and routinely characterized blacks by their country of origin. Had the boy been light-skinned, Charleston jurists would have said so.[8]

The boy lived with either his parents or his fictive kinsmen in a "village" of fifty to sixty huts. Just as the slave families on St. Thomas reflected an African heritage, the living arrangements were a rough recreation of a West African compound. But here too old world patterns changed to suit new world labor requirements. Overseers demanded that the huts be grouped not in a circle or semi-circle, but in long, regular rows, an arrangement, Oldendorp noted, designed to "facilitate order and supervision." Slaves sunk four long stakes into the ground. Carved into a fork at the top, each stake supported a series of horizontal limbs. Atop these rested the rafters of the roof, which came together in a crest. Craftsmen placed several more vertical stakes between the four corner posts and then wove pliable branches into the lattice. A plaster of quick lime and cow dung covered the branches and also served to construct a single interior wall, so that each hut was divided into two rooms. In most cases, a family of four slaves lived in each hut. Much to their dismay, however, missionaries observed that some men practiced polygamy and kept several wives, one to each hut, just as they had before being sold into a foreign land.[9]

---

8. Meier, "Oldendorp Manuscripts," 69. Robert V. Remini, *The Jacksonian Era,* 2nd ed. (Wheeling, 1997), 59, William W. Freehling, *The Road to Disunion: Secessionists at Bay, 1776–1854* (New York, 1990), and *The Reintegration of American History: Slavery and the Civil War* (New York, 1994), 40, and Charles Johnson, *Africans in America* (New York, 1998), 286, are only the most recent scholars to identify Vesey as a mulatto. Although no reliable description of Vesey's color exists, Charleston authorities never characterized him as a mulatto, as they were careful to do with several of his soldiers. As Sylvia R. Frey has observed, white South Carolinians "demonstrated an acute awareness of [African] ethnicity." See *Water From the Rock: Black Resistance in a Revolutionary Age* (Princeton, 1991), 27–28.

9. Hall, *Slave Society,* 76–77; Oldendorp, *History of the Mission,* 221.

Except during the rainy season, slave families prepared and ate their meals outside their huts. By tradition more than law, overseers parcelled out a weekly allowance of salted herring, flour, and corn meal. Little of this fare was fresh. Much of the herring came from the British New England colonies, and the wheat and corn arrived from the Southern mainland. Creative cooks relied on African recipes and local vegetables—typically red and green peppers—to produce a spicy pottage. Slaves also prepared mainland yams, cassavas, and potatoes to their own tastes. Like most slave diets elsewhere in the Americas, bondpeople on St. Thomas generally consumed a diet high in starch and deficient in meat and other sources of protein.[10]

At four in the morning the blowing of a conch shell, or *tuttue,* summoned the slaves to work. The *bomba,* or black driver, ushered what Oldendorp understood to be the "lowest but most numerous and necessary class of slaves," the *kamina,* or "field Negroes," toward nearby cane fields. A handful of older slaves stopped on the way to feed the livestock. After laboring for five hours, slaves paused for a half-hour breakfast. Women handed out what food they had brought, while newly-imported slaves who had not yet been adopted into a family, breakfasted on a few sugar canes. The *bomba* again cracked his whip and the slaves returned to work. At midday work stopped. Slaves returned to their huts to prepare the day's chief meal and escape the sun for a short time. Returning to the field after ninety minutes, slaves continued to plant and harvest cane until sundown. As an infant, the boy either rode on his mother's back while she labored in the tropical sun or lay close by on a sheep or calf-skin.[11]

For the slaves who planted the cane, the ultimate authority was not the *bomba*'s whip, but the law that allowed him to wield it. Governor Gardelin's comprehensive slave code of 1733 represented the fears and concerns of both Danish investors and provincial planters. Composed of nineteen clauses, Gardelin's code offered bondpeople little in the way of protection beyond a few nods at the basic essentials of food, clothing, and, if they were wed in the eyes of their

10. *Ibid.,* 79.
11. *Ibid.,* 73; Oldendorp, *History of the Mission,* 226.

master, freedom from separation. Black chattel were, after all, human property who could expect little beyond a few basic rights. Yet most of the code revealed that the slaves on St. Thomas behaved not as passive property but as assertive individuals. Running away, that is, the stealing of one's self, carried the penalty of losing a leg, unless the master chose to "pardon" the runaway. Pardons were typically granted, as masters had little use for crippled, one-legged workers. Instead, civil authorities ordinarily invoked the lighter penalty of 150 strokes of the whip and the removal of an ear. Collective action invited quick and savage retribution. Slaves convicted of trying to escape to maroon settlements in isolated villages high in the rugged hills around Crown Mount, lost their lives, but only after enduring torture with red-hot pincers. Oldendorp noted that the number of Danish soldiers on the island "was not great." But the small free population was "equipped with guns and committed to militia duty in an emergency." Even the handful of free blacks were allowed to carry arms. In times of danger, internal or external, "a company of Free Negroes" served as "town soldiers, and they are very useful during Slave disturbances." The boy, as he approached puberty, noticed these weekly "patrol[s] by men of this company." It taught him a hard lesson. Too many freedmen, hoping to better their precarious position, were willing to side with the master class against their own people.[12]

The child learned other lessons as well. If few bondmen were willing to risk life or limb in hopes of achieving limited freedom in marronage, there were safer methods of resisting the social death their owners planned for them. The island's population included African priests, "holy persons," as Oldendorp understood it, who "are the intimates of the gods who make their will known" to the black community. Even as the German missionary frowned on what he characterized as superstition, he was impressed by the practical application of African faith. The *bussalen* drew "no distinction between the effects of poison and those of black magic." Should a priest wish to kill an enemy, Oldendorp noted, "they would mix something into that person's food, which would cause him to die." In hopes of

12. Hall, *Slave Society,* 56–58; Oldendorp, *History of the Mission,* 156.

turning their labor force away from a religion of resistance to one of Christian docility, a few innovative planters ordered their *bombas* to herd the workers into Danish religious services. Moravians especially relied on black converts to spread the good word among the *kamina*. But if the whip could bring the slaves to Christ, it could not compel them to adopt a religion that would have them love their tormentors. Christianity "may be good for the Whites," one African retorted, but "it is not appropriate for the Negroes."[13]

Even the strongest magic—or the greatest Christian faith— could not subdue the worst tendencies of Atlantic slavery. In the fall of 1781, shortly after a series of rituals marked his passage into early manhood, the boy was roughly pulled aside by the *bomba*. With its golden age long behind it, St. Thomas had workers to spare. He was to be sold to another island. Soldiers and white overseers, all of them bristling with musket and sabre, marched 390 men and women down to the docks near the fort at Charlotte Amalie. As this number constituted approximately one out of every fifteen slaves on the island, most of them had to be recently imported Africans intended for reshipment. There they were loaded aboard the *Prospect,* a Massachusetts-based brigantine. The terrified child may not have noticed that some of the twelve cannon pointed inward toward the deck. But he noticed the tall, slender captain who watched as the slaves were chained below decks. And Captain Joseph Vesey noticed the handsome youth.[14]

13. Karen Fog Olwig, "African Cultural Principles in Caribbean Slave Societies: A View From the Danish West Indies," in Palmie, ed., *Slave Cultures,* 29; John F. Sensback, "'A Genuine Black Offering to Jesus': Black Moravians and the Genesis of a Transatlantic Afro-Protestant Movement," Paper delivered to the Institute of Early American History and Culture, June 1997; Oldendorp, *History of the Mission,* 176, 191.

14. Brig *Prospect,* [no editor], *Naval Records of the American Revolution, 1775–1788* (Washington, 1906), 421; Hamilton, *An Account,* 17. The date of purchase was obviously provided to Intendant Hamilton by Joseph Vesey long after the fact, although the time corresponds with what can be recovered regarding the captain's movements. Unfortunately, customs books for both Copenhagen and St. Thomas were destroyed in the 1920s by a clerk who regarded them as worthless. It is, therefore, impossible to discover on exactly what date Joseph Vesey bought Denmark. (Svend E. Holsoe to author, February 15, 1997, in author's possession.)

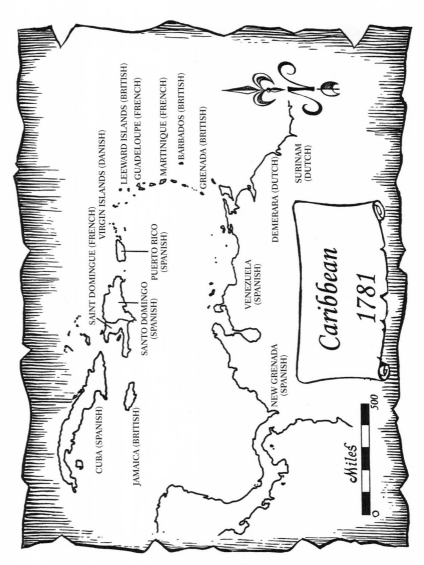

The Caribbean, 1781. *Map by the author.*

Born in the old port town of Warwick in the English colony of Bermuda, Joseph Vesey was thirty-four years of age when he first purchased the boy. Perhaps he saw something of himself in the child. Before his fourteenth year, both his father and mother had died; now, ironically, he was playing the role of death for a boy he guessed to be of the same age. Although Vesey still enjoyed the company of a large family in Bermuda—three older sisters, as well as an older brother named John—at the age of twenty he took to the sea. In 1767 he signed on with the *Rebecca,* a "prime Bermuda Vessel" involved in the Caribbean trade. Owned by Joseph Darrell, a wealthy South Carolina merchant, the small schooner supplied rice, wine, and Africans for the port of Charles Town. Vesey visited the city in July 1770, if not before, and in 1774 he invested his earnings in a lot of land that ran from Canal Street to Round O Road. By then he had advanced to the title of Master; he named his property "Capt. Vesey's Avenue."[15]

Despite his Bermudian birth, by the coming of the Revolution Vesey thought himself enough a Carolinian to side with the emerging patriot movement. Following the September 1774 meeting of the First Continental Congress in Philadelphia, the South Carolina General Committee—an ad hoc cadre of planters and merchants in the colonial assembly—called for the election of representatives to form a new government for the colony. Just as South Carolina delegates again readied to sail for Philadelphia for the Second Continental Congress the following May, word reached the city that fighting had already broken out between British regulars and Massachusetts militiamen at Lexington. Parliament retaliated with a naval blockade of the seaboard's leading ports, which served both to shut down Joseph Darrell's trading company and to draw Captain Vesey and the *Rebecca* into the conflict. In the fall of 1775, William Drayton,

15. Stephen C. Crane to John Lofton, January 27, 1983, Denmark Vesey File, South Carolina Historical Society (hereafter SCHS); Levinus Clarkson to David Van Horne, March 1, 1775, in William J. Morgan, ed., *Naval Documents of the American Revolution,* 8 vols. (Washington, 1964–1980), 1:118–19; R. Nicholas Obberg, ed., "Ship Registers in South Carolina Archives, 1734–1780," *South Carolina Historical Magazine* (hereafter *SCHM*) 74 (October 1973): 259–60; Land Deed, February 1774, JM Plats, #6346, SCDAH.

the leading member of the Secret Committee of Five (an executive created to protect the colony), ordered Vesey to take a detachment of troops and cruise the coast "to the northward of Charles-Town bar, in order to speak with and warn all vessels" that British warships guarded the harbor's entrance. Because Vesey had nearly a decade's experience running rum and slaves up Carolina rivers, the young captain was especially suited to guide patriot shipping "to some other port or inlet in this colony."[16]

The Revolution proved to be a lucrative venture for Captain Vesey. As a privateer and master of the "armed pilot boat" *Hawke,* Vesey was entitled to the lion's share of what he could drag into Southern ports. In early 1776, even before the congressional Declaration of Independence was adopted, Vesey's crew bested a British brigantine in the Mediterranean and dragged the captured prize up Stono River. But the war brought dangers as well. Upon his arrival in Charles Town, Vesey received orders to sail north to Philadelphia to pick up Christopher Gadsden and the other Carolina delegates in Congress. On the return voyage, the British man-o-war *Syren* suddenly appeared out of the icy rain and bore down upon the smaller pilot boat. Vesey sailed hard for the shore and beached his ship on the sandy coast of North Carolina. Before the British could land, Vesey, Gadsden and the crew fled into a nearby swamp and then journeyed overland to Charleston. But the *Hawke* now became an English prize.[17]

With his vessel lost but his reputation for courage intact, Vesey signed on as master of the *Providence.* With the help of a young midshipman named John Paul Jones, Vesey's crew captured the brig *Favourite* in September 1776.[18] But the *Providence* may have been

16. Fraser, *Charleston,* 139–41; William Henry Drayton to Joseph Vesey, November 4, 1775, in Morgan, ed., *Naval Documents,* 2:889.

17. Henry Laurens to Joseph Vesey, January 5, 1776, in Morgan, ed., *Naval Documents,* 3:647–48; Council of Safety, Minutes, January 3, 1776, in *ibid.,* 3:595–96; Edward Thornbrough, Journal, February 19, 1776, in *ibid.,* 4:16; E. Stanley Godbold, Jr. and Robert H. Woody, *Christopher Gadsden and the American Revolution* (Knoxville, 1982), 147–49.

18. John Paul Jones to Robert Morris, January 21, 1777, in Anna DeKoven, ed., *The Life and Letters of John Paul Jones* (New York, 1913), 131–32; "List of Officers

lost as well. In the fall of 1778, Vesey received a new letter of Marque and Bond in Annapolis, Maryland, authorizing the crew of his newest ship, the sloop *Adriana*, to plunder British shipping in the name of the republic. Evidently, Vesey's earlier prizes had paid handsomely. He was listed not merely as master of the *Adriana*, but he posted the $5,000 bond as well. Together with the Charles Town firm of North and Trescott, he claimed part ownership of the fifteen gun sloop.[19]

But as the war dragged on into the early 1780s, Vesey began to contemplate a return to his former profession. Marriage in 1779 to Fanny Dameron brought new responsibilities. (The death of his wife shortly thereafter only sent him in search of another, and on May 8, 1781, the captain wed Kezia Jones.) His latest and largest vessel, the *Prospect*, was fitted out in Boston with twelve cannon and a crew of sixty men. Massachusetts records indicate yet another letter of Marque was issued, but when his home port of Charles Town was occupied by the British in May 1780, Vesey decided that supplying the Caribbean with Africans would turn as handy a profit as plundering English shipping, and at far less risk to his ship and crew. The French entrance into the Revolutionary conflict meant that continental slavers-turned-warships were incapable of meeting the insatiable demand for laborers in the French sugar colony of Saint Domingue. It was this decision that carried Captain Vesey and the *Prospect* onto the shores of St. Thomas in September or October of 1781, and into the life of the boy.[20]

Seamen & Marines," in Morgan, ed., *Naval Documents,* 8:46; Bernard Gallagher to John Paul Jones, January 18, 1777, in *ibid.,* 7:993 note.

19. Stephen Crane to John Lofton, January 27, 1983, Denmark Vesey File, SCHS; Sloop *Adriana,* [no editor], *Naval Records,* 220.

20. Stephen Crane to John Lofton, January 27, 1983, Denmark Vesey File, SCHS; Carolyn E. Fick, *The Making of Haiti: The Saint Domingue Revolution From Below* (Knoxville, 1990), 26–27; David Eltis, *Economic Growth and the Ending of the Transatlantic Slave Trade* (New York, 1987), 49; Frey, *Water From the Rock,* 110–11; Hamilton, *An Account,* 17; Brig *Prospect,* [no editor], *Naval Records,* 421. (Because Kezia Jones Vesey gave birth to John Vesey in June 1782, Joseph Vesey was with her nine months before, perhaps in Norfolk, in September 1781. He therefore purchased Denmark in late September or early October 1871.)

Long accustomed to buying and selling African men and women like cattle, Joseph Vesey was normally indifferent to the cruelties of his chosen profession. But as he watched the crew prod his new purchases up the gangplank one boy caught his eye. There was something about the boy's "beauty, alertness and intelligence" that attracted his notice—or at least his desire to break the monotony of the voyage. Instead of having the child chained below decks, the captain adopted the boy as a "ship's pet and plaything." The captain gave him a new set of clothing and took him into his compartment to be used as a cabin-boy. Sexual abuse was hardly uncommon in such situations, but the child's later attachment to the tall mariner suggests that he was not raped or otherwise ill-used, at least by the captain.[21]

Undoubtedly the child expected to be retained in his new situation, but magnanimity was a rare commodity among slave traders. When the *Prospect* docked at Cap François, the captain, as he bluntly put it years later, "had no use for the boy." Armed crewmen returned their pet to the column of human freight disembarking the ship. The entire cargo of 390 slaves was turned over to Vesey's colonial agents, "Lory, Plombard, and Compagnie." Having so effortlessly parted with the child, probably more easily than he would have given up a stray dog or exotic bird, Captain Vesey pointed his ship toward St. Thomas and prepared to purchase another shipment of slaves.[22]

The terrified child, shackled together with dozens of older men and women, marched through the narrow streets, ankle deep in sandy black mud and corrupt water reeking of nautical smells. He was now a slave in the French colony of Saint Domingue, the most prosperous, and, for those who worked its plantations, the most deadly, of all the Caribbean sugar islands. By the 1780s, roughly

21. Grimké, *Right on the Scaffold*, 4; Hamilton, *An Account*, 17. On the use of boys as sexual partners on commercial, naval, and pirate vessels, see B. R. Burg, *Sodomy and the Pirate Tradition: English Sea Rovers in the Seventeenth-Century Caribbean* (New York, 1995 ed.), 121–26

22. Grimké, *Right on the Scaffold*, 4; Hamilton, *An Account*, 17; Cap François *Affiches Americaines*, April 24, 1782. I am grateful to Svend E. Holsoe for making a copy of this newspaper available to me. Cap François is now Cap Haitien.

400,000 slaves resided on Saint Domingue. The nearly 700 sugar plantations dominated the colony's economy. Indeed, Saint Domingue generated eighty percent more cane than its greatest rival, British Jamaica. Unlike its smaller neighbors who produced but a single crop, the colony boasted a diversified economy that included nearly 2,000 coffee plantations and 400 spreads of cotton and indigo. So great was the colony's agricultural output that Saint Domingue comprised fully one-third of all the foreign commerce of France; indeed, Captain Vesey probably received cotton and coffee, which he could easily barter in St. Thomas, as partial payment for his shipment of laborers.[23]

Having spent his childhood on an island of but 5,000 people, the boy on a happier occasion would have delighted in the sprawling city of Cap François. Samuel Perkins, an American shipper, marveled at docks "three quarters of a mile [long] filled with merchandise being shipped; all was bustle, noise, and cheerful labor." Of the colony's 24,000 white settlers, over half called Cap François home. The colony itself covered 12,000 square miles and encompassed the western half of the island the natives had once called Haiti and Christopher Columbus had rechristened Hispaniola; the Spanish colony of Santo Domingo occupied the eastern half of the island.[24]

As was the case in St. Thomas, many of those who owned the plantations lived on the other side of the Atlantic. Much of the land was owned by Paris financiers who employed large retinues of maritime agents and overseers to conduct the operations of their plantations. Even those planters born on the island, who styled themselves the *grand blancs,* hastened to earn their fortune so they could exchange Cap François for Paris; even those who could not afford permanent resettlement in France spent as brief a time on the island as their purse would allow. Either way, the result was a class of indifferent or absentee masters little concerned with life in Saint

23. Eltis, *Economic Growth,* 36–37; Thomas O. Ott, *The Haitian Revolution, 1789–1804* (Knoxville, 1973), 6; Fick, *Making of Haiti,* 22.

24. Martin Ros, *Night of Fire: The Black Napoleon and the Battle for Haiti* (New York, 1994), 11–12; Ott, *Haitian Revolution,* 6–10.

Domingue. They saw not the human face of slavery but merely numbers in a ledger book, which made it easier to rationalize a system in which brutal overseers habitually worked Africans to death. Paris investors saw no reason to encourage the natural reproduction of their laboring force so long as suppliers like Joseph Vesey were on hand with inexpensive replacements. As a result, the mortality figures for Saint Domingue were the highest in the Caribbean. The enslaved population would have disappeared had it not been for the constant importation of new Africans; during the 1780s, when the boy lived on the island, approximately 25,000 slaves were brought into the colony each year.[25]

Where the people of St. Thomas largely succeeded in rebuilding their extended families through fictive relationships and lived, as much as possible, in West African-style compounds, such creative familial reconstructions proved nearly impossible in Saint Domingue. Herded into the barracks-like slave quarters known as *cases a negres,* African men and women and children ate and slept according to the dictates of their owner, not according to the traditions of their homeland. Arranged in orderly military rows, the *cases* were windowless, straw-covered structures twenty-five feet long and twelve feet high. Some of the barracks had a single interior wall, but even when they did privacy was all but impossible as dozens of slaves resided in each hut. In front of the huts stood a tall rack, where the overseers hung extra whips, visible symbols of white authority and domination.[26]

Because of his youth, the boy did little more than light work on St. Thomas. But by the age of fourteen, children in Saint Domingue were sent to the fields, where they could expect to work until the day of their death. At five in the morning, the boy, asleep on a straw mat, was awakened by the crack of the overseer's whip. (Overseers in the French colony prided themselves on being accomplished "cutters" able to wield their whips so that they flayed the skin of their victim into neat ribbons.) The child worked in the cane fields

25. Fick, *Making of Haiti,* 16; Genovese, *World the Slaveholders Made,* 42; Ott, *Haitian Revolution,* 17; Rose, *Night of Fire,* 19.

26. *Ibid.,* 20; Fick, *Making of Haiti,* 31.

until eight, when he was fed a meager breakfast of manioc and beans. He then resumed work until noon. As on St. Thomas, overseers allowed slaves two hours rest to return to the barracks, but unlike on the Danish island the labor did not stop with sundown. During the grinding season, exhausted slaves staggered back from the fields only to find a long night's work ahead crushing cane in the sugar mills. Because of the mechanical requirements of sugar production, the plantations in Saint Domingue were almost as much an industrial enterprise as an agrarian one; older slaves often worked a twenty-hour day as they cropped, hauled, ground, and filtered the cane. Because the boy was but fourteen, the age at which children were first sent into the fields around Cap François, he performed no night labor. But whatever his job, the bright child was around overseers enough to begin to understand French, a language he soon spoke with "great fluency." Certainly he could see what his future held.[27]

In theory, the overseers' whip was restrained by the Code Noir, the Black Code of 1685. The code recognized only a rod or a whip as the legal instrument of punishment, although during the boy's brief residence on the island there was no restriction on the number of lashes cutters could employ. But over the course of the eighteenth century, as the colony grew more prosperous and the French government more insolvent, haughty kings and bourgeois investors alike became increasingly content to accept their profits in stony silence. The child witnessed cruelty and torture unequalled even in St. Thomas. Owners routinely branded their human property, and it would not be surprising to discover that the boy carried such an imprint throughout his long life. Equally common was the brutal practice of smearing salt, ash, or lemon into a beaten slave's open wounds. Bondmen caught attempting to flee into the mountains had their shoulders branded and their ears shaved off; a second attempt to escape the plantations led to the cutting of their ham-

27. Ott, *Haitian Revolution*, 15; Fick, *Making of Haiti*, 28–32; C. L. R. James, *The Black Jacobins: Toussaint Louverture and the Saint Domingue Revolution* (New York, 1963 ed.), 10; Second confession of Monday Gell, July 23, 1822, RGA, GM, SCDAH.

strings. Crippled slaves were of little use in the fields, but disabled men and visible scars on the backs of women served as deterrents for less stouthearted Africans.[28]

For the desperate, who could withstand neither the prospect of a brutal life in the cane fields nor the torment of the overseer's whip, there was always the possibility of suicide. Each year more than 2,000 newly-arrived Africans chose to deny their masters control over their lives by ending them. In most cases, older women or the occasional African priest administered locally-prepared poisons; other slaves hanged themselves from the rafters of their barracks. But the unusually bright boy found another way to escape Saint Domingue. Due perhaps to his growing facility with the French language, he somehow managed to understand that local law required all newly-imported slaves to be free of affliction or disease. Should the human product prove defective, local buyers had the right to return their purchase to the seller. During the late fall of 1781, the child began to display "epileptic fits." The disgruntled overseer promptly packed the boy off to Cap François, where the Royal Physician "certified that the lad" was unwell. The recent sale was "thereupon cancelled." The boy remained with the physician until the seller could return to claim him.[29]

On April 23, 1782, Joseph Vesey returned to Cap François with what a Saint Domingue newspaper described as a "tres-belle cargaison de Negres de la Cote-d'Or"—an exceedingly fine cargo of Gold Coast African slaves. Upon docking, he was surprised to learn that his former pet, who had displayed no signs of epilepsy during the voyage from St. Thomas, was unwell and had to be repurchased. He was also displeased. Finding a new consignee for an unhealthy boy would be no easy task. The most obvious course for the captain was to keep the child and again put him to work as a cabin boy. Vesey was a hard man but not much a fool; he retained the child even when the epileptic fits ceased as quickly as they had begun. He now perceived the artful boy might grow into a valuable servant.[30]

28. Genovese, *World the Slaveholders Made,* 43; Ros, *Night of Fire,* 17–20; Fick, *Making of Haiti,* 34–35.

29. Ros, *Night of Fire,* 19; Hamilton, *An Account,* 17; Grimké, *Right on the Scaffold,* 5.

30. Cap François *Affiches Americaines,* April 24, 1782; Hamilton, *An Account,* 17.

Charleston slaveholders in later years regarded the boy as a person of "superior power of mind & the more dangerous for it." Joseph Vesey saw only an untutored mind of uncommon native intelligence. Perhaps he admired the way a mere child of fourteen had outsmarted both a seasoned slave trader, a ruthless French overseer, and a royal surgeon. On the earlier voyage the boy had been a pet only, a diversion; now the captain began to appreciate the enormous value of a tall, muscular boy already conversant in two languages. The child was given his old wardrobe, and, befitting his new status, a new name as well: Telemaque. In Homer's ancient tale, Telemachus, the wandering son of Odysseus and Penelope, was shipwrecked on the perilous island of Ogyia, from whence he was rescued by Calypso, a savior who treated him kindly.[31]

The conceit that whites had the power to rechristen black children was typical of a Bermuda trader. But Telemaque may not have thought it so unusual. Many Africans carried more than one name. Among the Bakongo, young men adopted a new name when they assumed a new task. The Yoruba assigned a second name as a celebratory rite of passage. Undoubtedly, the boy had begun a new life, and so he may even have expected a new name to go with it. This tradition enabled many Africans to accept the new names given to them by their white masters, even if they sometimes retained their original name in the slave community as their appellation of choice.[32]

Presumably, Telemaque performed the typical duties of a cabin boy. The youth was responsible for keeping the captain's cabin tidy, his charts and maps stored safely away, his instruments polished. Many captains employed black linguists to translate orders to crew and human cargo alike; as the boy began to read and speak English under the captain's guidance, his value to the ship grew accordingly. Presumably also, as the *Prospect* was a slaver, Telemaque tried to remain above decks as much as possible. Because it carried nearly 400 slaves, the *Prospect* was a large vessel, roughly eighty feet in

31. Mary Lamboll Beach to Elizabeth Gilchrist, July 5, 1822, Beach Letters, SCHS; Grimké, *Right on the Scaffold,* 3.

32. Grimké, *Right on the Scaffold,* 3; Marvin L. Michael Kay and Lorin Lee Carey, *Slavery in North Carolina, 1748–1775* (Chapel Hill, 1995), 139; Mechal Sobel, *The World They Made Together: Black and White Values in Eighteenth-Century Virginia* (Princeton, 1987), 156–57.

length and twenty feet across. It displaced between 240 and 250 tons. But if, as was typical for a slaver that size, its depth was but twelve feet, the height of the slave deck would have been just over five feet. Like the chattel his new master carried, Telemaque was too tall to stand upright on the slave deck. More to the point, the Africans chained below the hatch served to remind Telemaque that he yet remained a slave, and that if he did not please his Calypso, he might rejoin them in the putrid hold at any moment.[33]

If life on the *Prospect* may be reconstructed from its physical dimensions, its course over the next months is not so easily recovered. Toward the end of 1781, just before Captain Vesey was forced to repurchase Telemaque, Copenhagen closed the slave trade in its three islands to all but a single Danish corporation, a practice consistent with the monopolist theories of that mercantilist age. Charleston remained under British occupation; in any case, buyers, not sellers, could be found in the Carolinas. If Vesey wished to continue feeding the voracious labor appetites of Saint Domingue, he would have to sail east for Africa. (Crossing the Atlantic posed little challenge for a man who had sailed the Mediterranean as a privateer in the patriot cause.) If Captain Vesey carried Telemaque to the coast of Africa—as the slave's later boast that he had "travelled through almost every part of the world, with his former master" would appear to confirm—he was not the only Boston-based merchant to cross the Atlantic. One observer on the African shore noted that numerous American slavers, "mostly from Boston," sailed the coast, trading New England rum for African captives.[34]

Captain Vesey's job was as difficult as Telemaque's was distasteful. To be the master of a slaver required special talents. Captains of any cross-Atlantic vessel needed to be experienced seafaring men,

33. Colin Palmer, *Human Cargoes: The British Slave Trade to Spanish America, 1700–1739* (Urbana, 1981), 47–48; Peter Wood, *Black Majority: Negroes in Colonial South Carolina From 1670 Through the Stono Rebellion* (New York, 1974), 174; Eltis, *Economic Growth,* 136.

34. John Lofton, *Insurrection in South Carolina: The Turbulent World of Denmark Vesey* (Yellow Springs, Ohio, 1964), 19–22; Second confession of Monday Gell, July 23, 1822, RGA, GM, SCDAH; James A. Rawley, *The Transatlantic Slave Trade: A History* (New York, 1981), 348–49.

but captains of slavers had to be both mariner and merchant. He needed to be familiar with the African coast, with Caribbean factors—agents who conducted business in behalf of European investors—and with American ports. Joseph Vesey was a novice in Africa, but not with Africans. Although captains were compensated by being allowed to carry cargo free of freight charges, Vesey was a shareholder in the *Prospect,* and so stood to turn a sound profit by getting his human baggage safely into Cap François. Because of the large number of Africans he carried, Vesey evidently had no single planter awaiting his arrival in Saint Domingue. Instead he probably continued to conduct business with Lory and Plombard, who marketed his wares in exchange for a commission of fifteen percent on the gross sale.[35]

In addition to owning a share of the cargo, Captain Vesey and his partners shared the heavy burden of insurance that slavers were forced to carry. Slave merchants typically insured the value of ship and cargo at eight percent. Because the *Prospect* carried a $20,000 bond, posted by Vesey and his two Boston partners, Jonathan Nutting and Ebenezer Woodward, the value of the vessel and the Africans below its decks may be estimated at $250,000. By the late eighteenth century merchant seamen like Vesey kept a close eye on their volatile cargo; insurance policies refused payment on losses incurred through natural death or on slave insurrections that took the lives of under ten percent of the entire value.[36]

When the *Prospect* reached African shores in the spring of 1782, its crew of sixty—large for a vessel of that size but unexceptional for a slaver—fell to its assigned tasks. As Joseph Vesey and several crewmen trained their muskets on the men and women filing out of the baracoons, other seamen hammered shackles onto the human cargo before chaining them in the hold. Male slaves, regarded as the more dangerous form of property, were chained in pairs, the right ankle of one man fastened to the left of another. As Telemaque

35. Daniel P. Mannix and Malcolm Cowley, *Black Cargoes: A History of the Atlantic Slave Trade, 1518–1865* (New York, 1962), 128; Rawley, *Transatlantic Slave Trade,* 258.

36. Brig *Prospect,* [no editor], *Naval Records,* 259–60; Rawley, *Transatlantic Slave Trade,* 421.

watched the small number of children brought on board (most of whom were allowed to remain at liberty), he doubtless prayed that no new pet would supplant him in his master's affections.[37]

Telemaque was not the only miserable passenger watching as the captives were forced below. By the 1780s, Atlantic crews were renowned for their international composition. Even on a ship outbound from Boston, Yankee sailors labored beside Englishmen, and Spanish and Portuguese dialects flew across the deck. If the Bermuda-born Vesey was a typical master, he employed not only a Caribbean cabin boy but hired free blacks to man his ship as well. Certainly freed Africans, more than most sailors, preferred employment in other types of deep-sea commerce; as one slave captain complained, "seamen in general have a great aversion to the Slave Trade." Black jacks even preferred the low pay of the British Royal Navy, in which fully one-quarter of the sailors were men of African origin. But steady work and honest wages were often hard to find in Atlantic ports, and surely more than a few Africans joined Telemaque aboard the *Prospect,* nestled precariously—both physically and psychologically—between people of their own ancestry in the hold and the tough, demanding captain above decks.[38]

By the time Captain Vesey weighed anchor and pointed his ship toward the Americas, Telemaque was well on his way to becoming a seasoned tar. Old salts on board taught him to wrap himself in a tattered piece of sail as a shield against the rats, and to hold his nose while he chewed rotten beef. But he never learned how to ignore the ever-present spectre of a slave uprising on the *Prospect.* Bloody slave mutinies—servile insurrections not on spacious sugar plantations but within cramped wooden walls—were common occurrences in the eighteenth century. Nervous tars told tales of Africans who would rather die and be tossed overboard than face the unknown horrors in a foreign land. They whispered of the slaves aboard the *Ferrar Galley,* who rose up and killed the captain, only

37. Palmer, *Human Cargoes,* 47; Rawley, *Transatlantic Slave Trade,* 259–60.

38. Marcus Rediker and Peter Linebaugh, *The Many-Headed Hydra: The Adventures of the Atlantic Proletariat* (Boston, forthcoming), chapter 2; Rawley, *Transatlantic Slave Trade,* 259.

to be crushed, and yet were determined enough to rise twice more before the beleaguered crew finally docked in Jamaica. Telemaque was the captain's boy, and saved from death in Saint Domingue because of it. He well knew, as one slaver put it bluntly, that a black "traitor to the cause of liberty is caressed, rewarded, and deemed an honest fellow." Yet he was also a slave, little different from the Africans chained below. Not for the last time in his life, Telemaque had to decide with whom he stood when it came time to fight for black freedom. That moment of truth never arrived on the *Prospect*. But the six months he spent aboard the ship taught him a hard lesson in the human dynamics of insurrection. In after years, "a pamphlet on the slave trade" fell into Telemaque's hands; its harsh words for the traffic in souls became a prized possession.[39]

Most likely, Telemaque and his captain made but a single voyage to Africa. In June 1782, Kezia Vesey bore her husband a son named John. Although Captain Vesey's presence was certainly superfluous to the birth, it is likely that having been at sea since September he would wish to be at his wife's side in the Virginia port of Norfolk for the birth of their first child. But other kinds of glad tidings awaited the captain. While Vesey was at sea the war had ended. At nearby Yorktown, a large British force surrendered to American and French forces on October 19, 1781; the disaster led first to the resignation of Lord North, the bellicose Tory Prime Minister, and then in March 1782 to the rise of the conciliatory Whig government of the Marquis of Rockingham.[40]

Following the signing of the preliminary treaty of peace in late November 1782, British forces made ready to evacuate the

39. Marcus Rediker, *Between the Devil and the Deep Blue Sea: Merchant Seamen, Pirates, and the Anglo-American Maritime World, 1700–1750* (Cambridge, England, 1987), 49; John Newton, *Thoughts Upon the African Slave Trade*, in David Northrup, ed., *The Atlantic Slave Trade* (Lexington, Mass., 1994), 85; Second confession of Monday Gell, RGA, GM, SCDAH. W. Jeffrey Bolster, *Black Jacks: African American Seamen in the Age of Sail* (Cambridge, Mass., 1997), 59, writes: "At least 155 documented slave mutinies occurred aboard ship, and an equal number of slavers are known to have been interrupted, or "cut off," by Africans."

40. Stephen Crane to John Lofton, January 27, 1983, Denmark Vesey File, SCHS.

still-occupied Charles Town. Preparing to leave with them were
5,327 black loyalists, former slaves many of whom had fought for
their liberty by picking up a musket in the name of Parliament
and King George. Over half were bound for the British colony of
Jamaica. The rest were destined for St. Lucia, London, and New
York City. On December 14, 1782, the British flotilla sailed out of
Charles Town harbor. Shortly thereafter, Captain Vesey, Kezia, her
son John, and Telemaque, together with thousands of returning refugees, alighted on Charles Town's docks.[41]

At the age of sixteen, Telemaque prepared to begin yet another
new life as a South Carolina slave. The quick-witted boy had learned
much during his turbulent childhood, and not just the rudiments of
three languages, either. No one could be trusted but his fellow
slaves. Those of his own ancestry, if free, were not to be relied upon;
the free black regiment in St. Thomas served as a reminder that too
many freedmen, and especially mulattoes, often bettered themselves
in the only way they could, by siding with their white benefactors
against the slave community. Even the man who flattered himself
the boy's Calypso was a potentially treacherous savior, a buyer of
souls who might sell his handsome pet if the price was high enough.
The boy had survived by his wits and luck and deception and an
abiding faith in the gods of Africa; therein lay the path to survival in
Telemaque's world.

41. James W. St. G. Walker, "Blacks as American Loyalists: The Slaves' War
for Independence," *Historical Reflections* 2 (Summer 1975): 62; Frey, *Water From
the Rock,* 179; Edward Ball, *Slaves in the Family* (New York, 1998), 236; Benjamin
Quarles, *The Negro in the American Revolution* (Chapel Hill, 1961), 128, 171.

Chapter Two

Stranger in a Strange Land 1783–1793

SOMETIME DURING the late spring of 1783 Joseph Vesey settled into his new business as a ship chandler—an importer and retailer of sundry commodities, naval stores, and Africans. Telemaque settled in with him. Although Vesey still owned his land near Canal Street, he wished to be closer to the heart of the city. On July 16, the captain leased (with an option to purchase) two town lots from John Christian Smith; one house, at 281 King Street, served as the Vesey household, the other building, four streets away on East Bay Street, became the captain's business office. To raise additional capital, Vesey sold the *Prospect* and prepared to liquidate his part interest in two other Caribbean slavers, the *Dove* and the *Polly*. In late September, the captain placed a card in the *South Carolina Gazette,* directing interested buyers in the schooners or their human cargo to apply at the establishment of "J. Vesey & Co." More than 100 "Prime Slaves," most of them from the British island of Tortola, were offered for sale on "every fair day" except Sunday. The captain set the sabbath aside for reflection and prayer.[1]

1. Donald R. Wright, *African Americans in the Early Republic, 1789–1831*

With that, the captain's name vanished from the "port news" section of the *Gazette*, which chronicled departures and arrivals in Charleston harbor. For the better part of the next two decades, 281 King Street was to be Telemaque's home. But his new occupation as an urban manservant in this strange and foreign land would prove quite different from his earlier lives as agricultural laborer and cabin boy. Town life and chattel slavery made for a poor partnership, and despite his often repugnant duties as a chandler's man, Telemaque discovered that Charleston's back-alleys and hidden courts concealed a thriving black community. On St. Thomas and Saint Domingue, community was to be found only in the huddled villages of slave huts. In Charleston, it existed outside the home, on the street corners, in the church basements, and in the illicit networks of goods and information. Although he remained but human property in the eyes of the law, Telemaque enjoyed a peculiar form of quasi-freedom in Charleston as an urban slave.

Telemaque's newest residence was a forlorn city at war's end. Situated at the conflux of the Ashley and Cooper rivers, Charleston—as it had recently been rechristened in an attempt to disguise its kingly appellation—then extended but four miles north up the peninsula. Several dozen crude quays, built atop the rough-hewn trunks of palm trees, stretched into the Cooper near the Customs House wharf. One disgusted visitor pronounced the city to be "very ugly." The waterfront was covered, she observed, "with reeking slime, over which large flocks of buzzards are incessantly hovering." Upon asking why the city did not exterminate the screeching irritants, the genteel lady was informed that the city actually imposed a fine of five dollars for shooting a black buzzard, "the unsalaried scavengers of the moister districts of the city."[2]

The city boasted a good number of elegant houses, nearly all of

(Arlington Heights, Ill., 1993), 101; Charleston Deeds, July 16, 1783, Vol. H-5, pp. 265–69, SCDAH; *South Carolina Gazette*, September 16, 27, 1783.

2. F. A. Michaux, *Travels to the West of the Allegheny Mountains in the Year 1802,* in Thomas D. Clark, ed., *South Carolina: The Grand Tour, 1780–1865* (Columbia, 1985), 35; Harriet Martineau, *Retrospect of Western Travel,* 2 vols. (New York, 1969 reprint of 1838 edition), 2:72

them embellished with elaborate outdoor galleries and porches to provide refuge from the sun and heat. But few were constructed of brick. City streets were planned with an eye to the future, and all were extremely wide. But due to the absence of nearby quarries, none of them was paved. Instead, residents spread sand and oyster shells on the sandy boulevards, which carriages ground into a fine silt. Young Telemaque gazed in wonder as horses waded past the office window in a sandy river of tumult and dust; merchants coming to conduct business with the captain sank "ankle-deep" into the sand. One annoyed visitor to Charleston observed that even "the most gentle wind fills the shops with it," and Telemaque spent more than a few hours trying to keep the office from resembling the strand.[3]

Both King and East Bay streets were but short distances to the city market, a series of five elongated open-air houses that stretched down to the harbor. To each side sat dozens of shops, their trades proclaimed from creaking sign boards that swayed in the warm breeze like hanged men. In both shops and market stalls Telemaque found an immense variety of meats and tropical delicacies—oranges from Spanish Florida, and pistachios and pineapples from Cuba—that were as plentiful as they were inexpensive. Buyers and sellers alike, however, had to move quickly to beat the buzzards to the exotic fruits. The protected scavengers had grown so tame, noted a nauseated German traveler, "that they crept about in the meat market among the feet of the buyers."[4]

As far as the city's merchant and planter elite was concerned, the turkey-sized nuisances were a minor annoyance. With the British evacuation, white Charlestonians hurried to rebuild their elegant society, just as a small army of slave laborers struggled to rebuild the war-torn city. Land speculators surveyed new lots north of Boundary Street, and Scottish merchants not only founded the South Carolina Golf Club in September 1786, they stole away from their shops to play their ancient game on Harleston's Green. No

---

3. Trautmann, ed., "South Carolina Through a German's Eyes," 21; Martineau, *Retrospect of Western Travel*, 2:64; Michaux, *Travels to the West*, 35.

4. Eugene L. Schwaab, ed., *Travels in the Old South*, 2 vols. (Lexington, Ky., 1973), 1:232; Karl Bernhard, *Travels Through North America, During the Years 1825 and 1826*, 2 vols. (Philadelphia, 1828), 2:9.

"A View of Charles Town," by Thomas Leitch, 1774, oil on canvas.
Depiction of Charles Town showing the city waterfront as seen

sooner had the redcoats abandoned the city than its free residents
also resumed their seasonal cycle of dinner parties, elegant balls,
horse races, card games, and deadly duels. "Dissipation—or to speak
more correctly—Idleness," complained Charles Manigalt, "is the
order of the day here."[5]

Idleness, of course, was hardly a word much familiar to young
Telemaque or the harried slaves who shoved past him in the sandy
boulevards. Everywhere Telemaque gazed he saw the ugly scars of
war, and if South Carolina needed to be rebuilt, it was African muscle that supplied the labor. Prior to the British occupation in 1780,
patriot forces habitually confiscated Tory property, including slaves,
to raise money to pay recruits and to purchase supplies. As a result

5. Fraser, *Charleston*, 175; Charles Sellers, *The Market Revolution: Jacksonian
America, 1815–1846* (New York, 1991), 274.

from across the Cooper River. *Collection of the Museum of Early Southern Decorative Arts; Winston-Salem, North Carolina.*

of the dislocation of war and the massive flight of slaves to British lines, cotton and rice went uncultivated. Returning to his home in the Sumter district, Captain Francis Richardson observed nothing but "general doom and destruction." Once thriving plantations had shrunk "into small truck patched; stock of every description had been taken for the use of the British army; fences gone." Nor was the war over for everyone. Several marauding bands of heavily-armed black loyalists, dubbed the "Black Dragoons," remained active in parts of the state well into 1783.[6]

The desperate need to rebuilt their plantation world forced

6. Philip D. Morgan, "Black Society in the Lowcountry, 1760–1810," in Ira Berlin and Ronald Hoffman, eds., *Slavery and Freedom in the Age of the American Revolution* (Charlottesville, 1983), 112–13; Frey, *Water From the Rock,* 206–7; Robin Blackburn, *The Overthrow of Colonial Slavery, 1776–1848* (London, 1988), 116.

white Carolinians to crack down not merely on the "Black Dragoons," but to reimpose those labor controls that had fallen into disuse during the British invasion. Colonial acts codifying unfree labor, of course, dated back to the dawn of the eighteenth century and remained on the statute books. As early as 1712, ordinances required slaves traveling into or about Charleston to carry a "ticket," that is, a pass from their master, specifying their reason for being away from their owner's watchful eye. Slaves caught without a ticket were whipped "on the bare back not exceeding twenty lashes." The comprehensive twenty-four page slave code of 1740, commonly known as the "Negro Act," covered every possible aspect of slave life and made it abundantly clear where *all* Africans stood in the social order. The code drew few distinctions between bondpersons and free blacks, as it empowered rural patrollers or city watchmen to stop and interrogate any black on sight. So sure were colonial legislators that Africans were meant to be slaves that the lengthy bill mentioned free blacks only four times, and in two of those instances mandated that freedmen be treated as human property in the courts.[7]

For urban slaves like Telemaque, the most visible sign of white authority was the Workhouse, formally known as the House of Correction. Built on Magazine Street in 1768, the imposing brick structure fulfilled the role that overseers played on the rice plantations. If discipline on rural plantations was a private affair, the Workhouse warden symbolized public control in the crowded city. Night watchmen sent the slaves they rounded up during the night to the Workhouse, and sensitive masters, one resident noted, frequently ordered "refractory slaves" to the Workhouse "with a note from the owner directing a specified number of lashes to be given." A visitor to Charleston discovered "about forty individuals of both sexes" awaiting "correction." The "whipping-room," constructed of double

---

7. "An Act for the Better Ordering and Governing of Negroes and Slaves," 1712, in Thomas Cooper and David J. McCord, eds., *The Statutes at Large of South Carolina* (Columbia, 1840), 7:352–65; "Negro Act," 1740, in Joseph Brevard, ed., *An Alphabetical Digest of the Public Statute Law of South Carolina* (Charleston, 1814), 2:202. On the lack of distinction drawn between free and enslaved blacks, see Robert Olwell, "Becoming Free: Manumission and the Genesis of a Free Black Community in South Carolina, 1740–1790," *Slavery & Abolition* 17 (April 1996): 1–2.

walls filled with sand to muffle the screams of inmates, housed a crane, "on which a cord with two nooses runs over pullies." The warden chained the feet of slaves to the floor, and then hoisted the crane until their bodies were "stretched out as much as possible." Slaves took the beating, but masters paid a price for their squeamishness; each visit to the Workhouse cost twenty-five cents.[8]

In theory, the ownership of another might be an individual matter, but the imperatives of human property forced the state to routinely intervene in the private affairs of the ruling race. William Mazych, the master of Indian Fields, found himself indicted by a Charleston court when it was discovered that he had neither lived on his plantation for the required seven months of each year nor kept an "overseer or a white person in his employ." None of this is to imply, of course, that all Carolina masters relied on the courts or the Workhouse to supervise their enslaved laboring force. One visitor to the region, St. John de Crevecoeur, was unnerved to find a dying slave suspended from a tree in an enormous iron cage, while flapping vultures picked at his flesh. The slave murdered an overseer, Crevecoeur's host calmly explained, and the gruesome sight would prove a terrible reminder to less courageous bondmen.[9]

Presumably, Captain Vesey never inflicted either public or private violence upon Telemaque's body; after all, in later years, the boy chose to adopt the captain's surname. But life as a manservant on King Street was often difficult, frequently distasteful, and even psychologically cruel. As a chandler's man, Telemaque was responsible for helping to receive imported goods from incoming ships, cataloging items in the Bay Street office, and even, as his ability to read and write English neared perfection under the captain's tutelage, to conduct minor transactions in his master's absence. Due to

8. Norrece T. Jones, Jr., *Born a Child of Freedom, Yet a Slave: Mechanisms of Control and Strategies of Resistance in Antebellum South Carolina* (Middleton, Conn., 1990), 76–77; Elizabeth B. Pharo, ed., *Reminiscences of William Hasell Wilson* (Philadelphia, 1937), 8; Bernhard, *Travels Through North America*, 2:10. After 1802, when Denmark was a free man, recalcitrant slaves were flogged at the new Charleston District Jail, which adjoined the Workhouse.

9. Bills of Indictment, January 19, 1822, Court of General Sessions, Charleston District, SCDAH; Sellers, *Market Revolution*, 274.

the obvious need to rebuild the region's shattered economy, Charleston escaped the post-war recession that visited much of the republic throughout the mid-1780s. The immense volume of agricultural and building materials that flooded into the harbor—ploughs, hoes, marble, lumber, stone, bricks, nails—illustrated the determination of white Carolinians to resume their plantation empires. For a businessman like Vesey, who imported small commodities into a region that was generally incapable of producing basic supplies, the first years after the Peace of Paris brought new riches.[10]

Unlike many merchants, who pooled their capital to purchase the entire cargoes of the larger ships from London or Liverpool, Vesey partnered with one or two other small chandlers, such as Edward North or a Mr. Blake, and procured select goods from the smaller Caribbean vessels. Certainly Vesey did well in his ventures; perhaps he preferred to deal with familiar cargoes and the merchants he had known from his days in the West Indies. From Saint Martin came rum and sugar. From "Turks Island" came 1000 bushels of salt, and from the Dutch colony of Saint Eustatius, Vesey imported gin. Most of the amounts paid out were small, and Vesey—or his enormous, quick-witted manservant—always settled in cash. Assuming Telemaque collected many of these items for his master, his responsibilities carried him to the city treasurer, where he paid the import duty on the captain's consignment, and then to the customs house off East Bay Street with a signed manifest in hand to check in the cargo. Telemaque's presence in the customs house surely irritated some merchants, but other businessmen employed literate bondmen in the same manner, and few merchants wished to anger the stern former slaver; in May 1784, only one year after arriving in Charleston, a notice appeared in the *Gazette* that Vesey planned to take legal action against those yet "indebted to him for Negroes sold last year," and several months after that he successfully sued a fellow chandler for "Four Hundred Pounds Sterling," about $1,600.[11]

On occasion it was Telemaque's lot to perform a far more loath-

10. R. Nicholas Olsberg and Helen C. Carson, eds., *Duties on Trade at Charleston, 1784–1789* (Columbia, 1970), 9.

11. Mary Lamboll Beach to Elizabeth Gilchrist, July 25, 1822, Beach Letters, SCHS; Schooner *Nancy*, Duties on Trade at Charleston, Manifests and Entries,

some duty. Some of the assorted merchandise the captain imported were people, and it was Telemaque's unhappy assignment to receive the human cargo as well as the inanimate freight. In October 1784, after but one year in Charleston, Joseph Vesey imported "3000 Gallons" of rum and "1 Negroe Woman" from Guadaloupe on the brig *Le Vigilant*. Two years after, the captain purchased "sundry non-Enumerated Goods" from Bermuda, including four adult "wench[es] and Child at the Breast." Having been sold as a child into Saint Domingue, Telemaque understood all too well the terrors of arriving in chains in a strange land, but now he himself was an unwilling participant in the traffic in humans.[12]

Captain Vesey was hardly unique in importing both human and dry goods. Between the end of the war and 1787, when the Atlantic slave trade was temporarily prohibited in South Carolina, merchants like Vesey paraded nearly 9,000 slaves across Charleston docks. Most came from the Gambia River region, as well as Martinique, Jamaica, and Spanish Florida. In the years after Telemaque's death, the importation of African Americans from other parts of the United States virtually became a separate economic enterprise, and the city constructed a slave mart at 6 Chalmers Street. But in Telemaque's day the merchants who purchased slaves imported other items as well, and their shops could be found all along the city's business district from State Street to East Bay. Petty chandlers like Vesey had their human stock brought directly to the docks, while larger importers unloaded their cargoes just outside the harbor on Sullivan's Island. But the harsh realities of the Atlantic trade were never far from view; Africans sometimes mutinied within sight of land, and dead

---

December 1, 1784, SCDAH; Sloop *May,* November 9, 1784, *ibid.*; Sloop *Betsey,* August 21, 1787, *ibid.*, Olsberg and Carson, eds., *Duties on Trade at Charleston,* 6; *South Carolina Gazette,* May 8, 1784; Joseph Vesey vs. William Davis, September 17, 1784, South Carolina Court of Common Pleas, Judgement Roll 96, Vol. 11A, SCDAH. For an example of the way larger merchants pooled their resources to purchase an entire cargo, see "ship Olive-branch," in which Joel Poinsett and twenty-four partners bought every item in the ship's hold. Duties on Trade at Charleston, Manifests and Entries, May 13, 1785, SCDAH.

12. Schooner *Active,* December 11, 1786, Duties on Trade at Charleston, Manifests and Entries, December 11, 1786, SCDAH; Brig *Le Vigilant,* October 30, 1784, *ibid.*

bodies thrown from slave ships often washed into Charleston harbor. Visitors found the sight ghastly, but locals learned to ignore the problem except when the bobbing corpses became so numerous that "nobody [could] eat any fish."[13]

When it suited his needs, Captain Vesey bought and sold urban slaves as well. In the fall of 1786, Vesey paid 111 guineas for "a Negro Man named Sam." The captain probably retained Sam as a house slave, as his high price indicates literacy or a marketable skill. But on another occasion, as the holder of a mortgage, Vesey made good on a debt owed him by liquidating four slaves, "Sylvia a Wench," and her three children, "George a boy & two Girls Sappho & Lindy."[14]

"[H]e would not like to have a white man in his presence [as] he had a great hatred for the whites," Telemaque swore in later years, and it is hardly difficult to imagine why. Every weeping African woman he met at the docks in his role as a chandler's man reminded him of his own precarious existence. Telemaque's feelings toward his master were complicated at best; slavery produced few slavish personalities but more than a few psychologically disfigured slaves, and Telemaque's relationship with the captain evidently contained equal parts love and loathing. The captain rescued the boy from the sugar fields in Saint Domingue, taught him to read, and treated him as more of a servant than a slave. Yet a slave Telemaque remained, and his duties on East Bay Street served as a grim reminder that the captain too often personified the heartless greed of white Charleston. Certainly it was hard for young Telemaque to ignore the wealth Joseph Vesey gained through his occasional traffic in Africans. The 1790 census listed Vesey as a "chandler," but only four years later the city recorder paid him the compliment of elevating his occupation to that of "merchant."[15]

13. Olsberg and Carson, eds., *Duties on Trade at Charleston*, 8; Steven H. Deyle, "The Domestic Slave Trade in America," Ph.D. dissertation, Columbia University, 1995, 114; Winthrop D. Jordan, *White Over Black: American Attitudes Toward the Negro, 1550–1812* (Chapel Hill, 1968), 366–67; Edmund Drago and Ralph Melnick, "The Old Slave Mart Museum, Charleston, South Carolina: Rediscovering the Past," *Civil War History* 27 (June 1981): 140.

14. Bill of Sale, September 21, 1786, Vol. 2Q, p. 513, SCDAH; Bill of Sale, September 2, 1789, Vol. 2Q, p. 758, *ibid.*

15. Examination of William Paul, June 26, 1822, in Kennedy and Parker, eds.,

However distasteful some of Telemaque's responsibilities may have been, his life as an urban slave was far different from that of rural bondmen. On the plantations, the relationship between master to slave could be characterized as seigneurial, for the dependent black working class held some claims to the means of production, yet they were compensated not in cash but, in theory, in support and protection. In the countryside, owner and laborer struggled for domination within the context of a harsh, premodern union not unlike that of lord and serf. The patriarchal relationship between the two, despite the fact that slaves were engaged in a form of exploitation designed to produce a profit for the master, was primarily social rather than economic. Relations of exchange between white planters and white importers like Joseph Vesey may have been market-oriented, but relations of production between owner and bondperson manifestly were not.[16]

To be sure, no Carolina planter who produced for export could be totally free of the economic or social sway of Atlantic capitalism. But the desire to maintain and defend unwaged labor both kept a capitalist mentality at bay and hindered the growth of precisely those market mechanisms necessary for a well-rounded capitalist economy. More than simply an economic investment, slave labor provided the foundation for a premodern society that grew increasingly distinct from that of the Northern Atlantic world as it contin-

---

Official Record, 85–86; Carroll A. McElligot, ed., *Charleston Residents, 1782–1794* (Bowie, Md., 1989), 42, 52. Nicholas Halasz, *The Rattling Chains: Slave Unrest and Revolt in the Antebellum South* (New York, 1967), 119, suggests that Denmark Vesey "was consumed with self-disgust for his former status as the eager henchman of a trader" and that this self-loathing somehow developed into a "hatred [of] his own race." There is no evidence, of course, that Telemaque was at any time an "eager" participant in the captain's business or that he blamed anybody but white Charlestonians for the slave trade. Certainly there is no extant evidence that he hated all blacks.

16. The view that unfree labor produced a nonmarket *society* fundamentally different from that of the capitalist North can be found in the complicated and sophisticated writings of Eugene D. Genovese, especially *The World the Slaveholders Made: Two Essays in Interpretation* (New York, 1969); Genovese, *In Red and Black: Marxian Explorations in Southern and Afro-American History* (New York, 1968); and Genovese and Elizabeth Fox-Genovese, *Fruits of Merchant Capital: Slavery and Bourgeois Property in the Rise and Expansion of Capitalism* (New York, 1983).

ued to develop in the years after the Revolution. The need to discipline and justify unfree labor, in short, gave rise to a hierarchical society founded upon paternalism—an ongoing process of negotiation and violence that many scholars regrettably reduce to a simplistic model of accommodation—which produced an agrarian ideology linking whites and blacks with mutual responsibilities and obligations in a decidedly precapitalist relationship.[17]

Slavery in Telemaque's Charleston, however, was an altogether different matter. If Carolina planters largely succeeded in restoring the old colonial controls over their agrarian labor force in the decades after the Revolution, urban masters found it all but impossible to monitor their bondpeople as closely as they wished. The ability of one man to own another was based not merely upon colonial statute and the brute force of the Workhouse, but upon supervision, and the sandy boulevards and back-alleys of Charleston rendered constant surveillance a futile task. Whereas plantation slaves labored under the watchful eye of a small percentage of masters—in rural South Carolina nearly three quarters of the white population did *not* own slaves—urban conditions encouraged a broad diffusion of ownership. Most city dwellers, like Joseph Vesey, retained very few domestic slaves. But approximately seventy-five percent of Charleston families owned at least a single slave. Most slaves, like Telemaque, spent part of the day apart from their master's home or business. "City air makes free," Medieval peasants once said, and Africans in North America did not disagree. "A city slave is almost a freeman, compared with a slave on the plantation," one bondman observed.[18]

The physical separation of black and white characterized much of life on the countryside, but Charleston's cramped peninsular space did not allow for traditional plantation arrangements, in which

17. I have briefly discussed the ways in which slave society resisted the coming of modern capitalism in "Markets Without a Market Revolution: Southern Planters and Capitalism," in Paul A. Gilje, ed., *Wages of Independence: Capitalism in the Early American Republic* (Madison, Wis., 1997), especially 51–52.

18. Richard C. Wade, *Slavery in the Cities: The South, 1820–1860* (New York, 1964), 20; Frederick Douglass, *Narrative of the Life of Frederick Douglass* (New York, 1979 ed.), 50.

secluded slave cabins were strung together far behind the big house. Instead, most urban slaves lived in close proximity to their owner— surely too close to please either master or slave—either in separate slave quarters within an enclosed compound adjacent to the main residence, or in the case of less wealthy masters, in the master's home. Joseph Vesey's house on King Street was far from an elegant mansion, and Telemaque lived either in a small servant's room or in a low attic. Charleston's growing free black population, however, resided farther north on the peninsula in the Hampstead suburbs, where housing was cheaper. Only freedom altered living arrangements by allowing Africans to escape the relentless white surveillance in removing to the straggling neighborhoods beyond Boundary Street and the city proper.[19]

Telemaque's responsibilities, like those of many urban slaves, often carried him away from the captain's hearth and sovereign gaze. But during the long daylight hours spent at King or East Bay streets, Telemaque enjoyed little of the free air for which urban areas were so justly celebrated. Unlike plantation slaves on the countryside, who achieved a measure of cultural autonomy during the evening hours in the slave quarters, urban domestics worked no regular schedule. The captain employed his able slave in a variety of ways, from chandler's apprentice to personal manservant. Although the Vesey household included several other bondpersons, Telemaque spent his seventeen years at 281 King Street at the constant beck and call of Joseph's white family. As an urban domestic of all trades, Telemaque could claim no moment of the day or night as his own time.[20]

This was one of the few disadvantages; in most other ways life in town was preferable to that of the countryside, and slaves, when given the choice, favored life in Charleston over labor on the plantations. Few slaves anywhere were literate, but learning was more common in the cities. Joseph Vesey was hardly the only entrepre-

19. Michael P. Johnson and James L. Roark, *Black Masters: A Free Family of Color in the Old South* (New York, 1984), 226–27; Wade, *Slavery in the Cities,* 55–59.

20. Gary B. Nash, "Forging Freedom: The Emancipation Experience in the Northern Seaport Cities, 1775–1820," in Berlin and Hoffman, eds., *Slavery and Freedom,* 21; John W. Blassingame, *The Slave Community: Plantation Life in the Antebellum South* (New York, 1979 ed.), 251.

neur whose business suffered if left in the hands of unlettered servants. Telemaque's responsibilities, together with the long years spent in a predominantly white household, forced him to speak English, the language of business and prestige. On the plantations across the Ashley River, communication between African laborers and the white minority was limited to orders barked by overseers, and acceptance of the English language was a prolonged process. Rural slaves spoke Gullah, a common language forged out of diverse linguistic traditions. But by the late 1780s, Telemaque lost most of his youthful African and Cariolisch words through disuse; English now came more naturally than any other tongue.[21]

Urban bondmen also tended to be better dressed than their rural brothers. Plantation slaves typically received but one new set of coarse clothing each year, and more than a few urban tradesmen also dressed their slave assistants in unrefined "Negro cloth," simple "Blue, Brown and Green Plains" linens imported from Wales. But no merchant south of Broad Street wished his dinner guests to be greeted by a shabbily-dressed slave, and if Telemaque occasionally accompanied his master on business, he surely did not arrive at the customs house in rags. Elegant apparel for slaves, however, was a violation of the Negro Act. The slave code of 1740 included dress regulations intended to maintain and emphasize social stratification between white and black through the symbol of dress. Slaves were forbidden to "wear any sort of apparel whatsoever, finer [or] of greater value than negro cloth." But the law was unenforceable and unenforced. No doubt the habitual immaculacy of Telemaque's adult years derived from his days as a bond apprentice.[22]

Little imagination was required to envision the risk posed by elegant slaves strolling the boulevards in cast-off evening apparel; every citizen decried the practice even as they tolerated it in their own parlor. In the same way, white Charlestonians turned a blind eye to the private tutors and well-intentioned church groups who

21. Charles W. Joyner, *Down By the Riverside* (Urbana, 1984), 216; Blassingame, *Slave Community*, 312.

22. Charleston *City Gazette*, October 1, 1799; "Negro Act," 1740, in Brevard, ed., *Alphabetical Digest*, 2:242; Charleston *Southern Patriot*, September 12, 1822; Wood, *Black Majority*, 232.

taught slaves how to read on Saturday afternoon or following Sunday services. The Negro Act stood silent on the question of black literacy, yet the folly of revealing a larger world of information to human chattel was obvious to all but the most naive master. But many town masters required at least semi-literate bondmen for their trade, and in any case the precarious nature of urban controls made it difficult for white authorities to crush black initiative. As a literate slave, Telemaque may have taught others to read. Perhaps it was in this fashion that he first met Peter Poyas. A literate and highly-skilled ship carpenter, Poyas was raised outside the city on the Ball family's Windsor plantation. In 1784 he lived and labored beside his new owner, James Poyas, a master ship-wright. Both lord and slave worked near the docks at 35 South Bay Street but resided at 49 King Street, not far from Joseph Vesey's home. Poyas became young Telemaque's closest friend, and in later years, his greatest confidant.[23]

If the fragile nature of slave controls in Charleston allowed Poyas and Telemaque the benefits of a thriving slave community, black autonomy in the city only grew stronger, ironically, as servitude became more securely fastened upon the countryside. In an attempt to buttress slave prices and stabilize the state's delicate economy, the South Carolina legislature temporarily suspended the Atlantic slave trade in 1787. But six years later, while visiting Catherine Greene's Mulberry Grove plantation, Connecticut-born Eli Whitney devised a simple machine for extracting seeds from the common but previously unprofitable short-staple cotton. The result was that upcountry cotton could now compete with its sea-island rival for the expanding British market. Almost overnight the forests of piedmont South Carolina gave way to hundreds of new plantations, which in turn heightened demands for the restoration of the slave trade.[24]

23. Janet Duitsman Cornelius, *When I Can Read My Title Clear: Literacy, Slavery, and Religion in the Antebellum South* (Columbia, 1991), 38; Eugene D. Genovese, *Roll, Jordan, Roll: The World the Slaves Made* (New York, 1974), 563; *Directory and Stranger's Guide, 1822* (Charleston, 1822), 70.

24. Frey, *Water From the Rock*, 213; John B. Boles, *Black Southerners, 1619–1869* (Lexington, Ky., 1984), 61; Constance McL. Green, *Eli Whitney and the Birth of American Technology* (New York, 1956), 45, 93.

The resumption of the Atlantic trade had implications for the city as well as the upcountry. Once more, Sullivan's Island became the leading entrepôt, a hellish Ellis Island for Africans, most of whom were purchased from Angola and the Gambia River region of West Africa. Nearly 10,000 Africans passed through Charleston each year on their way to the upland plantations. Between Telemaque's arrival in 1783 and the federal suppression of the Atlantic trade in 1808, roughly 100,000 Africans disembarked in South Carolina. This forced migration was of critical significance. The proportion of native Africans in the state's slave population declined after 1760, but now it rose again to twenty percent, the highest of any region in mainland North America. In the countryside and city alike, this massive incursion bestowed upon the slave community a renewed degree of cultural coherence, in part because nearly sixty percent of all Africans came from but two coastal regions. Enough Africans remained in Charleston to revitalize a sense of black distinctiveness, and hence cultural autonomy, and to militate against the growth of paternalism in Charleston, which required not only a landed elite determined to uphold the pose of benevolence, but an American-born laboring class with no personal memory of freedom.[25]

Worse yet, from the perspective of control, some of the Africans imported into Charleston arrived infected with the disease of liberty. Although their numbers were small compared to the thousands purchased from Angola, many of the blacks who reached South Carolina were refugees from the slave rebellion in Saint Domingue. Inspired in part by the ideological currents that washed about the Atlantic basin in the late eighteenth century, the uprising posed a dangerous challenge to slaveholding regimes on the mainland. When in 1789 France exploded into revolution, the colony's 20,000 free mulattoes, the *gens de couleur,* seized the moment to advance their claims for political equality. Frustrated by the refusal of the Paris Assembly to grant them citizenship, and enraged at the intransigence of the wealthy white planters, a mob of wealthy mulattoes murdered three

25. Wright, *African Americans in the Early Republic,* 23; Powers, *Black Charlestonians,* 288; Morgan, "Black Society in the Lowcountry," 129; Genovese, *World the Slaveholders Made,* 97.

whites near Port-au-Prince in the spring of 1790. This increasingly bloody division among the ruling elite paved the way for a revolt by the black majority of nearly 408,000 slaves. On the evening of August 22, 1791—later known as the Night of Fire—hundreds of slaves under the command of Boukman Dutty, a plantation driver and voodoo priest, simultaneously put the torch to the same sugarcane they had previously nourished with their sweat and blood.[26]

Early on in the conflict, control of the rebel forces fell to Toussaint, a forty-eight-year-old house servant and folk doctor on the Breda plantation. Like Telemaque, Toussaint learned to read and write as a young man, a skill denied to most Dominguan slaves just as it was to Carolina bondmen. As he rose to power, the black general—increasingly known to his men as Toussaint Louverture, the soldier who always found his opening—inspired enslaved Americans with an ideology of revolutionary violence and a model of black heroism, resiliency, and self-reliance. By fighting for the principles of liberty that white patriots once proclaimed, the Dominguan slaves reminded their Carolina brethren that freedom might be theirs as well if another Toussaint arose from the streets of Charleston.[27]

With refugees and Dominguan planters fleeing in every direction, many of them carrying what slaves they could with them, news of the revolt could hardly be kept from mainland bondpersons, especially those in Southern ports. So great was interest in the rebellion that Peter Freneau, editor of the *City Gazette,* printed hundreds of additional copies of his daily newspaper to meet the voracious demand for information regarding the island. Much to his dismay, Freneau later discovered that bond apprentices at his press pirated several hundred copies for circulation within the black community. Shortly thereafter, Swiss immigrant James Negrin tried to cash in

26. Philip D. Curtin, *The Rise and Fall of the Plantation Complex: Essays in Atlantic History* (Cambridge, England, 1990), 166; Frey, *Water From the Rock,* 228; Fick, *The Making of Haiti,* 92.

27. Eric Foner, *Nothing But Freedom: Emancipation and Its Legacy* (New York, 1983), 41–42; Alfred N. Hunt, *Haiti's Influence on Antebellum America: Slumbering Volcano in the Caribbean* (Baton Rouge, 1988), 101; Monroe Fordham, "Nineteenth-Century Black Thought in the United States: Some Influences of the Saint Dominguan Revolution," *Journal of Black Studies* 6 (December 1975): 115–26.

on what for whites was a nearly morbid fascination with the Caribbean revolt by publishing a hastily-penned biography, *Life of Toussaint.* The book sold well enough, but Charleston authorities deemed
it likely to "incite domestic insurrection" and imprisoned the unfortunate Negrin on the charge of rebellion. Negrin emerged from
jail after eight months, only to discover that his landlord had seized
his furniture and printing press to cover back rent. Having learned
a lesson about the limits of the first amendment in a slave society,
a chastened Negrin sold no more copies of his biography, but for
Charleston blacks eager for any information about their hero, the
seed had been planted.[28]

One black Charlestonian who could not read enough about
the island revolution was Telemaque. As a former resident of the
French colony, Telemaque rejoiced at the news that the sugar plantations he remembered all too well were now in the hands of African workers. One of the young slave's acquaintances, Jack Purcell,
later recalled that Telemaque "was in the habit of reading to me all
the passages in the newspapers that related to S[ain]t Doming[ue],"
as well as "every pamphlet he could lay his hands on, that had any
connection with slavery." On a separate occasion, a slave named
Bacchus encountered Telemaque carrying a "large Book" with a letter or document in it, which Bacchus understood came "from some
free Country off [the coast], may be S[ain]t Doming[ue]."[29]

Surrounded as they were by a potentially dangerous black majority, lowcountry planters required little imagination to envision
themselves as the next victims in this bloody saga. "When we recol-
lect how nearly similar the situation of the Southern States and
S[ain]t Doming[ue] are in the profusion of slaves," worried Governor Charles Pinckney, "a day may arrive when [we] may be exposed
to the same insurrections." When white emissaries from the belea-

28. Julius S. Scott, "The Common Wind: Currents of Afro-American Communication in the Era of the Haitian Revolution," Ph.D. dissertation, Duke University, 1986, 284; Frey, *Water From the Rock,* 228; Marina Wikramanayake, *A World
in Shadow: The Free Black in Antebellum South Carolina* (Columbia, 1973), 148.

29. Confession of Jack Purcell, in Hamilton, *An Account,* 42; Richmond *Enquirer,* September 3, 1822; Confession of Hammet's Bacchus, no date, William and
Benjamin Hammet Papers, Duke University Library (hereafter DUL).

guered colony approached South Carolina in search of financial assistance, the General Assembly appropriated £3,000 to assist the French colonists in isolating the contagion of black rebellion before it reached American shores. The undisguised glee and ill-concealed delight of black Charlestonians over each new victory by Toussaint warned Carolina masters, observed Thomas Pinckney, the governor's cousin, of the ominous "example of S[ain]t Doming[ue]" on the mainland slave population.[30]

Black revolutionary fervor only increased in the summer of 1793, when a second wave of Caribbean refugees and their slaves broke upon Charleston's shores. In June, slave rebels in Saint Domingue captured the Plaine du Nord and with it Telemaque's former home of Cap François, a campaign that took the lives of over 10,000 white colonists. In early July, French warships ferried refugees into Charleston and other American ports. Sympathetic whites again rushed to assist "the distressed Inhabitants," for most were "destitute of the Means of Subsistence." But once more white authorities worried about the influence of refugee slaves in their midst, and with good reason; between 1791 and 1795 French masters brought as many as 12,000 Dominguan slaves into the United States. Few came willingly, and most regarded Toussaint as a liberator. At least two refugee bondmen became close friends with Telemaque, whose fluency in French allowed him to converse with the new arrivals. Louis Remoussin lived at 11 Stroll's Alley with his owner, Charles Cromwell, a French captain, and Patrick Datty, a cook, resided with his owner, Julia Datty, a refugee who made a marginal living by teaching French to merchants' daughters.[31]

With victorious slave armies just off the mainland serving as inspiration, it did not take long for ever-present slave unrest to revolutionize into servile rebellion. Even before the second wave of refu-

---

30. [Thomas Pinckney], *Reflections Occasioned by the Late Disturbances in Charleston* (Charleston, 1822), 7; Merton Dillon, *Slavery Attacked: Southern Slaves and Their Allies* (Baton Rouge, 1990), 42–43; Frey, *Water From the Rock*, 231–32.

31. William Moultrie to General Assembly, November 30, 1793, RGA, GM, SCDAH; David P. Geggus, *Slavery, War, and Revolution: The British Occupation of Saint Domingue, 1793–1798* (New York, 1982), 305; *Directory and Stranger's Guide, 1819* (Charleston, 1819), 35–36.

gees, Carolina residents began to fear that their human property were plotting for their freedom. Newspapers reported that urban slaves had suddenly become "very insolent," as if they believed that events would soon allow them to abandon the polite mask of subservience. Only "an excess of humanity," editorialized the *Columbian Herald,* blinded white Charlestonians to the dangers of allowing white refugees to carry their slaves into the state. The only solution was the expulsion of all blacks who had arrived from Saint Domingue since 1791. The legislature refused that drastic step but did clamp down on future importations. In 1794 the General Assembly barred entry of free blacks or mulattoes from any part of the Americas except the United States. Nine years later, the state took the final step and banned any "person of colour, whether bond or free" from entering South Carolina if they had previously resided in "any of the French West India islands."[32]

This embargo on information came too late. In August of 1793 disquieting news arrived from Virginia that evidence from Williamsburg revealed a massive conspiracy that stretched as far as Charleston. An elusive preacher known only as Garvin—most likely Gowan Pamphlet, the free minister of the Williamsburg Baptist Church—dropped a letter addressed to the "Secret Keeper" of Norfolk. The letter indicated that slaves in Richmond and Norfolk were stockpiling weapons and powder in preparation for a concerted revolt, and that a good number of Carolina slaves were aware of the plan. "Since I wrote you last I got a Letter from our Friend in Charleston," insisted the "Secret Keeper" of Richmond, and "he tells me he has [en]listed near Six thousand Men." On a yet-to be appointed night, the rebels planned to "begin with fire [and] Clubs and shot [and] we will kill all before us." Virginia authorities, at least, were certain that events in the Caribbean led to this dangerous moment. Chesapeake bondmen, a correspondent warned the South Carolina governor, "say the Negroes of Cap François have obtained their Liberties by this method."[33]

32. Scott, "Common Wind," 289–90; Wikramanayake, *A World in Shadow,* 18; Jordan, *White Over Black,* 382; Brevard, ed., *An Alphabetical Digest,* 2:261.

33. Secret Keeper Richmond to Secret Keeper Norfolk (copy), no date, RGA, GM, SCDAH; James Wood to William Moultrie, August 1793, *ibid.*; William Nel-

Increased vigilance and enlarged militia patrols put a quick end to the "Secret Keeper" conspiracy, but as always, Carolina bondpeople found the greatest succor in small acts of rebellion, such as family formation. By affirming the privilege of kinship before their owners' very gaze, slaves reenforced the central importance of family ties. The determination to establish healthy families through marriage was itself an act of resistance that proclaimed the enslaved community's refusal to be characterized as the barbarous property their masters insisted them to be. Slaveholders might disparage the depth of romantic attachment in their human property, but they understood all too well that black familial ties ultimately challenged the absolute power of the master class, just as they fostered pride and community among the enslaved.[34]

After five years' residence in Charleston, Telemaque was well known to both the white and black communities, but increasingly, by different names. The Vesey family, as well as other whites, continued to summon him by the appellation the captain had imposed upon him years before, but in the black community, his name was slowly being corrupted. Caribbean-born slaves found his classical name hard to pronounce and simply shortened it to "Telmak." From there it was but a short step, and perhaps initially a humorous reference to the island of his birth, to corrupt it further to "Denmark." Perhaps because it symbolized his place of origin, Denmark was the name he came to prefer. As he neared the age of twenty, Telemaque began to consider the prospect, and the difficulty, of marriage. Were he a free man, Denmark would only have to ask his would-be bride and consult her parents. But as the property of Joseph Vesey, Denmark had to obtain the additional permission of his master, and that of his prospective wife as well.[35]

---

son to Thomas Newton, August 8, 1793, *ibid.*; Peter Oram to William Moultrie, August 16, 1793, *ibid.*

34. Sharon Ann Holt, "Symbol, Memory, and Service: Resistance and Family Formation in Nineteenth-Century African America," in Larry E. Hudson, Jr., ed., *Working Toward Freedom: Slave Society and Domestic Economy in the American South* (Rochester, N.Y., 1994), 197.

35. Hamilton, *A Report*, 17; Brenda E. Stevenson, *Life in Black and White: Family and Community in the Slave South* (New York, 1996), 227.

Provided that proper deference was paid to their authority, few masters voiced any objection to slave marriages. Captain Vesey obviously did not. As Christians, white Charlestonians believed marriage, like slavery itself, to be ordained by the Bible. To permit their slaves to cohabitate without benefit of a marriage ceremony was to sanction sin within their household. Wise masters also understood that stable black families meant a secure social order; the threat of selling a spouse into the Carolina upcountry was enough to mold the most disobedient slave into a complaint servant. The Negro Act of 1740, however, refused to recognize the legality of slave marriage. If few masters doubted the essential humanity of their slaves, neither were they inclined to extend them the sort of legal protection that would distinguish them from other forms of property. As a result, South Carolina law actively subverted the emergence of a male-dominated nuclear slave family; indeed, what enslaved Carolinians called "marriage" was technically but a consangual relationship secured only by bonds of affection. Because black children inherited the status of their mothers, the Negro Act defined slave families as matrilineal. Children of slave women automatically became slaves, regardless of their fathers' legal status. Assuming black fathers to be dependent servants with no income of their own, the Act accorded husbands no legal claim to their children and made no demands of financial support.[36]

It was not legislative action, however, threatening though it was, that posed the most formidable barrier to servile marriage in Charleston. It was the pattern of urban slaveholding itself. On the large plantations across the Ashley, young men experienced little difficulty in finding a bride of the same age in a nearby cabin; roughly two-fifths of agrarian slaves lived in two-parent dwellings. But in Charleston, prospective grooms like Denmark rarely found a wife within the same household or even on the same street. The diffuse nature of urban slaveholding not only sent young men across the city in search of a partner, it also meant that upon marriage they would not live under the same roof as their wife. Settling for an "abroad" wife, a spouse who lived in her master's house away from

---

36. Joyner, *Down By the Riverside*, 137; Stevenson, *Life in Black and White*, 161.

her husband's domicile, was the most common arrangement in Charleston. Slaves might obtain their masters' permission to marry, but few whites allowed their house servants the luxury of permanently residing in the home of another. The best Denmark could expect would be the customary visits on mid-week and Sunday, together with the few fleeting moments he and his bride might steal along the way.[37]

Such unfavorable if necessary arrangements meant that few urban slave families enjoyed a nuclear structure. Instead, black parents in Charleston revived African traditions of extended, even matrifocal families, in which fathers were at best a remote figure and women assumed preeminent influence over their offspring. Denied control over the family's meager financial resources and refused the privilege of residing with their wives and children, slave husbands lacked the coercive power that white husbands possessed. In the big house, the ideal of patriarchy held sway. But slave children who saw their fathers but once or twice a week, and then only for a few short hours, instinctively recognized their mother, or even other slaves of either gender in their master's house, as the person to whom they owed obedience and respect.[38]

Denied the legal authority granted to masters like Joseph Vesey, Denmark's relationships were hidden from the church register and city recorder and so remain shrouded in mystery. His first wife was named Beck. But in what year they married and at what date they parted is unclear. Although African women married young and, like many women in pre-Victorian societies, engaged in sexual experimentation prior to matrimony, Beck may have been Denmark's senior. She already had at least one child from a previous relationship, a daughter named Sarah. Beyond that little is known about her. In later years, she lived as a slave near the corner of Coming and Bull streets, but she had been bought and sold numerous times over the course of her long life. Once she had been owned by John Paul, a grocer who lived

37. White, *Somewhat More Independent*, 88–89; Frey, *Water From the Rock*, 33–34; Sobel, *The World They Made Together*, 161–63.
38. Graham R. Hodges, *Slavery and Freedom in the Rural North: African Americans in Monmouth County, New Jersey, 1665–1865* (Madison, Wis., 1997), 17; Stevenson, *Life in Black and White*, 227.

at 47 Broad Street. Before that, she may have been owned by John White, who in 1806 sold "one Negro Woman named Beck with her three Children Sarah, Nancy & William" to David Lamb for $700. But while Denmark indeed had a daughter, her name is unidentified, and later records say nothing about a son named William. Perhaps instead she was the "Negro Wench Named Beck" whom John Barker sold, together with "her Son Robert," to James Evans in 1808 for a paltry $400.[39]

Whoever was her master, Beck remained married to Denmark long enough, and saw him often enough, to give birth to at least three of his children, and perhaps several more. Sandy Vesey, "a fat black fellow [who] looked very much like Denmark," was almost certainly born before 1800. As a young man, Sandy was the property of John J. Schnell, a grocer who lived at 74 Church Street; Schnell presumably purchased Sandy from John Paul, who was also a grocer. Even if Denmark did not reside with Sandy, he certainly exerted a great deal of influence over his son. Like his father, Sandy "could read" and write. He would be the only one of Denmark's children to be deeply involved in the 1822 conspiracy. Denmark had at least two other sons, both of them probably Beck's children. One was named Polydore Vesey. The other went by the name of Robert Vesey, who inherited his father's later profession of carpenter and builder.[40]

Whether Beck bore Denmark any other children is unknown. Due to a diet low in protein, nonexistent prenatal care, and long hours of toil until the last moments of pregnancy, the infant mortality rate for the enslaved population was a ghastly 350 per thousand births (roughly twice that of white infants). Put another way, approximately one in three slave infants did not survive their first year, and over half of all slave children in the United States died before

---

39. Testimony of William Paul at trial of Denmark Vesey, June 26, 1822, in Kennedy and Parker, eds., *Official Record,* 85; Bill of Sale, September 10, 1808, Vol. 4A, p. 97, SCDAH; Bill of Sale, December 9, 1806, Vol. 3X, p. 307, SCDAH. (William Paul identified Vesey as Sarah's father-in-law, but if Denmark "married her mother Beck," he would have been her step-father.)

40. Bacchus, second confession, July 13, 1822, RGA, GM, SCDAH; Bacchus, third confession, July 17, 1822, *ibid.; Directory and Stranger's Guide, 1819,* 83; Philadelphia *Christian Recorder,* October 14, 1865.

reaching the age of five. Even taking into account the robust health that ran in the Vesey family—Denmark and Robert both survived far beyond the average life expectancy for either black or white males in antebellum America—Beck surely buried at least one of her infants, and probably more.[41]

The fact that Sandy was literate, and that Robert chose to follow his father's profession, indicates that Denmark was hardly the negligible father that urban conditions too often fostered. Even as a young man, his domineering, even overpowering personality compensated for the long hours he was forced to spend away from Beck and his children. But child rearing in the Charleston slave community was a nearly impossible task. Although Beck's children were unfettered with the comical or classical names that signified the master's interference, a good many owners presumed the right to name their slaves' children, who were, after all, as much their property as a dog or cat. Such claims often proved confusing to slave children who frequently found themselves torn between the imperious demands of their white master and the authority of their parents. Masters expected to be promptly obeyed without question, but parents believed they should have the first claim on their children's attention. One slave father, not too different from Denmark in this regard, impressed this lesson upon his son when the child answered the master's voice instead of the parent's call. "You are my child and when I call you, you should come immediately," the father insisted, "if you have to pass through fire and water."[42]

This unending dispute between owner and father for the attention of a slave child served as an apt metaphor for the larger and equally unceasing negotiation—if such a sterile word can describe this often violent process—between the free and the enslaved communities of Charleston. The master class, with its laws and militias and workhouses, quite literally held the whip hand, but the black

41. Wright, *African Americans in the Early Republic*, 69.
42. Joyner, *Down By the Riverside*, 217; Wilma King, *Stolen Childhood: Slave Youth in Nineteenth-Century America* (Bloomington, Ind., 1995), 14–15; Wilma King, "'Rais Your Children Up Rite:' Parental Guidance and Child Rearing Practices among Slaves in the Nineteenth-Century South" in Hudson, ed., *Working Toward Freedom*, 147.

majority tenaciously refused to be transformed into the obedient servants their owners wished them to be. The problematic nature of urban slavery itself, with its limited controls and inviting back-alleys, served to weaken the bonds of patriarchy, just as the renewed importation of Africans strengthened the black community by re-invigorating the cultural traditions of the old world. Finally, the nearby revolt in Saint Domingue, a place Denmark had once called home, emboldened the slave community by reminding them that freedom might be theirs as well, if they were courageous enough to rise when the moment proved right.

With slave controls nearly as neglected as the city's docks, and with the disquieting example of Toussaint Louverture murdering their peaceful slumber, nervous Carolinians increasingly assured themselves that if given the choice, the slaves who cleaned their homes and cooked their meals favored servitude over freedom. Pre-Revolutionary planters had harbored few doubts about their slaves' unhappiness with their lot, but in the waning moments of the eighteenth century, anxious Charleston masters began to embrace comforting theories about the "extreme indulgence and kindness which characterises the domestic treatment of our slaves." Living amidst a hostile and potentially revolutionary black majority, Charleston masters could do no other; the reality of their situation was too terrifying. "The negroes of the Southern states of this country," editorialized the *Southern Times,* "are better off and better contented, than the labourers of many other civilized countries." Henry William De-Saussure also "denied that in this country [slavery] is a system of cruelty in practice."[43] But if the unrest of the early 1790s forced whites to embrace such soothing absurdities, the growing economic autonomy of the enslaved community would force the master class to find new ways to restrain the activities of their servants as the decade wore on.

· 43. Kenneth Greenberg, "Revolutionary Ideology and the Proslavery Argument: The Abolition of Slavery in Antebellum South Carolina," *Journal of Southern History* (hereafter *JSH*) 42 (August 1976): 381; Hamilton, *An Account,* 29; Columbia *Southern Times,* April 12, 1830; [Henry William Desaussure], *A Series of Numbers Addressed to the Public, on the Subject of the Slaves and Free People of Colour* (Charleston, 1822), 6.

Chapter Three

—————————◯—————————

Nor a Lender Be
1794–1799

THE AGREEMENT WITH the yard foreman concluded, Polydore Faber stripped off his shabby waistcoat and set to his labors. Faber, an acquaintance of Denmark's, was "a hearty, sound, strong, intelligent, sober and honest" man; all of which is to say, that were he a free man of European descent, Faber would have done very well for himself. But Polydore was a slave, and so he did very well for another, his master Catherine Faber. The widow Faber, who lived an impoverished existence at 25 Montague Street, had few sources of income. But as Polydore was "an excellent sawyer of Lumber [and] a Rope Maker," she allowed him to hire his time around the lumber yards at Gadsden's Wharf. In exchange for this privilege, Polydore turned over to his aged mistress the lion's share of his wages, twelve dollars each month.[1]

Polydore lived the peculiar life of a slave for hire, a practice common to the urban South. The leasing of bondmen like Polydore enabled masters like Catherine Faber to profit from their surplus

---

1. Petition of Catherine Faber, November 18, 1822, General Assembly Petitions, 1822, SCDAH; *Directory and Stranger's Guide, 1819, 42.*

slaves, while it allowed white Charlestonians with short-term labor needs to fill them for a modest cost. Largely peculiar to the cities—only six percent of rural slaves were on hire, compared to in-excess of thirty-one percent in Charleston—the hiring of bondpeople allowed slaves to acquire small amounts of cash. This acquisition of money, and in some cases, even of property, facilitated the emergence of a thriving underground economy, through which slaves participated in the market economy of the urban South. This illegal traffic, perhaps even more than the servile unrest brought on by the revolution in Saint Domingue, threatened the security of the master class by creating an illicit network where blacks achieved a level of economic autonomy, a network in which information moved as easily as stolen goods. For concerned authorities, it would later come as no surprise that a majority of those implicated in the conspiracy of 1822 (including Polydore Faber) were skilled slaves who hired their time.[2]

Under the law, the master class enjoyed unlimited control over the labor of their African servants. But theory and practice were rarely the same thing, and masters in and around Charleston typically allowed their slaves to use a portion of their time and labor for their own account. Most urban masters believed, perhaps unwisely, that granting their slaves a small amount of control over their day would hardly bring about the overthrow of unfree labor. Some penurious owners even encouraged black entrepreneurship as it meant they could spend less on food and clothing for their human prop-

2. Peter Kolchin, *American Slavery, 1619–1877* (New York, 1993), 110. The literature on the informal, or internal, slave economy is growing rapidly. Several historians suggest that an overemphasis on this underground economy neglects the obvious fact that slaves were dependent agricultural laborers. See, for example, Michael Mullin, *Africa in America: Slave Acculturation and Resistance in the American South and the British Caribbean, 1736–1831* (Urbana, 1992), 126–58; Gary B. Nash, "Slavery, Black Resistance, and the American Revolution," *Georgia Historical Quarterly* 77 (Spring 1993): 68–69; Peter Coclanis, "Slavery, African-American Agency, and the World We Have Lost," *Georgia Historical Quarterly* 79 (Winter 1995): 880–81. One does not have to slight the bloody mechanisms of control, however, to recognize the extraordinary determination of black Southerners to survive in a hostile world, and this chapter borrows from pioneering studies by Betty Wood, Loren Schweninger, John Campbell, Philip Morgan, and Robert Olwell, all cited below.

erty. Bondwomen from across the Cooper River, for example, who were responsible for selling their masters' produce in town, often brought vegetables grown in small garden plots to sell for their own personal profit. As occasional participants in the urban market economy, Carolina slaves temporarily enjoyed the same privileges accorded to the white minority, the right to barter their labor—or in this case, the fruits of their labor—for a needed commodity, or even for cash.[3]

Slave marketeers worked outside the law. The Negro Act of 1740 allowed bondpersons into the Charleston city market only for the limited purposes of buying or selling commodities on behalf of their owners, and it enjoined "any shopkeeper, trader, or other person" from dealing in items not "particularly enumerat[ed]" by masters under penalty of a $200 fine. But except in times of war or slave unrest, white authorities permitted any slave traveling with a "ticket" to enter the market houses. Few white retailers turned down a modestly-priced basket of fresh foodstuffs, regardless of origin, for fear that their competitors in the next stall would purchase the illicit goods and undercut their price. So long as slave marketeers returned to their masters' property by nightfall, white peddlers—and the politicians who coveted their block of votes—welcomed rather than discouraged ambitious slave suppliers.[4]

Some prudent rural slaves managed to build their illicit networks away from the gaze of white authorities. Plantation slaves along the Carolina waterways often bartered the crops or livestock they raised to white and free black boatmen. One rice planter on the Combahee River observed numerous "ped[d]ling boats which fre-

3. John Campbell, "As 'A Kind of Freeman'?: Slaves' Market-Related Activities in the South Carolina Up Country, 1800–1860," in Ira Berlin and Philip D. Morgan, eds., *Labor and the Shaping of Slave Life in the Americas* (Charlottesville, 1993), 243; Robert Olwell, "'Loose, Idle, and Disorderly': Slave Women in the Eighteenth Century Charleston Marketplace," in David Barry Gaspar and Darlene Clark Hine, eds., *More Than Chattel: Black Women and Slavery in the Americas* (Bloomington, Ind., 1996), 99–100.

4. Brevard, ed., *An Alphabetical Digest*, 2:248–49; Wade, *Slavery in the Cities,* 143. In 1817 the penalty imposed on those who "Deal or Trade With Negro Slaves" was increased to a fine of $1,000 and a jail sentence from one month to one year. See Cooper and McCord, eds., *Statutes at Large,* 7:454,

quent the river [for] the purpose of trading with the Negroe Slaves."
But most enterprising plantation slaves chose to hawk their wares in
the city. According to one white observer, on Sundays, the day when
most slaves were not required to perform labor for their masters, an
"immense number of canoes of various sizes," some of which "could
transport upward of one hundred men," poured into Charleston
from across the rivers and from the coastal "Islands," carrying "vegetables, stock of every kind and the staple of the country."[5]

If white retailers had every reason to encourage this illegal trade,
planter-legislators sought to control and limit it. When the traffic in
stolen cattle became so prevalent that lowcountry planters complained, state lawmakers responded in 1790 with an ordinance that
required bondmen who transported slaughtered beef to market to
"produce the Hides" or some other evidence of rightful ownership.
But black initiative was not so easily denied, especially among unwaged laborers who believed they had the right to recompense
themselves from their masters' corral or larder. Some enterprising
upcountry slaves even insisted that their owners obtain goods for
them that were unavailable from local shopkeepers. Peter Bacot's
slaves used the money they earned in the local village market to purchase, through Bacot's intervention, coats, shawls, and even dress
patterns from Charleston shops.[6]

Bacot saw little harm in filling his slaves' orders, but more discerning masters worried about the impact of the informal economy
on their patriarchal control. Henry Laurens, for one, feared the
underground market's ability to provide his bond servants with a
source of cash or bartered goods that did not require them to approach him, cap-in-hand, and request the goods with the proper
deference. Planters like Laurens correctly perceived the Charleston
marketplace—and its capitalist orientation—as an assault on the
seigneurial social order from which they derived their patriarchal
authority. So too, perhaps, did the slaves, who viewed their right to

5. Loren Schweninger, "Slave Independence and Enterprise in South Carolina, 1780–1865," *SCHM* 93 (April 1992): 105; A Narrative of the Conspiracy, in
Kennedy and Parker, eds., *Official Report,* 38–39.

6. Schweninger, "Slave Independence and Enterprise," 106; John Campbell,
"As 'A Kind of Freeman,'" 271.

acquire money and property as a challenge to the hegemony of the master class. One slave, Hercules LeCount, told a surprised visitor to the region that his owner "did not own or even claim a cent worth" of the cash he earned by selling his foodstuffs in the city. Prince Wilson agreed. Although human property himself, he was "the only one who has any legal right to the property" he acquired away from his master's fields.[7]

Charleston slaves were especially adamant on this point. Rural bondmen like Prince Wilson might cultivate small "provisions grounds" next to their cabins for sale in the city, but their actual journeys to Charleston were at best infrequent. But Polydore Faber and other city slaves spent at least a portion of *every* day away from the daunting gaze of their master; of the many differences between urban and plantation slavery, it was this relative freedom of movement that was the most noticeable to visitors to the South. Consequently, for enterprising bondmen like Faber, their proximity to the market buildings and the consistent shortage of skilled laborers in Charleston allowed him to use his talents to good effect. The Workhouse stood as the visible symbol of white authority, but in the city no plantation overseer kept a watchful eye on a gang of laborers. Instead, employers competed with one another for slave craftsmen, and bondmen like Faber, with a reputation for honesty and hard work, shopped about for contractors and even inquired into the reputations of whites who offered them employment.[8]

Rural masters, of course, required a good number of skilled slaves. Every large plantation employed slave blacksmiths, carpenters, and weavers. But Northern visitors to Southern ports like Charleston witnessed bondmen and women performing every imaginable task; indeed, urban slaves worked in a variety of skilled enterprises closed by law or tradition to their free black counterparts in the North. Slaves along the docks, sweating in orderly chaos, loaded and unloaded trading vessels. Hotel proprietors retained a

7. Robert Olwell, "'A Reckoning of Accounts:' Patriarchy, Market Relations, and Control on Henry Laurens's Lowcountry Plantations, 1762–1785," in Hudson, ed., *Working Toward Freedom*, 38; Philip D. Morgan, "The Ownership of Property By Slaves in the Mid-Nineteenth Century Low Country," *JSH* 49 (August 1983): 410.

8. Wade, *Slavery in the Cities*, 148; Boles, *Black Southerners*, 129.

number of slaves to cook, clean, and handle baggage. Racing en-
thusiasts, which every wealthy Carolinian professed to be, bought
Africans who showed promise as jockeys or who had experience
grooming horses in the land of their birth. Even the city government owned slaves. A small team of three slaves smoothed the
sandy streets and kept them free of refuse. By the very nature of
their labors, all of these bondpersons spent time away from their
masters' homes, and almost all found ample opportunities to earn
illicit wages.[9]

The vast majority of Charleston's skilled slaves, however, fell
into one of two categories. Most, like Denmark, served their masters
in a domestic capacity. Trained as manservants, cooks, butlers, coachmen, valets, and grooms, they labored inside their owners' homes.
But on Sundays or late afternoons when their tasks were finished,
they wandered down to the wharves, seeking temporary employment
as porters and carters. As a literate slave and a talented linguist of
immense size, Denmark could easily find short-term work along the
docks in any number of occupations. The next largest category was
that of slave artisan. Artisan ownership was commonplace in Southern towns, and especially so in Charleston, the largest slave city in
the republic. In the 1790s, more than half of all white artisans retained at least a single bondman as an apprentice. In select trades,
the percentage was even higher. Sixty percent of Charleston carpenters held slaves, and some of them ran their entire businesses using
gangs of bond carpenters; a full twenty-five percent of carpenters
possessed more than ten bond artisans, who they employed in small
groups at construction sites around the city.[10]

Despite long hours and often dangerous work high above the
city streets, carpenters like Faber—indeed, all manner of slave
craftsmen—enjoyed the reputation for being the proudest and most

9. Betty Wood, *Women's Work, Men's Work: The Informal Slave Economies of
Lowcountry Georgia* (Athens, 1995), 107; Wade, *Slavery in the Cities,* 33, 37–38, 45;
Boles, *Black Southerners,* 126.

10. Wood, *Women's Work, Men's Work,* 118; Ira Berlin and Herbert G. Gutman,
"Natives and Immigrants, Free Men and Slaves: Urban Workingmen in the Antebellum American South," *American Historical Review* 88 (December 1983): 1185–86,
note 17.

self-reliant of all bondmen. The prestige accorded to slave mechanics and craftsmen arose not only from the intricate nature of their
work, which often allowed for demonstrations of African artistry,
but also from their ability to move freely about the city, control their
own pace of work, and labor beside other bond artisans, while most
domestic servants had little opportunity for contact with their fellows until after their tasks were completed. During his journeys
about the city in the captain's behalf, Denmark came to know a good
number of these craftsmen. Harry Haig and Jack, known also as
Jacob Glen, both labored as carpenters beside their artisan masters.
Jack's master owned a lumber yard on Tradd Street, and Harry lived
at 150 Meeting Street with his owner, David Haig, a cooper; Denmark also became acquainted with another of Haig's skilled slaves,
Nero, who was also a cooper.[11]

On occasion, Charleston's bond artisans rose to the top of their
profession and all but managed their owners' businesses. One of
Denmark's close friends, Adam Robertson, served as foreman at his
master's South Wharf rope making operation (known as a rope
walk). Adam's owner, John Robertson, was a "merchant and navy
agent" with a good many investments, indeed, too many to manage
himself. Adam early on demonstrated both an unusual aptitude for
his craft as well as the capacity to manage other men, gifts that
wiser minds might regard as inherently dangerous in young slaves.
John Robertson saw only greater efficiency and increased profits
and put Adam's talents to use as manager of the "Rope Walke Negroes," which endowed him with enormous influence over the other
slaves in Robertson's employ.[12]

Young Adam was Charleston born and bred, but several of the
men who worked under him were Africans, and when the day's
labors drew to a close all retired together to Robertson's elegant
home on Meeting Street. There, in the claustrophobic attic, all distinctions between skilled and unskilled, between native-born and

11. Kenneth M. Stampp, *The Peculiar Institution: Slavery in the Antebellum
South* (New York, 1956), 58–59; Genovese, *Roll, Jordan, Roll,* 392–93; *Directory and
Stranger's Guide, 1819,* 47, 49.

12. *Ibid.,* 80; John Potter to Langdon Cheves, July 15, 1822, Cheves Papers,
SCHS.

African, promptly vanished. Whatever their occupational or cultural differences, Robertson's men were united by their common condition as human property. Contrary to myth, skilled bondmen displayed little disdain for their less privileged brethren, and the high regard in which the "Rope Walke Negroes" held Adam rarely translated into envy. To suggest, as many historians have, that Adam's story proves that only American-born slaves became skilled workers, or that acculturated bondmen lost all traces of their African past, is to suggest that no craft artisans existed in Africa, or that the ability to learn the English language and gain the respect of the master class was to somehow eradicate all vestiges of an African past. Adam's influence over his men stemmed not only from his natural power of command, but from the fact that he remained connected to the African heritage of his parents or grandparents.[13]

It so happened that enterprising masters with visions of business grandeur often acquired more slaves than they found they could readily employ, especially if their business experienced a sudden setback. In that eventuality, urban slaveowners routinely hired out their slaves to their more prosperous but short-handed white neighbors, a practice, as noted before, far less prevalent in the countryside. The brief employment of a slave artisan by a temporary master was a recent development in American slavery, but hardly an illogical one. Since white Carolinians owned the very bodies of African men and women—and not merely their labor or time, as would be the case in indentured servitude—slaves had to submit to the fact that their service could be arbitrarily redirected to suit the needs of their owners or the fluctuating requirements of the Charleston economy. If masters could turn a profit by having others labor in their behalf, as John Robertson had done, it made equal sense to assume that masters also enjoyed the right to gain additional revenue by temporarily transferring that labor power to other whites.[14]

In rare cases, the period of hire could reach fifty weeks, beginning on the first day of January and stretching to seven days before

13. Genovese, *Roll, Jordan, Roll*, 393; Sterling Stuckey, *Slave Culture: Nationalist Theory and the Foundations of Black America* (New York, 1987), 43.
14. Wood, *Black Majority*, 205; Wade, *Slavery in the Cities*, 38.

Christmas. But most urban masters leased their human property out for as little as a few days. White Charlestonians in need of ready capital typically initiated the process, but under the urban hiring system, skilled slaves often bargained with their masters for the right to hire out as if they were free wage laborers. Agreements between masters and slaves varied, but in most instances masters retained the lion's share of the money their slaves earned, while the slaves kept but one-third of the cash paid to their master. Even so, bond artisans pushed their owners hard for the right to hire out. The practice put cash—albeit a paltry amount—in their pockets and carried them away from their masters' gaze long enough to visit their wives and purchase goods for their children at the city market (thereby strengthening the informal slave economy of lowcountry Carolina). Though no less a slave in the eyes of Charleston authorities, bondmen for hire enjoyed a measure of independence virtually unknown in the countryside.[15]

The practice was lucrative for the owner but dangerous to social stability. Although skilled slaves comprised the majority of the hired work force, Charleston's docks offered less skilled bondmen ample opportunities to earn quick wages; together skilled and unskilled slaves made up better than seventy percent of all laborers in Charleston. Some owners accompanied the slaves they intended to hire to the wharves each morning, but it was impractical for masters to loiter along the docks to negotiate a new agreement every few hours. Instead, after reaching an initial agreement, Charleston masters left their servants to their own devices, provided that they returned home at the end of the day with an adequate sum in their pocket. Most likely, Joseph Vesey rarely hired Denmark out; the old captain owned few slaves and a servant as bright as Denmark could always be put to good use in the East Bay office. But many of Denmark's acquaintances routinely hired out. One of them was Caesar, an "active drayman" who carted goods about the city and virtually passed as a free

15. Clement Eaton, "Slave-Hiring in the Upper South: A Step Toward Freedom," *Mississippi Valley Historical Review* 46 (March 1960): 677–78; Mary Beth Corrigan, "'It's A Family Affair:' Buying Freedom in the District of Columbia, 1850–1860," in Hudson, ed., *Working Toward Freedom*, 168.

man. Caesar paid his aged owner, Naomi Smith, "two dollars per month" for the privilege of hiring out. Beyond that, he bought his own "Clothing & Support[ed] himself at his own Expense" and patiently saved for the day that he would have cash enough to buy his freedom.[16]

Over time, a body of law arose to meet this new variety of unfree labor. A standard contract specified the time of hire and required the lessor to cover clothing and medical bills. State law also compelled every slave who hired out to wear a badge marking him as a masterless man. The badge law categorized slaves into three groups. Badges for "handicraft tradesmen" were the most expensive at six dollars, while badges for "carters, draymen, porters, or day labourers" cost four dollars. Emblems for slave "fishermen or fisherwomen" were the least expensive. In hopes of limiting the perilous custom of hiring out, state law forbade masters from purchasing more than six badges each year. But because the price of even the cheapest badges was roughly what a skilled slave might earn in a week or two, the law provided an inadvertent incentive to maximize the profit gained from each badge purchased by hiring each slave out for as many weeks as possible and so actually encouraged the practice.[17]

If the badge law did little to discourage the hiring of slaves, it nonetheless had the effect of turning every white Charlestonian into a watchman or constable. The badges indicated that the wearer was a slave, and not a member of the city's small free black population. Each badge carried a visible number, which was recorded by the city clerk, together with the slave's name and occupation, at the time the owner bought the emblem. Owners who tried to save a few dollars by ignoring the law were fined twenty dollars for each offense. But while the badge law provided for a modicum of control over the city's large hired population, it did little to suppress the practice. So common was the custom of slave hiring that even the city government participated in it. Charleston not only employed

16. Berlin and Gutman, "Natives and Immigrants," 1187; Wood, *Women's Work, Men's Work,* 107; Petition of Naomi Smith, November 16, 1822, General Assembly Petitions, 1822, SCDAH.

17. Wade, *Slavery in the Cities,* 40–42, 46; Johnson and Roark, *Black Masters,* 175.

Slaves, and later, free blacks, were forced by law to wear identification tags. Each tag contained information denoting the person's free or slave status, occupation, identification number, and year the badge was purchased. *Courtesy of The Charleston Museum, Charleston, South Carolina.*

leased slaves to assist the buzzard population in cleaning the streets, the city even hired bond firemen to staff one of the two volunteer fire companies in an attempt to keep city taxes low. (Bond firemen, of course, received a lower wage than their white counterparts.) State legislators in Columbia might seek to limit the practice, but confused white Charlestonians understandably believed the custom carried an official stamp of approval when it was so brazenly practiced by the city government.[18]

Although it was not unheard of, few women hired their time, and there is no evidence that Beck was ever far from her master's voice. Some Charleston bondwomen hawked bread and cakes on streetcorners, but often the same domestic skills that would in a later century drive impoverished black women into the homes of their wealthy white neighbors—the ability to wash, iron, cook, and scrub—kept slave women closely tied to their masters' townhomes. Charlestonian slave owners expected six days hard labor from their bondwomen. From the lighting of the morning's fires through the washing of the evening dishes, slave women spent almost every waking moment serving their owners' white families. Even assuming women like Beck cared to exchange her long-awaited Sunday visits with Denmark for a few pence, slave women for hire faced stiff competition from Charleston's free black women.[19]

As dangerous to social stability as was the practice of slave hires, worse still, from the perspective of racial supervision, was the fact that masters often found it convenient to allow their bondmen to hire their own time, in effect, to choose their own masters. Instead of finding a position for their surplus slaves, masters allowed trusted bondmen to secure their own employment, negotiate their own wages, and come and go as they pleased provided an agreed-upon amount landed in the owners' purse at the end of each month. Whatever a skilled craftsman could make beyond the sum he owed his master was his to keep. So while slaves who were leased by their masters retained but a small portion of their earnings, ambitious bond artisans who put in long hours enjoyed the possibility of keeping the bulk of their earnings. "At the Christmas holidays," observed a visitor to the South, the "cities and towns are alive with negroes, in their best attire, seeking employment to come."[20]

18. Powers, *Black Charlestonians*, 12–13; Johnson and Roark, *Black Masters*, 175.

19. Philip D. Morgan, *Slave Counterpoint: Black Culture in the Eighteenth-Century Chesapeake and Lowcountry* (Chapel Hill, 1998), 250; Wood, *Women's Work, Men's Work*, 117; Corrigan, "It's A Family Affair," 168.

20. Genovese, *Roll, Jordan, Roll*, 392; Robert S. Starobin, *Industrial Slavery in*

Charleston masters who responded to the revolution in Saint Domingue by assuring themselves that mainland slaves were plump and satisfied were, not surprisingly, cheerfully oblivious to the hazards of self-hire. As far as they could see, self-hire was all to their advantage. The practice required no more exertion on their part than the sending of their slaves out into the city streets, yet it deposited cash into their pocket. Indeed, canny businessmen bent on turning an easy profit demonstrated no more inclination to submit to the remonstrances of state legislators when it came to their slaves than they did in later decades when it came to federal interference in their peculiar institution. As long as their skilled bondmen earned the sums they demanded in exchange for the right, they saw little reason to put a stop to it; a few masters even flogged their slaves if they failed to keep their part of the agreement. As several Charleston bondmen confided to Johann Bolzius, a visiting pastor, the need to raise quick cash often forced them to resort to theft. Most masters, they insisted, "neither knew nor cared how the money handed over to them had been made."[21]

If Carolina authorities frowned on the practice of slaves being hired out by their masters, they flatly refused to sanction an innovation as perilous as self-hire. State law and city ordinance alike banned the practice. But the fines were so paltry, complained Thomas Pinckney, "that the execution of these laws [was] frustrated by public inattention." Masters caught allowing their slaves to hire their own time paid twenty dollars for each infraction. But Charleston lacked a daytime constabulary force to control the practice, and as Pinckney observed, so "many proprietors" engaged in the practice that the laws were all but unenforceable. Only a very few discerning whites saw the danger in allowing chattel slaves to behave as free entrepreneurs. "The evil is he buys the control of his own time from his owner," one Carolinian remarked. Critics focused on the lack of "discipline and surveillance" inherent in self-hire, but they might well have added that most bond craftsmen, while at first content to

---

the Old South (New York, 1970), 135; Eaton, "Slave-Hiring in the Upper South," 672; Boles, Black Southerners, 129.

21. Wood, Women's Work, Men's Work, 101, 107–8.

turn part of their earnings over to their masters, soon wished to pocket their entire salary. As one of Denmark's confidants bragged on the eve of the conspiracy, "he would pay [his master] no more wages, [for] what would the Whites want with wages, [as] they would soon be no more."[22]

If frustrated critics of self-hire found that their shrill warnings failed to put a stop to the practice, it was because white skilled labor remained a scarce commodity. Black artisans determined to raise the agreed-upon sum that would allow them to continue their quasi-free existence frequently resorted to undercutting the prices asked by skilled whites. White artisans responded first by complaining to city authorities, and then by abandoning the state. "Jobbing Negroe Tradesm[e]n" who worked on "their own Account," protested one craftsman in 1783, enjoyed several unfair advantages. Because most black artisans had to pay neither room nor board, they could afford to accept a smaller sum than their free competition. Busy merchants also tended to leave it to their domestic servants to hire the carpenters and bricklayers who repaired their elegant homes, and house slaves, as a group of skilled whites complained, invariably "prefer men of their own color and condition." The result was the gradual emigration of impoverished skilled whites north to Philadelphia or New York, and a black "monopoly" on craft labor.[23]

The constant reallocation of craft labor through the hiring of surplus bondmen from one temporary master to another may have rendered servile labor—an inefficient, antiquated form of labor organization—more compatible with the requirements of urban capitalism, but in the process white masters carelessly ignored fundamental principles of control. If white craftsmen complained about the impact of black competition on their wages, planter commentators discussed the problem not in economic terms, but in statements that implied fear of insubordination and insurrection. When human chattel were employed as free wage earners, one discerning

22. [Pinckney], *Reflections*, 8–9; Wade, *Slavery in the Cities*, 50–52; Confession of Ferguson's Frank, June 1822, RGA, GM, SCDAH.

23. Schweninger, "Slave Independence and Enterprise," 114; Powers, *Black Charlestonians*, 14.

critic observed, they ceased to behave like human chattel. Charleston law, for example, forbade slaves from congregating unsupervised in large numbers, but slaves employed along the docks in effect did so every morning. One astonished visitor to the city, upon observing independent black activity in the Charleston markets, blurted out, but "they are your slaves," as if the cash changing hands left the issue in some doubt.[24]

Planter visitors to the city were right to be concerned. Urban traditions of hired slaves introduced cash into a labor relationship that was supposed to be based upon paternalism. Though the economy of rural South Carolina could be described as seigneurial, a primitive variety of capitalism—a mode of production characterized by free wage labor, or in the context of Charleston, semi-free hired bondmen, and the separation of the black working class from the means of production—had begun to appear in the seaport. The sound of a few coins clinking in the pockets of slaves for hire was also the sound of paternal authority being torn asunder. Although slaves who hired their time had to surrender most of their earnings to their owner, some of their wages remained in their possession, and what little they retained accorded them an incalculable degree of psychological and economic independence. For men raised to believe that the acquisition of any sort of property was impossible, cash was a new and potent symbol of liberty and self-sufficiency.[25]

Masters who seized the greater portion of their slaves' earnings, or failed to observe the deceit behind their servants' polite mask of obedience, little understood the liberating power of cash. Nor did they notice that the growing desire for cash on the part of their slaves fueled an illicit trade in stolen goods. Indeed, the more planter polemicists railed against the practice of slaves earning wages, the more the black community was determined to obtain this forbidden fruit. Unwaged rural slaves who carried their produce to the city

24. Olwell, "Loose, Idle, and Disorderly," 103; Powers, *Black Charlestonians*, 14,
25. E. P. Thompson, "Patrician Society, Plebian Culture," *Journal of Social History* 7 (Summer 1974): 385; Rediker, *Between the Devil and the Deep Blue Sea*, 168, 200; Clement Eaton, *The Growth of Southern Civilization, 1790–1860* (New York, 1961), 270; Larry E. Hudson, Jr., *To Have and To Hold: Slave Work and Family Life in Antebellum South Carolina* (Athens, 1997), 180.

markets on Sunday thought it no sin to supplement their meager earnings by selling items they found left unguarded on the docks— or on their masters' estate. Dilapidated groghouses located in back alleys so infamous that even night watchmen passed them by, housed women always ready to purchase stolen items, or men who made a living by hiring slave rivermen to resale purloined items along Carolina's inland waterways.[26]

Like the illicit trading of produce from the countryside, the traffic in stolen items endangered white hegemony little enough. Free blacks who sold forged passes allowed a few slaves to occasionally slip away from Charleston harbor, but in most cases the slaves and freemen who traded in stolen goods preferred to buy or sell small items that were easy to hide in secret caches. Charleston authorities lacked the manpower to search every boat or wagon entering the city, and rural masters across the Cooper or Santee Rivers learned to ignore the random disappearance of an ax or a hog in the name of maintaining plantation morale. But as an illicit network of communication available to shrewd slaves, the underground economy had the potential to prove disastrous to white control—should a leader arise who wished to use it for purposes other than trafficking in stolen goods.[27]

A greater issue, or at least a more obvious one, was that hiring out placed urban bondmen in contact with the sort of whites whom the patrician class suspected were not exactly supportive of racial controls. Like most seaport towns, Charleston concealed a rich tavern subculture consisting of, as one commentator defined it, "apprentices, servants, slaves, and perhaps some journeymen, laborers, and sailors." This back-alley culture was not in itself revolutionary, for it did not consciously challenge the Southern social order; working people merely wished to gather for a drink or song at the end of the day, and they naturally tended to congregate with those they had labored beside before the sun set. But neither could this waterfront subculture be described as deferential, and the slaves who

26. Wood, *Black Majority,* 216–17; Schweninger, "Slave Independence and Enterprise," 107.

27. Loren Schweninger, "The Underside of Slavery: The Internal Economy, Self-Hire, and Quasi-Freedom in Virginia, 1785–1865," *Slavery and Abolition* 12 (September 1991): 8.

raised their tankard when John Igueshias, a Spanish seafarer, shouted that "he disliked every thing in Charleston but the negroes and sailors" implicitly challenged established notions of the proper relationship between the master race and the unfree. Because much of the money hired slaves earned was used, according to one critic, "in drunkenness and debauchery," city authorities feared that the irreverent words of white sailors or unskilled laborers might transform obsequious bondmen into the "willing instruments of any delusive plan of mischief which may be presented to them."[28]

Many of the complaints about Charleston's street-corner culture came from gentlewomen who merely found the sight of black frolics distasteful. More than a few refined Charlestonians disapproved of the "gangs of drunken and riotous negroes lounging, pitching cents, playing marbles, cursing, and blaspheming" in the hidden courts that spilled out onto the sandy boulevards. But others saw hidden dangers in these noisy assaults on genteel slumber. Waterfront taverns provided covert meeting places for slaves who wished to fence stolen property, purchase a dagger, or obtain a forged pass, and the free blacks and middling whites who operated these secluded grog shops were hardly above trafficking with bondmen if the price was equitable. White shopkeepers, one critic charged, actually "became courteous to the negro and submit to an equality of sociability," an ominous breach of Southern etiquette.[29]

Charleston authorities were especially alarmed at the number of immigrants and transients who passed through the city on the way to other Atlantic ports. Although a good number of foreign nationals settled in the city and quickly adopted Southern attitudes toward racial control, too many immigrant workers remained deeply hostile to the idea of unwaged labor. Foreign seamen who fled hierarchical peasant societies were hardly predisposed to identify with the haughty Carolinian planter class, and London-born artisans who had listened to violent denunciations of "wage slavery" almost from

28. Thompson, "Patrician Society, Plebian Culture," 397; Marcus Rediker, "The American Revolution and Cycles of Rebellion in the Eighteenth-Century Atlantic," Paper presented at the United States Capitol Historical Society, Washington, 1989; Kennedy and Parker, eds., *Official Report*, Appendix, v–vi; [Pinckney], *Reflections*, 9.

29. Wood, *Women's Work, Men's Work*, 136; Powers, *Black Charlestonians*, 23–24.

the cradle had little use for aristocrats who earned their living off the sweat of others. Typical of these men was Jacob Danders, a German peddlar "of low stature" given to eloquent, if alcohol-inspired outbursts about the cruelty of servitude. Not surprisingly, the City Council routinely sought, and routinely failed, to close down interracial "dram shops." But when one tavern was raided by the night watch, two others, more cleverly concealed, opened nearby, leaving one frustrated editor to suggest that the problem be halted at the source. "[L]et the owners of Negroes shut out, as far as they can, all undue means of furnishing their people with money—the fuel by which the dram shop fire is fed."[30]

Regardless of whom they met or where they spent their wages, slaves were required by law to return to their masters' homes at the end of the evening. Many did not. Charleston was compact enough that hired bondmen could usually return to their owners' house each night, but black craftsmen set to their labors the moment the sun rose, and masters often allowed their trusted slaves to find a room near their place of temporary employment. In the same way that most white shopkeepers did business with slaves if the compensation was adequate, white tenants with a spare room to let and a mortgage to settle rarely paid as much attention to the color of the rentor as they did to the authenticity of the coin. Although yet slaves in the eyes of the law, bondmen who lived away from their masters severed the few remaining ties to their owners. Advocates of tighter slave controls in the wake of the Dominguan revolution found the practice appalling. The ability of hired slaves to rent rooms, observed a group of Columbia mechanics, had "serious and alarming consequences." The least of which was the "pernicious" model of black autonomy living out provided to "other slaves."[31]

The state legislature flatly prohibited masters from allowing their slaves to live away from their house or plantation. As early as 1740, in the aftermath of the Stono River insurrection, colonial legislators forbade slaves "to rent or hire any house, room, [or] store

30. Berlin and Gutman, "Natives and Immigrants," 1189, 1195–97; Kennedy and Parker, eds., *Official Report,* Appendix, vi–vii; Charleston *Southern Patriot,* July 19, 1822.

31. Wood, *Women's Work, Men's Work,* 129; Schweninger, "Slave Independence and Enterprise," 114–15.

[on] his or her own account." But as with the equally illegal tradition of self-hire, living out was hard to prevent in the cities, and except in times of alarm few masters saw much hazard in allowing trusted servants to live close to their place of labor. Despite the unsanitary conditions of most back-alley rentals, no slave wished to exchange the squalor of freedom for a cleaner attic in his owner's house. "The negroes appear to think," sighed one Charleston mistress, "that even if they receive wages, [they] are not free as long as they live with their old masters."[32]

Among those who lived away from their master was one George Wilson. Wilson was a "dark mulatto of large frame" and a pious, devoted slave. Affection for his master, Major John Wilson, together with his literacy and industry as a blacksmith, won George not only the right to "work at his trade, paying to his owner a reasonable amount of wages," but to live away from the major's Broad Street home as well. Denmark came to know Wilson quite well, but they were never close. Denmark rarely trusted the sort of slave who professed to be happy with his condition.[33]

Somewhat more suited to Denmark's temperament and views was Monday Gell, a skilled craftsman who also lived away from his master. An African-born Ibo, Gell learned to "read and write [English] with facility" upon being sold into Charleston. Gell's owner was John Gell, who ran the livery stables at 127 Church Street. Like George Wilson, Gell played the role of the devoted slave, although with Monday it was merely an act, and Denmark quickly befriended Gell as he already had Peter Poyas. Because of his skill as a harness-maker, a skill he perhaps brought with him from West Africa, together with his pretended reverence for his master, John Gell allowed Monday "all the substantial comforts of a free-man." Monday was permitted to hire himself out, and at length, to rent a home and even run a business on Meeting Street in the heart of Charleston.[34]

At about the same time that Denmark met Monday Gell, change

32. Brevard, ed., *An Alphabetical Digest*, 2:243; Wade, *Slavery in the Cities*, 74–75.

33. Pharo, ed., *Reminiscences of Wilson*, 6; W. Hasell Wilson to Rev. Robert Wilson, no date, Charleston Library Society (hereafter CLS).

34. *Directory and Stranger's Guide, 1822*, 42; *Niles' Register*, September 7, 1822, p. 11; Charleston *Courier*, August 23, 1822; Hamilton, *An Account*, 21.

arrived in Joseph Vesey's household in the person of Mary Clodner. Mary, also known as May, was described by one white Charlestonian as "a free East Indian" woman. But Euro-Americans were notoriously inept at characterizing people to the east of Africa, and Mary could have hailed from any port between Persia and Java. Clearly, she was dark enough that a clerk in the land office felt the need to observe that she was free, but her unusual, even romantic background—the Indian population in the United States was then virtually nonexistent—caught the eye of the old captain, whose second wife, Kezia, had passed away several years before. Mary's dark skin barred the path to legal marriage, but by 1796, when the wealthy immigrant purchased an elegant plantation called the Grove on the Ashley River, the clerk noted that "Mary Clodner [was] commonly called May Vesey."[35]

To better conduct his business, Joseph Vesey formally retained his King Street home. But the couple clearly spent time both in the city and on Mary's plantation just north of Charleston. Around 1798, Mary evidently gave birth to a son, whom she named Joseph Vesey after her common-law husband. Perhaps to help her during her confinement, the elder Joseph sent Denmark to reside at the Grove. Living as they did in a major Atlantic port, white Charlestonians were accustomed to unusual sights, but the family at the Grove—a former sea captain from Bermuda, his East Indian mistress, a giant, imperious domestic slave, and an Euro-Indian child church records would later describe as "a free person of color"—comprised as exotic a household as that of Edmond Dantes.[36]

For all that, Denmark's life was about to become stranger still. Despite his new duties at the Grove, Denmark—or Telemaque, as

35. Carl J. Vipperman, *William Lowndes and the Transition of Southern Politics, 1782–1822* (Chapel Hill, 1989), 26; Lease, July 26, 1796, Charleston Deeds, P-6, pp. 467–68, SCDAH.

36. *Directory and Stranger's Guide, 1794,* 40; Register, 1810–1857, p. 260, St. Philip's Protestant Episcopal Church, Charleston, South Caroliniana Library, Columbia (hereafter SCL). The Register records the marriage of "Joseph Vesey, free person of color" to Sarah Duprat in 1818, which means that Joseph was most likely born between 1796 and 1798. At that time Captain Joseph Vesey was the only person with that surname in Charleston.

his mistress continued to call him—spent many of his hours in Charleston, either helping the captain in his East Bay office or visiting friends like Peter Poyas and Monday Gell. Like many a slave and working man, Denmark amused himself by occasionally buying a lottery ticket and dreaming of the life his fantasy riches could buy him. On September 30, 1799, he chanced upon a handbill announcing the "East-Bay Lottery," which would "commence drawing" on October 7. Denmark bought a ticket, number 1884, and probably thought no more about it. For the next twelve days, no winner emerged, but on November 9, 1799, the Charleston *City Gazette* announced that the "Thirteenth Day's Drawing" was ticket 1884. The top prize was $1,500, a princely sum that hired slaves like Polydore Faber would take ten years to acquire.[37]

Denmark's first thought was of freedom. His winnings would allow him to buy his freedom, and that of Beck as well. In 1799 prime fields hands sold for $500; bright, literate domestic bondmen in the prime of their life might go for twice that. Money enough would remain to start a small business. For the better part of two decades, Denmark had served the captain and his wives faithfully. Neither Joseph nor Mary had cause to deny him his wish, and neither did. Once more luck was on his side. The state Assembly was then considering draft legislation that gave a panel of "five indifferent freeholders" the authority to veto individual acts of manumission, but the bill was not yet law. In 1799, South Carolina masters yet enjoyed the liberty to free any slave by deed or will.[38]

Considering Denmark's long service, the Veseys might well have accepted a modest sum for their house slave, but the old slave trader was never a soft-hearted businessman. Instead, the captain and his wealthy mistress agreed upon a price of $600. On De-

37. Grimké, *Right on the Scaffold*, 5; Charleston *City Gazette*, October 1, November 9, December 4, December 9, December 11, 1799. The "Thirteenth Day's Drawing" of November 9 was the only $1500 winner in 1799.

38. Hamilton, *An Account*, 17; W. Augustus Low, ed., *Encyclopedia of Black America* (New York, 1981), 764, for the price of South Carolina field hands; Donald J. Senese, "The Free Negro and the South Carolina Courts, 1790–1860," *SCHM* 68 (April 1967): 142; On the law of December 20, 1800, see Brevard, ed., *Alphabetical Digest*, 2:255–56; and Cooper and McCord, eds., *Statutes at Large*, 7:440–43.

cember 31, 1799, the last day of the eighteenth century, Denmark handed Mary Clodner more than one-third of his winnings, and Mary handed Denmark his freedom papers. With the stroke of a pen, Mary "manumitted, released and from the yoke of Servitude set free and discharged a certain negro man named Telemaque." Joseph Vesey "personally appeared" and signed the document as witness.[39]

After seventeen years a Charleston slave, Denmark prepared to begin yet another new life, this time as a free man of color. If the captain's dating was accurate, Denmark was thirty-three years of age, old in a time when most African American males lived only to their mid-thirties.[40] But the powerful and determined freedman had no intentions of dying young. Like Monday Gell and other slaves who hired their talent and muscle and conscientiously saved for the future, Denmark anticipated a long and prosperous life. Inspired by the aspirations of friends like Polydore Faber, who pocketed their wages and rarely saw their owners—and perhaps by his own occasional self-hire along the docks—Denmark had already achieved a degree of psychological and economic independence from the master class. All that remained was to use his remaining $900 to buy his family and start a business. Perhaps caught up in the optimism of the moment, he believed that might not be difficult. But if he could not purchase their freedom, he would have to find another way.

39. Emancipation Deed, December 31, 1799, Miscellaneous Records, Vol. 3M, pp. 427–28, SCDAH.

40. Between 1820 and 1830, the life expectancy for black males, slave or free, was 34.1 years. See Jack Ericson Eblen, "New Estimates of the Vital Rates of the United States Black Population During the Nineteenth Century," *Demography* 11 (May 1974): 304, 309.

Chapter Four

Freedom
1800–1817

ON JANUARY 1, 1800, the first day of the new century, Denmark strolled the streets of Charleston a free man. Brawny, sophisticated, and literate, if no longer young in a century when black men grew old long before their time, the newly-freed man had great expectations regarding his future. He was, in the words of Archibald Grimké, a Charleston mulatto and Denmark's earliest biographer, "in possession of a fairly good education—was able to read and write, and to speak with fluency the French and English languages." As a former cabin boy, he had sailed the Atlantic and "obtained a wealth of valuable experience" that few Charlestonians could match.[1] Were he a white man with $900 to his name, there would be no impediment to what he might accomplish; Andrew Jackson, born on the South Carolina frontier in the year of Denmark's birth, began his plantation empire in the Tennessee wilderness with far less capital.

But a white man he was not. Over the next seventeen years of his life—the same amount of time that he had endured as a Charleston slave—Denmark would discover that freedom was a precious

1. Grimké, *Right on the Scaffold*, 6.

commodity that Euro-Americans reserved for themselves. No matter how hard he labored or how desperately he tried to prove his worth to the master class, most white Carolinians regarded ambitious former slaves as a danger to the social order. Restrictive city ordinances designed to drive free blacks from the state circumscribed his earning potential, as did the inexpensive labor supplied by bondmen who hired their time. As a dark-skinned freeman, Denmark would even find that most of Charleston's free community of color—the majority of whom were of mixed ancestry—looked not to the black community as a source of solidarity but rather sought to cultivate their former masters and white fathers (who were often one and the same) in hopes of sustaining their elite status. As a former slave in a slave society, as a man of Africa in a light-skinned free community, Denmark was condemned to remain a stranger in a strange land.

On that New Year's Day, the total free African-American population for the entire state stood only at 3,185. Put another way, just 2.1 percent of Carolina's black population had discovered the hidden path to freedom. If unfree labor was on the decline in the border South—in that same year, 15.6 percent of Maryland's African-American population was free—slavery was firmly entrenched in the lower seacoast states.[2]

That meant that an unusually small number of Carolina blacks of Denmark's day were permitted to experience his first unique act of freedom: the taking of a surname. Although plantation slaves occasionally adopted family names for use among themselves, few masters wished to bestow upon their human property the sense of dignity a surname implied. In the kinship-conscious South, family connections conferred respect and rank; but slaves were denied both. Kinship among slaves had no standing in the law. For most African-Americans, therefore, the adoption of a surname was a defiant act of personal liberation. For black fathers, it served as a public announcement of patrilineal authority in a country that defined the status of black children by the condition of their mother. For

2. Ira Berlin, *Slaves Without Masters: The Free Negro in the Antebellum South* (New York, 1974), 47; Low, ed., *Encyclopedia of Black America*, 764.

Denmark, who was both a father and a son, the taking of a surname reversed the process of his family's enslavement, just as the removal of Ashanti names had once symbolized the sale of his parents into captivity in St. Thomas.[3]

Not surprisingly, most freedpersons chose to put as much linguistic distance as possible between themselves and their former masters. Very few embraced their previous owner's surname; to the north in Philadelphia, only nineteen of the 270 bondpersons liberated between 1770 and 1790 selected the family name of their old master. But Philadelphia, with its rapidly growing free black community, was decidedly not Charleston. With so few free people of color in the Southern coastal region, white Carolinians would be Denmark's main customers and clients, regardless of what profession he might choose. A wealthy patron, or at least a linguistic tie to an established businessman like Captain Vesey, could help immeasurably. Perhaps even now Denmark felt strangely bound to his old Calypso, who had rescued him from the sugar islands and now agreed to his liberation. Whatever his motivation, Denmark Vesey was the name he settled upon, and Vesey became the surname his sons inherited.[4]

For a good many Southern freedmen, Northern cities, and particularly Philadelphia, beckoned with their thriving black communities and economic opportunities. Perhaps, however, Vesey believed that the captain's name and the better part of two decades in Charleston presented a more realistic chance of success than starting over in an unknown city. Undoubtedly his family also tied him to South Carolina. He almost certainly attempted to purchase Beck and their children, but evidently his remaining lottery winnings were insufficient to compel John Barker to sell a black woman to her husband. That meant that although free and reasonably wealthy, Vesey could neither liberate his family nor even reside in the same house with them.

3. Charles Joyner, *Down By the Riverside: A South Carolina Slave Community* (Urbana, 1984), 221; White, *Somewhat More Independent*, 192; Gary B. Nash, *Forging Freedom: The Formation of Philadelphia's Black Community, 1720–1840* (Cambridge, Mass., 1989), 80.

4. Boles, *Black Southerners*, 43; Nash, *Forging Freedom*, 85; John C. Inscoe, "Carolina Slave Names: An Index to Acculturation," *JSH* 49 (November 1983): 550.

The forced separation of husband and wife inflicted enormous psychological trauma on even the strongest of marriages. Too often, such cross-city relationships, in which white master and not black husband laid first claims on a woman's time and attention, snapped under the pressure of anger and resentment. Not long after obtaining his freedom, the relationship between Vesey and Beck began to deteriorate. The gulf between his initial expectations as a freeman with ready capital and the cruel reality of his wife's continuing servile status inevitably proved too great. Never permitted the distinction of a state-sanctioned marriage, Vesey now used what bondpersons typically regarded as a dehumanizing legal flaw—the absence of a marriage license—to escape an unhappy relationship that had been irreparably damaged by white authority.[5]

Yet Vesey neither abandoned his family nor neglected his responsibilities to his children. Long after his first marriage collapsed, Vesey employed his step-daughter Sarah (Beck's child from an earlier relationship) as a "cook" in his household. Sarah was in later years the slave of John Paul, a grocer who lived on Broad Street, and the wages she received from her step-father allowed her to purchase those goods her master denied her. Vesey also remained close to his sons, especially Sandy, whom John Paul had sold to John Schnell, a fellow grocer who resided at 74 Church Street. Presumably, Vesey later trained his son Robert, the future architect, in the art of woodworking, and as adults, both Sandy and Robert bore the surname of Vesey.[6]

Even so, the determined and imperious Vesey quickly earned the reputation for being as demanding of the women in his life as he was protective of his children. Eighteenth-century men, whether of African or European descent, were imbued with patriarchal notions of family structure. The one trait that the two Veseys—captain and carpenter alike—shared was the belief that it was their paternal responsibility to dominate their households. Vesey's close friend Monday Gell later observed that while the slave community regarded

5. Kolchin, *American Slavery*, 126; Stevenson, *Life in Black and White*, 255.

6. Testimony of William Paul at trial of Denmark Vesey, June 1822, in Kennedy and Parker, eds., *Official Report*, 85; *Directory and Stranger's Guide, 1819*, 83.

him "as a man of great capacity," they also thought him "possess[ed of] a bloody disposition." Even Gell, Vesey's oldest confidant, could not with certainty recall how many women Vesey had been involved with. "He had," Gell once remarked," in the course of his life, several wives."[7]

Modern historians have speculated that Vesey practiced polygamy. No evidence exists to support the theory, although it is certainly possible. Whether his origins lay in Africa or in St. Thomas, Vesey would have been quite familiar with the ancient practice of wealthy men taking as many wives as they could support. Both traditional African religions and Islam, which began to arrive on the Gold Coast in the mid-eighteenth century, sanctioned the custom. Christian concepts of monogamy helped to extinguish the practice in the Americas, although in some parts of the South it was probably more widespread than historians have commonly thought. The scarcity of marriageable men in urban centers and coastal areas depopulated by the internal slave trade, together with the rise of matrifocality—in which the forced absence of bond fathers gave mothers a dominant role over their children—occasionally allowed for the continuation of old world mores, especially in lowcountry South Carolina, where the bond population included large numbers of West African natives.[8]

Although certainly possible, polygamy was probably not the case here. In a time of high female mortality, especially among urban bondwomen, Vesey could easily have united with the "several" wives

7. Confession of Monday Gell, July 23, 1822, RGA, GM, SCDAH. In Kennedy and Parker, eds., *Official Report,* 98, the words "several wives" is misprinted as "seven wives." John Lofton, who was unable to use the original documents compiled in the Governor's Report, repeated the claim that Vesey had seven wives. See his *Insurrection in South Carolina,* 76.

8. In addition to Lofton, cited above, William Freehling, *Reintegration of American History,* 41, suggests that Vesey practiced polygamy, as does John O. Killens in his novel *Great Gittin' Up Morning* (Boston, 1972), 27. On polygamy in North America, see Stevenson, *Life in Black and White,* 233; Claire Robertson, "Africa Into the Americas? Slavery and Women, the Family, and the Gender Division of Labor," in Gaspar and Hine, eds., *More Than Chattel,* 11–12; Lorena S. Walsh, "A 'Place in Time' Regained: A Fuller History of Colonial Chesapeake Slavery Through Group Biography," in Hudson, ed., *Working Toward Freedom,* 30 note 52.

Gell knew about and yet remain monogamous. After all, Vesey far exceeded the average life expectancy for black males in antebellum America, and his thirty-nine-year residence in Charleston granted him more than enough time to sequentially marry two or three women. Vesey's unfortunate luck in falling in love with slave women meant that his wives' masters—despite his own freedom and initial prosperity—could destroy these fragile consangual relationships at any moment.

Vesey's second relationship may have been with a Charleston woman named Dolly, the slave of Elizabeth Taomer. Several years after his death, Dolly and her four children were sold for $1,100 by the deceased Taomer's heirs to John and Thomas Gates. One of Dolly's children, Charlotte, was a girl. The rest were boys; the oldest, named Denmark, is the only other person with that name to appear in Charleston's antebellum public record besides Vesey. In West Africa, children typically carried the forenames of their grandparents. But by the late eighteenth century, Africans in the South began to adopt the Euro-American tradition of naming the oldest son after his father. Because fathers were more likely to live apart from their children in matrifocal Charleston, naming a boy for his father served as a defiant announcement of paternal authority (when in reality very little authority could be exerted). By Vesey's day, more than one in four slave households included a son who carried his father's forename. Very few daughters, on the other hand, bore their mother's name; their residence in their mother's household adequately established the maternal tie.[9]

Toward the end of his long life, Vesey married yet again, proba-

---

9. Bill of Sale, September 3, 1825, Vol. 5A, p. 547, SCDAH; Cheryll Ann Cody, "Naming, Kinship, and Estate Dispersal: Notes on Slave Family Life on a South Carolina Plantation, 1786–1833," *William and Mary Quarterly* 39 (January 1982): 203; Sobel, *World They Made Together*, 156; Herbert S. Gutman, *The Black Family in Slavery and Freedom, 1750–1925* (New York, 1976), 190–91. Dolly's remaining sons were named London and Gabriel. Although Gabriel was a common name, it also perhaps indicated that the literate Vesey was aware of the black Virginia revolutionary, who was hanged in 1800. In Robert Jordan's novel *The Fallon Pride* (New York, 1981), 97, interestingly enough, Vesey is quite familiar with Gabriel, whom he calls his "hero."

bly for a third time. Susan Vesey was born a slave around 1795 but somehow obtained her liberty during the course of her life; perhaps her husband bought her freedom following their betrothal.[10] Assuming they married around 1815, as Susan approached the age of twenty, Vesey would have been in his late forties. Susan was at least twenty-eight years younger than her husband, and only twenty-seven-years-old at the time of his execution. In 1821, tax collectors listed her under the name "Susan Vesey" and characterized her as a "free negro" residing at 20 Bull Street. Vesey's friend Bacchus later remembered seeing Susan "at Denmark's house," where she and "two or three [other] women" took in laundry and "ironing."[11]

As the only one of Vesey's women to carry his surname, it may be that upon obtaining her liberty, Susan and Denmark ritualized their union in one of Charleston's established churches. A small number of wealthy free mulattoes obtained a legal marriage license from the state, but more commonly, the document they obtained came not from secular authorities but an established clergyman. The records of the two churches that Vesey is known to have attended—the Second Presbyterian Church and Charleston's African Methodist Episcopal congregation—are respectively incomplete and nonexistent. Yet it is likely that as free people, Susan and her husband had their marriage solemnized in one of the city's churches.

White authorities later insisted that "to his numerous wives and children," Vesey "displayed the haughty and capricious cruelty of an Eastern Bashaw." The judges who sentenced him to hang for the crime of abolitionism were hardly, of course, unbiased observers. There was more than a touch of hypocrisy on the part of white Carolina patriarchs—who rarely behaved with liberal charity where their wives were concerned—in denouncing Vesey as "impetuous and domineering."[12] Yet their judgment cannot be completely dismissed, for it is similar to Monday Gell's forthright characterization

10. Carter G. Woodson, ed., *Free Negro Heads of Families in the United States in 1830* (Washington, D.C., 1925), 157. (In 1830 census takers listed Susan Vesey as "age 35–36," which means she was born around 1795.)

11. State Free Negro Capitation Tax Books, Charleston, 1821, p. 30, SCDAH; Second confession of Bacchus, July 13, 1822, RGA, GM, SCDAH.

12. Hamilton, *An Account,* 17.

of Vesey's relationship with women. As a militant abolitionist, Vesey was a radical, but he must be understood in the context of his own day, and not by late twentieth century standards. Very few men generally characterized as radical during the age of revolution, from Thomas Jefferson to Georges Danton to Simón Bolívar, wished to challenge traditional conventions regarding family structure or much desired to turn the world of gender upside down. Had Vesey, who from his earliest years was raised amidst black and white patriarchal ideals, *not* attempted to dominate his wives, he would indeed have been a most extraordinary man.[13]

Men of Vesey's generation, however, saw little contradiction in being both domineering *and* loving husbands and fathers. Charleston males of both races believed that a father who failed to achieve mastery over his household failed to fulfill his paternal responsibilities and thus did his sons little favor. Vesey not only dominated his sons, he taught them to be domineering in turn. Although free and relatively "satisfied with his own condition," Vesey confided to Monday Gell that "all his children were [born] slaves, [and] he wished to see what could be done for them."[14] But in teaching his sons to stand up for themselves, Vesey flaunted conventional black wisdom. Prudent slave parents advised their children to be courteous to the master race, for a passive demeanor was a valuable survival technique in the slave community. "Learn them to be Smart and deacent and alow them to Sauce no person," Carolina slave Robert Woodfin urged his wife. But the fact that his children belonged to other men "ate into Vesey's mind," as Archibald Grimké put it, and so when he was allowed to visit them he encouraged his sons to deport themselves with the same pride and self-respect that he exhibited—advice that quite nearly resulted in the death of two of his sons.[15]

Nevertheless, his marriage to Susan lay in the future. Even as

13. Erica Jong's fictional eighteenth century heroine *Fanny* (New York, 1980), 407, said it best: "Alas, most Revolutionaries are none where Women are concern'd."

14. Confession of Monday Gell, July 23, 1822, RGA, GM, SCDAH.

15. Wilma King, "Rais Your Children Up Rite," in Hudson, ed., *Working Toward Freedom*, 144–45; Grimké, *Right on the Scaffold*, 6.

his relationship with Beck began to fail, Vesey was forced to put aside his private cares and attend to the basic necessities of life. As a free man, he now had no place to live. Most likely, he initially boarded with another freeman or a slave for hire, a typical living arrangement for newly liberated people.[16] Thanks to his lottery winnings, Vesey had money enough to establish a separate household. But given his as-yet lack of a chosen occupation, together with his hopes of purchasing Beck and their children, prudence dictated residing with a black family until he was better prepared to join the free world. Only in later years did Vesey rent a house of his own, a modest, one-floor structure at 20 Bull Street. Despite published claims made in 1822 that Vesey died a rich man worth nearly $8,000,[17] there is no evidence that he ever owned a *single* piece of property. The house on Bull Street was owned first by attorney George Cross, and later, toward the end of Vesey's life, by Benjamin Ireland, a white carpenter. The fact that Susan Vesey ironed shirts for her white neighbors indicates that together the Veseys earned but a modest income.[18]

Vesey probably settled on Bull Street only after deciding to become a carpenter. Because of the city's growth and the rise of a shipbuilding industry, skilled carpenters—both bond and free—were in great demand. In the month that Vesey won the lottery, Charleston

16. Nash, "Forging Freedom," in Berlin and Hoffman, eds., *Slavery and Freedom,* 35.

17. Charleston *City Gazette,* August 21, 1822.

18. *Directory and Stranger's Guide, 1822,* 109; Wylma Wates to Charles E. Lee, August 29, 1980, Denmark Vesey House File, Charleston County, National Register, SCDAH. Although the city of Charleston now identifies a house currently numbered 56 Bull Street as being the home of Vesey, archivist Wates and architectural restoration consultant Edward F. Turberg demonstrate that the building is not only in the wrong place but was built several decades after Vesey's death. "As a result of my investigation of the house at 56 Bull Street," Turberg writes, "I feel certain that the present structure was not on the site during the residence of Denmark Vesey." The "latter building relates more closely with neighboring houses constructed after 1830 and before 1850 than any other period." See Turberg to Beckie Johnson, May 14, 1980, Denmark Vesey House File, Charleston County, National Register, SCDAH. Wates's research suggests that 20 Bull Street was four or five houses east of the private home currently numbered 56 Bull Street.

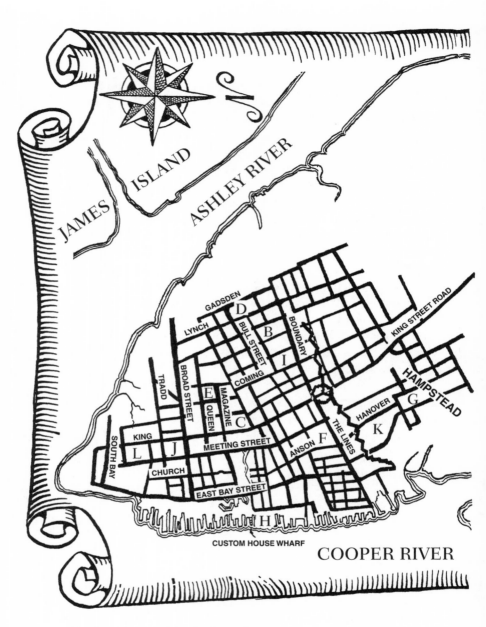

Charleston, 1822. *Map by the author.*

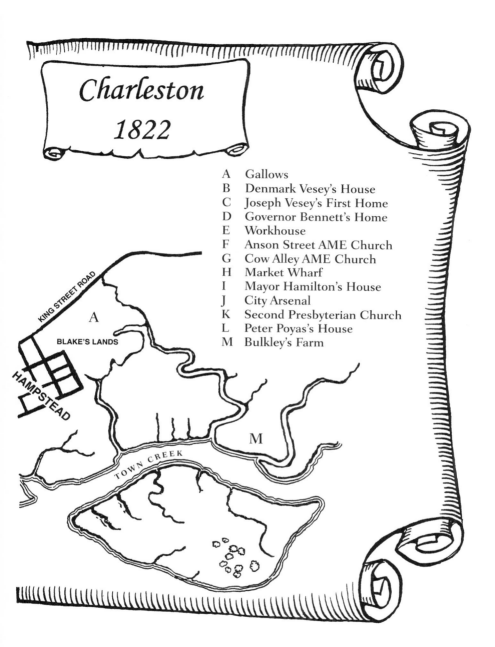

Charleston
1822

A Gallows
B Denmark Vesey's House
C Joseph Vesey's First Home
D Governor Bennett's Home
E Workhouse
F Anson Street AME Church
G Cow Alley AME Church
H Market Wharf
I Mayor Hamilton's House
J City Arsenal
K Second Presbyterian Church
L Peter Poyas's House
M Bulkley's Farm

KING STREET ROAD

BLAKE'S LANDS

A

HAMPSTEAD

M

TOWN CREEK

newspapers ran advertisements calling for "Twenty Negro Carpenters and Thirty Axmen" to clear timber on Bull's Island for the manufacture "of the frames of two or three brigs or schooners." Freemen who could wield a hammer or pull a saw earned a respectable $1.50 per day. Thomas Bennett, a successful merchant and politician, constructed his lumber mills on the west end of Bull Street, where the avenue poured into the Ashley River. The mills made Bull Street a natural home for men who earned their livelihood in construction. Vesey's neighbors included free mulatto carpenters Richmond Kinloch, Benjamin Marchant, and Robert Smythe. But as Charleston was segregated along lines of class more than race, he lived but a few doors away from white tradesmen as well; Benjamin Ireland, his future landlord, resided nearby, as did rising young attorney James Hamilton.[19]

Money enough Vesey had, but as yet no skill. His early training as a chandler's man was useless now; bright young men with very dark skin had no prospects in Charleston's commercial world, except as chattel. Presumably, Vesey spent some of his remaining winnings to obtain an apprenticeship with an established craftsmen. Perhaps he worked for one of his white neighbors; perhaps instead he apprenticed under "a Free Black" carpenter like Saby Gaillard, who resided two streets south at 3 Wentworth. Certainly the two men grew very close over the years, and in 1822 Gaillard would pay a high price for his friendship.[20]

Because early nineteenth-century builders constructed homes and small shops from handed-down knowledge and local tradition rather than detailed scale drawings, inexperienced youths found apprenticeship in carpentry a quick and easy path to becoming a master craftsman. If Vesey indeed acquired his skills under the tutelage of an established carpenter-contractor like Gaillard, he not only learned to wield the tools of his trade. He was trained also to sketch

19. Charleston *City Gazette*, November 9, 1799; Lofton, *Insurrection in South Carolina*, 76; Wylma Wates to Charles E. Lee, August 29, 1980, Denmark Vesey House File, Charleston County, National Register, SCDAH.

20. *Directory and Stranger's Guide, 1819*, 45; *Directory and Stranger's Guide, 1822*, 104; State Free Negro Capitation Tax Books, Charleston, 1821, p. 12, SCDAH; Charleston *Mercury*, July 23, 1822.

crude plans that showed the placement of doors and windows, and to gauge the price of materials and wages of whatever number of hired-journeyman laborers he might require to complete a commission.[21]

As a free black, Vesey had to purchase a special license to conduct business (which white Carolinians were not obliged to procure). He opened his own establishment, hiring other free men of color to work in what he grandly called his "shop," the front room of his cramped Bull Street home. Having come by his fortune and freedom rather late in life, Vesey threw his enormous energies into his fledgling enterprise. According to Israel Nesbitt, the great-grandson of Vesey's friend Robert Nesbitt, Denmark labored "every day at de trade of carpenter" and "soon become much [re]spected" and "esteem[ed] by de white folks." Even James Hamilton later conceded that as a businessman Vesey was "distinguished for [his] great strength and activity." In the eyes of the black community, Hamilton added, Vesey "was always looked up to with awe and respect."[22]

Awe and respect, unhappily, neither paid the rent nor fed Vesey's hungry families. Despite his freedom, Vesey soon discovered that the shackles of slavery still bound him close to poverty. Free carpenters, black and white alike, faced economic competition from bond craftsmen who hired their time, and it was a competition free tradesmen lost more often than not. Because they typically resided with their masters, slave carpenters—who were more numerous in Charleston than either free black or white woodworkers—paid neither rent nor taxes nor licensing fees. Yet freemen like Vesey and Gaillard paid all three, and so they struggled just to put a plate of food before their children. White artisans responded to unwaged

21. Jack Larkin, *The Reshaping of Everyday Life, 1790–1840* (New York, 1988), 106–8; William J. Rorabaugh, *The Craft Apprentice: From Franklin to the Machine Age* (New York, 1986), 60. Conventional wisdom holds that Denmark learned carpentry while still a slave, but no evidence exists to support the theory that Joseph Vesey ever hired him out. Indeed, the captain's thriving business surely kept Denmark tied to his master's economic interests. Carpentry was simply the most common enterprise for unskilled young men to enter.

22. Higginson, *Black Rebellion*, 265; Israel Nesbitt in Rawick, ed., *American Slave*, Supplement, Series 1, Vol. 11:261; Hamilton, *An Account*, 17.

competition and the subsequent marginalization of their labor by abandoning Charleston for Philadelphia or New York. But that option was not available to a man whose slave families chained him to South Carolina. Instead, the Veseys sought to compete with cheap, bond labor by working six days a week, taking in ironing, and trying their luck: long after winning his freedom in 1799, Vesey persisted in scanning "the Newspaper for Lottery Reports as he had tickets in one."[23]

If craftsmen like Vesey looked to the white community to ameliorate their condition, they were to be sadly disappointed. Too many prominent citizens enhanced their incomes by hiring out their surplus laborers, and too few white Charlestonians much cared about the economic conditions facing former slaves. Indeed, as more dark-skinned men like Vesey entered the ranks of freedom, a position previously held only by the mixed-race offspring of the planter class, the white community began to rethink the relative autonomy they once had accorded the small number of freemen. Proslavery polemicists like E. C. Holland increasingly denounced "the existence of Free Blacks among us, as the greatest and most deplorable evil." Vesey hoped that his industry and ambition would win him benefactors in the business district, and in some instances it did, but political theorists like Holland regarded struggling black artisans as little more than "a perpetual source of irritation" to the master class. "Our slaves, when they look around them and see persons of their own color enjoying" rights and "privileges beyond their own condition," Hollard fumed, "naturally become dissatisfied with their lot." Because many white Carolinians regarded the ambitions of former slaves as a basis for trouble, it made scant sense to enforce city ordinances against hiring out if such enforcement only served to add to free black prosperity.[24]

If anything, the men who drafted Charleston's city ordinances

23. Thomas Holt, *Black Over White: Negro Political Leadership in South Carolina during Reconstruction* (Urbana, 1977), 60–61; Rorabaugh, *Craft Apprentice,* 185; Wikramanayake, *A World in Shadow,* 72; Examination of Evans's George, August 3, 1822, RGA, GM, SCDAH.

24. Wright, *African Americans in the Early Republic,* 144; E. C. Holland, *A Refutation of the Calumnies Circulated Against the Southern and Western States* (Charleston, 1822), 83.

openly conspired to drive freemen like Vesey out of the state. Ironically, free black marketeers, unlike their enslaved counterparts, could not peddle their produce without first purchasing a license. No freeman, unless he was a fisherman, could own a boat, an ordinance that prevented black pilots and seamen from starting their own business. Charleston even placed a limit on how much a freeman like Vesey could earn in a single day. All of these codes were occasionally evaded; black carpenters frequently earned more than the $1.00 per day set by the City Council. But the fines for those who evaded the law were stiff—five dollars for each infraction or confinement in the Workhouse—and city fathers invariably resorted to strict enforcement in times of slave unrest or national danger. As Archibald Grimké, himself subject to some of these restrictions, said of Vesey: "Wherever he moved or wished to move he was met and surrounded by the most galling and degrading social and civil conditions and proscriptions."[25]

As if burdening newly-liberated men—who typically walked out of their masters' doors with nothing more than the clothes on their backs—with licensing fees was not hinderance enough, the state legislature added to their burden by levying a special tax on their freedom. Like the city ordinances that restricted their access to lucrative occupations, the special tax was designed to drive liberated bondpeople from the state's borders. First passed by the colonial Assembly in 1756, the levy on "all free Negroes, Mulattoes and Mestizos" (persons of Afro-Spanish or Afro-Native descent) varied in rate from year to year. By Vesey's day, the state required payment of two dollars per year on both men and women between the ages of fifteen and fifty. For tax collectors, actually finding Charleston's free blacks at home was no small task, for many freedpersons made it their business to avoid white authorities. But like the occupational restrictions that kept them near-paupers, the tax remained on the books. For Susan Vesey, the tax served as a yearly reminder that she was officially unwelcome in what was probably the state of her birth.[26]

Hindered in his business endeavors by white authorities, Vesey

25. Wikramanayake, *A World in Shadow,* 102; Grimké, *Right on the Scaffold,* 7.
26. Berlin, *Slaves Without Masters,* 97; State Free Negro Capitation Tax Books, Charleston, 1811, 1821–1822.

relied on the goodwill of his white clientele and his own hard-won reputation for industry. Almost certainly, Vesey followed the example of many former slaves by relying upon the patronage (and business contacts) of his former master. When Mary Clodner Vesey died in late 1801, the old captain moved back into Charleston, where he remained a respected merchant. Because Mary died intestate, "the goods, rights, and credits of the said deceased," including her plantation on the Ashley River, all passed "unto the said Joseph Vesey." The captain was never one for solitary mourning, and now that he was a man of considerable fortune Charleston's elite took proper notice. On October 9, 1803, the captain acquired his fourth wife, Maria Blair, a wealthy widow.[27]

A decade later, as the aged captain approached his sixty-eighth year, he and Maria purchased a handsome plantation of 200 acres in Christ Church Parish, although they retained a townhome at 41 Anson Street. At about the same time, Joseph Vesey, his son by the late Mary Clodner—as yet identified by city authorities as a free man of color—married a freewoman named Sarah and established a residence nearby at 37 Market Street. Because Denmark had to depend upon both Joseph Veseys for patronage, he often had to resume his distasteful old role of dutiful family retainer. The necessity of remaining in the good graces of the white business community meant that prudent free blacks had to maintain their cultural distance from the often-rowdy slave community. In short, because they could achieve little more than a marginal existence, former slaves, despite their reputation as dangerous symbols of black liberty, proved to be a conservative force in Charleston society.[28]

Denmark Vesey was the exception to that rule, but then Den-

27. John B. Boles, *The South Through Time: A History of an American Region* (Englewood Cliffs, N.J., 1995), 218–19; Mary Clodner Vesey, January 15, 1802, Letters of Administration, Probate, RR, p. 360, Charleston County, SCDAH; Charleston *Times*, October 10, 1803.

28. *Directory and Stranger's Guide, 1819,* 93; Land Deed, February 16, 1815, John McCrady Plats, #5565, SCDAH; State Free Negro Capitation Tax Books, Charleston, 1821, SCDAH, 30. This Sarah Vesey could not have been Beck Vesey's daughter, who belonged to John Paul in 1822. At the time of her marriage to Joseph

mark Vesey was ever the atypical freeman. It was not merely that his size and multilingual brilliance stood him apart from most Charlestonians, it was that by virtue of his African parents, Vesey's dark appearance was strikingly different from the overwhelming majority of Carolina freemen, most of whom were mulattoes. Over the course of the eighteenth century, a three-caste system of racial stratification emerged in Charleston that gave the port a uniquely Caribbean appearance. Perched atop the city's racial hierarchy was the white minority; African laborers and their descendants occupied the bottom rank. Precariously balanced in between were the light-skinned freepersons of color, most of whom had been granted their freedom by their white fathers. Painfully aware that they owed their special privileges to sexual transgressions of the master class, the free browns—as they styled themselves—sought to strengthen their delicate position by eagerly assimilating into white society. As a dark-skinned man of Africa who literally gambled his way into freedom, Vesey was an anomaly among Charleston freemen.[29]

Like Vesey, many of the freemen were refugees from the Caribbean. Some were the offspring of privileged servants who migrated from the British islands of Barbados and Jamaica as domestics to the early Carolina settlers. But most arrived from Saint Domingue during Vesey's early years as a Charleston slave. The prosperous French colony had been home to a socially-powerless caste of wealthy *gens de couleur*, many of whom—as young Telemaque was certainly quite aware—were themselves wealthy sugar planters and slaveholders. As a flood tide of refugees from the rebellious island—free mulattoes and Africans alike—began to wash into Charleston harbor, the light-skinned emigrés made common cause with native-born browns in hopes of distinguishing themselves from the liberated Africans by publicly emphasizing their mixed ancestry.[30]

Vesey in 1818, Sarah was listed as a "free person of color." See Register, 1810–1857, St. Philip's Protestant Episcopal Church, Charleston, SCL, p. 260.

29. Powers, *Black Charlestonians*, 58–59; Holt, *Black Over White*, 61.

30. E. Horace Fitchett, "The Origin and Growth of the Free Negro Population of Charleston, South Carolina," *Journal of Negro History* 26 (October 1941): 434; Berlin, *Slaves Without Masters*, 58.

To illustrate, perhaps even to exacerbate, the extent of African American disunity in the Palmetto state, the Reverend Thomas
Frost, the white pastor of St. Philip's Protestant Episcopal Church,
encouraged several brown members of his flock to create an exclusive mulatto fraternal organization. Founded by five "free brown
men" on November 1, 1790, the Brown Fellowship Society became
the ultimate symbol of racial schism. By its charter, the Society was
open to no more than fifty men; each had to pay a prohibitive initi-
ation fee of fifty dollars in addition to monthly dues. The general
fund supported aged members who were too ill to work. Upon their
death, members were guaranteed an impressive funeral and intern-
ment in the Society's private cemetery. But social advancement and
economic security for the colored elite, not philanthropy for the
slave majority, was the goal of the organization. Despite its motto of
"Charity and Benevolence," the Society existed for the purpose of
drawing biologically-constructed lines of demarcation between the
wealthy browns and Charleston's sizable black community, whether
bond or free.[31]

For ambitious freemen like Vesey, the Society's rhetoric, perhaps
even more than its very existence, was galling. Determined to maintain their tenuous position between the white minority above them
and what they derisively dubbed "the backward race" below,[32] the
browns manipulated every conceivable social opportunity to ingrati-
ate themselves with their fathers and former masters and prove that
they were a self-segregating and trustworthy caste. The master race
held the whip hand, "and as our [colored] fathers allided themselves
with them," conceded one Society member, the browns "had their
influence and protection." Browns assiduously avoided the city's
emerging black churches and instead flocked to congregations dominated by white parishioners. Because of the role it played in the So-

31. Michael P. Johnson and James L. Roark, "'A Middle Ground': Free Mulattoes and the Friendly Moralist Society of Antebellum Charleston," *Southern Studies*
21 (Fall 1982): 247–48; Johnson and Roark, *Black Masters*, 212; Holt, *Black Over
White*, 65. (In this study, the contemporaneous terms "colored" and "brown" are used
in reference to African Americans of mixed ancestry, whether mulatto, quadroon, or
octoroon.)

32. Holt, *Black Over White*, 65–66.

ciety's founding, browns traditionally purchased pews in St. Philip's Episcopal Church; among its congregants could be found the old captain's mixed-race son Joseph Vesey, who was married before its altar in 1818.[33]

On rare occasions, some prosperous mulattoes successfully passed over into the white community. The family of Gideon Gibson, a free man of color, was only one example. Gibson's mixed-race daughter married an English immigrant of considerable means, and after his death, she remarried one of the richest planters in the Carolina lowcountry. The life of James Pendarvis also demonstrated how wealth could wash away the stain of Africa. James was the son of Saint Paul's Parish planter Joseph Pendarvis and Parthena, Joseph's black mistress. The younger Pendarvis married a respectable but poor white woman named Catherine Rumph, and both of their daughters married prosperous white planters.[34]

The next step in all of this was as predictable as it was tragic. In a slaveholding society, the ownership of other persons connoted both upper-class status and demonstrated fealty to the established order. Shortly after being emancipated themselves, the free colored aristocracy began to purchase Africans. Admittedly, a few dark-skinned freedmen owned bond servants, and some modern accounts wrongly accuse Denmark Vesey of becoming a slave owner.[35] But in Charleston, fully eighty-five percent of those African Americans who owned slaves were free mulattoes. Outside the city, Pendarvis owned 150 slaves. Most Charleston browns nested together around Coming Street, but even in Vesey's Bull Street neighborhood, the ownership of slaves by prosperous mulattoes was commonplace. Robert Smythe, the wealthy mixed-race carpenter who lived a few doors away at 15 Bull Street, owned six slaves. Sophia Kinloch, the mulatto wife of Vesey's associate Richmond Kinloch, purchased a twelve-year-old black girl to help her with the domestic chores. The fact that afflu-

33. Johnson and Roark, *Black Masters,* 217; Koger, *Black Slaveholders,* 166; Register, 1810–1857, St. Philip's Protestant Episcopal Church, Charleston, SCL, p. 260.

34. Philip D. Morgan, *Slave Counterpoint: Black Culture in the Eighteenth Century Chesapeake and Lowcountry* (Chapel Hill, 1998), 488–89.

35. David Clark, "Denmark Vesey: Portrait of a Rebel," Charleston *Post and Courier,* September 30, 1996.

ent mulattoes ruthlessly assisted the master race in the destruction
of black families taught the slave community that their light-skinned
neighbors were questionable allies at best. For Denmark Vesey, who
had first learned this unhappy lesson as a boy on St. Thomas, the
fact that many men would do whatever they thought necessary to
survive in their unforgiving world was a reminder that he would always have to be on his guard, even on Bull Street.[36]

The determination of wealthy mulattoes to identify with their
fathers' caste was evidenced in other ways as well. The free brown
aristocracy not only owned slaves, on occasion they even fought to
protect Charleston's social structure. Conscious of the fact that their
mixed ancestry made them suspect in the eyes of many proslavery
theorists, who devoutly believed that African blood was both dis-
similar and inferior to the fluid in Euro-American veins, Carolina
mulattoes sought to prove their worth in times of crisis. During the
War of 1812, at a time when Chesapeake slaves fled toward the British invaders, Charleston mulattoes helped man the defense of the
city. Five years later, in 1817, the Brown Society publicly expelled
a member who was implicated in a slave conspiracy. The cost of
white protection, one Society member admitted, was that the colored elite "had to be in accord with [whites] and stand for what they
stood for." As recompense for their service against Britain, city magistrates exempted free mulattoes from the ordinance requiring the
attendance of a white man at any meeting of more than six people
of color.[37]

Due as much to temperament as to pigmentation, Vesey had little to do with Charleston's mulatto caste. He lived among them,
conducted business with them, and paid his respects as they strolled
past the porch of his modest Bull Street home. But he rarely socialized with them, and they rarely socialized with him, or anybody who
resembled him. Free mulattoes like Richmond Kinloch not only

36. Robert L. Harris, Jr., "Charleston's Free Afro-American Elite: The Brown
Fellowship Society and the Humane Brotherhood," *SCHM* 82 (October 1981): 304;
Koger, *Black Slaveholders,* 173; Johnson and Roark, *Black Masters,* 204; Powers,
Black Charlestonians, 50.

37. Holt, *Black Over White,* 66; Robert Brent Toplin, "Between Black and
White: Attitudes Toward Southern Mulattoes," *JSH* 45 (May 1979): 196.

married free mulatto women, they gazed condescendingly on free-men like Vesey who married unfree and unwisely. Because he lacked the requisite single drop of "European blood," Vesey and his African fellows could neither join their Society nor dine at their table. George Wilson, an acquaintance of Vesey's and a Brown Society member, once conceded that he had "never seen" either Vesey or Monday Gell "at my Society," for as sons of Africa, they "would not have been admitted."[38]

The tiny number of African freemen found themselves in a most difficult position. Slaves who hired their time around the city cut deeply into Vesey's meager profits, yet the wealthy mulattoes who lorded themselves above him in Charleston's peculiar caste system proved to be of little assistance. Some mulatto tradesmen conducted business with him, and perhaps one of their number even accepted Vesey as an apprentice. But when they had the op-portunity, free mulattoes kept their transactions among themselves; the Brown Fellowship Society, which barred its doors to him, existed for the self-improvement and economic advancement of themselves alone. Mulattoes looked to their former masters for protection and assistance, and their resulting willingness to inform against the black majority only reenforced the suspicion in the white commu-nity that industrious exslaves like Vesey ultimately served as a dan-gerous model of black resilience. "An amalgamation of the races produced us," sighed one Society member, and the hostility of blacks and the suspicion of whites was "the whirlpool which threatens to swallow us up."[39]

As a result, even after winning his freedom, Vesey continued to associate with the slave community of which he had so long been a

38. Johnson and Roark, *Black Masters,* 213–15; Kennedy and Parker, eds., *Offi-cial Report,* 116. Kimberly S. Hanger suggests that in New Orleans, the only other Southern port with a sizeable free African-American population, free people of color also tended to choose a spouse "with similar skin coloring. Of the ninety-three marriages recorded in the black registers between 1777 and 1803 in which both parties were libres, seventy-one (over three-quarters) involved partners of the same phenotype." See *Bounded Lives, Bounded Places: Free Black Society in Colo-nial New Orleans, 1769–1803* (Durham, N.C., 1997), 94–95.

39. Fraser, *Charleston,* 199–200.

part; after all, his first two wives and all of his children remained property. But Charleston's was not a static slave community. Following the invention of the cotton gin, upcountry agriculturalists pressured the state Assembly to reopen the portal to the Atlantic slave trade, which the legislature had slammed shut in 1787. Lowcountry planters had laborers enough, and state politicians feared the national opprobrium that was sure to follow if South Carolina became the only state to return to African shores. But with the federal prohibition of the traffic looming on the horizon, the state threw open its ports to forced immigration in 1803. By January 1, 1808, when the federal ban went into effect, slavers carried 39,075 more Africans into the state. The impact on Charleston and the surrounding countryside was stunning. In 1820 the region was home to 57,221 slaves and but 19,376 whites. The always tiny free African-American community of 3,615—most of whom were of mixed ancestry—became even less statistically significant when compared to the tidal wave of bonded labor.[40]

This latest influx of chained emigrants meant that dark-skinned freemen, already locked out of the parlors and bedchambers of the brown aristocracy, were fastened ever more closely to the slave community. As the Brown Society exhibited little fellowship toward the psychologically-traumatized newcomers, it fell to rival organizations like the African Association, of which Monday Gell was a leading member, to assist in the cultural transition of enslaved Africans into Carolina's perilous society. Many dark-skinned freemen even wed newly-arrived bondwomen; a few free black men circumvented the laws restricting emancipation by purchasing (but not liberating) their wives and children. Most newly-imported Africans remained slaves while occasional siblings and parents somehow discovered the path to freedom. Vesey's young friend William Garner, for example, a Charleston drayman and the property of the widow Garner, watched his brother Jack Lopez earn his liberty.[41]

40. Jordan, *White Over Black*, 318–19; Donald G. Morgan, *Justice William Johnson: The First Dissenter* (Columbia, 1954), 128; Frey, *Water From the Rock*, 213; Deyle, "The Domestic Slave Trade in America," 25.

41. Kennedy and Parker, eds., *Official Report*, 116; Powers, *Black Charlestonians*, 49; Charleston *Courier*, July 26, 1822.

Socially ostracized by his mulatto neighbors along Bull Street, Vesey instead associated with Rolla Bennett, the property of politician and entrepreneur Thomas Bennett. To better oversee his lumbermill on the Ashley River, Bennett acquired a handsome residence at 19 Lynch Street (now Ashley) on the corner where it intersected with Bull. Together with slaves Peter Poyas and Monday Gell, Rolla became Vesey's oldest friend and closest confidant.[42]

As with many of those who would later be involved in Vesey's conspiracy, frustratingly little can be discovered about Rolla Bennett. Most likely he was born in Charleston. Literate and articulate, and highly assimilated into Euro-American society, Rolla ran his master's household as the "confidential servant" and chief domestic. Thomas Bennett had long owned Rolla when Vesey first met him on Bull Street; perhaps Bennett owned Rolla since birth.[43] One white Charlestonian described him as "quite a young man" at the time of his death in 1822, which made Rolla at least several decades younger than Vesey. In 1819, Rolla took up with Amaretta LaRoche, the former companion of his close friend Joe LaRoche. Despite the fact that Amaretta had given him two children, Joe later claimed that "he was very glad to get rid of her," for she had "a very blood thirsty character." But Thomas Bennett saw in Rolla only a loyal domestic and a man of remarkable self-possession, perhaps because Amaretta lived abroad from her new husband. So confident was Thomas Bennett of Rolla's devotion, that when the future-governor's public duties carried him to the state capital of Columbia, he "entrusted to" Rolla's protection "the safety of his family."[44]

Because the enterprising carpenter remained a slave without a master, Vesey retained his precautionary habit of avoiding white authorities whenever possible, no matter how benign they might be.

42. *Directory and Stranger's Guide, 1819,* 25; *Directory and Stranger's Guide, 1822,* 25.

43. Narrative, in Kennedy and Parker, eds., *Official Report,* 43.

44. Mary Lamboll Beach to Elizabeth Gilchrist, July 5, 1822, Beach Letters, SCHS; Testimony of Joe LaRoche at trial of Rolla Bennett, June 19, 1822, in Parker and Kennedy, eds., *Official Report,* 64 (see also 43); Testimony of Mr. LaRoche at trial of Rolla Bennett, June 22, 1822, RGA, GM, SCDAH; John Potter to Langdon Cheves, July 20, 1822, Cheves Papers, SCHS.

As a free tradesman who resided in Charleston for more than two decades, Denmark Vesey should have made numerous appearances in the city's public record. Instead, he appeared only sporadically. Three times—in 1800, 1810, and 1820—Vesey dodged federal census takers as they marched through his neighborhood, quill pen in hand. Only once, in 1822, did Vesey's name and address appear in Charleston's annual *Directory and Stranger's Guide,* the city's business and population index. (Listed in the "colored" section of the guide, he was identified only as a "carpenter [at] 20 Bull" Street.) Not surprisingly, the proud freeman never graced the pages of the extant free black tax books, the special burden placed on those few who had somehow managed to become free. In 1821, Susan Vesey answered the taxman's knock and dutifully paid her levy, but according to the public record, her elusive husband was nowhere to be found.[45]

Far from opening his door to intrusive white authorities, Vesey spent his rare free moments pondering ways to resist the indignities that the white and mulatto communities daily heaped upon him. Words had always come easily to him, and when he could obtain them, he pored over the antislavery books and pamphlets that black seamen smuggled into Southern ports. One of his friends, John Enslow, stopped by Vesey's home to find him reading "a Book about the complexion of people." It was "the climate of Africa" that made "them Black," he lectured an impressed Enslow, but the rays of the African sun hardly made them "inferior to Whites on that account." Most likely, Vesey had obtained a copy of Abbe Henri-Baptiste Gregoire's *An Enquiry Concerning the Intellectual and Moral Faculties, and Literature of Negroes.* Translated into English in 1810, Gregoire's monograph found a receptive audience in the Northern free black community; Vesey obviously believed the abbe's enlightened theories on "color and climate" had critical implications for South Carolina's slave regime.[46]

45. *Index to the 1820 Federal Census* (Austin, 1972), 91; Ronald V. Jackson, ed., *South Carolina 1810 Census Index* (Bountiful, Utah, 1976), 147; *Directory and Stranger's Guide, 1822,* 109; State Free Negro Capitation Tax Books, Charleston, 1821, SCDAH, p. 30.

46. Confession of Enslow's John, no date, William and Benjamin Hammet Papers, DUL; Henri Gregoire, *An Inquiry Concerning the Intellectual and Moral Faculties, and Literature of Negroes,* Graham Hodges, ed. (New York, 1997 ed.), 6.

In his quest to prove himself the equal of any man, Vesey was as tireless in rhetoric as he was industrious in business. Prudent black Carolinians donned the mask of obedience as a survival technique, but the aging giant refused to defer to the master class, and he regarded it his responsibility to encourage others to act as he did. Upon seeing a companion bow to a white man in the street, Vesey archly observed that "all men were born equal, and that he was surprised that anyone would degrade themselves by such conduct." He "would never cringe to the whites," he snarled, "nor ought anyone who had the feelings of a man." Startled by the unexpected rebuke, Vesey's friend sputtered that he was but a slave. Then "[y]ou deserve to remain slaves," came the haughty reply.[47] Timid bondmen found such lessons dangerous, even insulting, coming as they did from a freeman. Many "blacks stood in great fear of him," insisted Pompey Bryan. "I always endeavored to avoid him."[48]

But Vesey practiced what he preached. Protected by his size as much as by his status as a free tradesman, Vesey sought every opportunity to verbally confront representatives of the master race—if not necessarily the planter class. Particularly in waterfront taverns and working-class grog shops, where slaves and white workingmen drank shoulder to shoulder, Vesey often shocked both races by loudly advancing "some bold remark on slavery." Depending on the response his words elicited, Vesey grew "bolder still" and denounced the peculiar institution with a fury that would have earned less intimidating freemen a trip to the Workhouse.[49]

Even Vesey's physical demeanor and habitual immaculacy of wardrobe indicated his defiance of Charleston's racialist code of appropriate deportment. Slaves learned early in life to avoid the master's gaze, a practice inherited from Africa, where avoiding eye contact was a nonverbal acknowledgement of another's strength and authority. But Vesey boldly stared into the eyes of the white men he met in the streets—or more accurately, given his great height, he stared down at them—in a calculated act of insolence that defied both European and African standards of etiquette. So too did his

---

47. Narrative, in Kennedy and Parker, eds., *Official Report*, 19.
48. Confession of Pompey Bryant, June 1822, RGA, GM, SCDAH.
49. Narrative, in Kennedy and Parker, eds., *Official Report*, 19.

apparel. Southern bondmen, not unlike medieval peasants, wore drab, tattered clothing to symbolize their inferior rank; the 1740 Negro Act forbade slaves to "wear any sort of apparel whatsoever, finer [or] of greater value [than coarse] negro cloth." Vesey was no longer a slave, and Charleston's bond domestics frequently flouted the law against fine clothing. But the Negro Act—as its very title indicated—drew few distinctions between bond and free, and where the law failed, there were invariably white mobs to enforce black submission. Few white toughs, however, cared to attack a colossus who would certainly fight back, and so Vesey strolled the sandy streets in garments that defied both Carolina mores and his own meager income. Vesey never forgot that equality in all things, and not merely freedom alone, marked the antithesis of slavery.[50]

For all that, Denmark Vesey was only one man. Few freemen sought to join his lonely crusade to topple Charleston's caste system through elegant clothing, intimidating glares, enlightened science, or bold words hurled across a crowded tavern. Certainly the wealthy mulattoes who peopled the Brown Fellowship Society refused to endorse his methods. Painfully aware of the fact that they too, despite their white patrons and patronage, stood condemned in the eyes of proslavery theorists for the crime of carrying even a hint of African blood, Vesey's light-skinned neighbors sought to earn the respect of the master class through their conservative respectability.[51] Rebuffed by the free colored population, Vesey remained a vital part of the slave community. Like Charleston's bondpersons, Vesey found no peace in this world, and so like them, his gaze increasingly turned toward the heavens.

---

50. White, *Somewhat More Independent*, 202; "Negro Act," 1740, in Brevard, ed., *Alphabetical Digest*, 2:242; Shane White and Graham White, "Slave Clothing and African-American Culture in the Eighteenth and Nineteenth Centuries," *Past & Present* 148 (August 1995): 154–55; David Brion Davis, *Revolutions: Reflections on American Equality and Foreign Liberations* (Cambridge, Mass., 1990), 29.

51. Boles, *Black Southerners*, 136–37, correctly observes that as free blacks were well aware of their precarious position in Southern society, they tended to be a conservative force and were "more likely to report rumored slave rebellions than, like Denmark Vesey, to lead one."

Chapter Five

Building the House
of the Lord
1817–1821

CHURCH BELLS DISTURBED the slumber of the port, as drowsy white Charlestonians hastened to dress for Sunday services. For a small city, Charleston was home to numerous churches and temples, all of them erected with money earned from the sweat of Africans, and all of them designed to point the way to heaven. In status-conscious South Carolina, Sunday mornings provided ample opportunities to parade visible signs of social rank, from purchased pews toward the front of the churches to the expensive dresses worn by merchants' wives. But in the city's mean houses, black Charlestonians also donned their finest clothes, garments they reserved for Sunday alone, in open defiance of state laws regarding servile dress. One German visitor, accustomed to seeing enslaved Carolinians shabbily attired, was astonished "to walk in the main street after church on Sunday and see Negro men and their beauties tricked out in their Sunday best."[1] But what visitor Clara Von Gerstner attributed to

    1. Wood, *Woman's Work, Men's Work*, 134; Frederic Trautmann, ed., "South Carolina Through a German's Eyes: The Travels of Clara Von Gerstner, 1839," *SCHM* (July 1984): 222.

"vanity," and what white authorities regarded as an act of calculated insolence, was instead a reverential determination to honor God by donning clothing that befitted the morning. Not for the first time in western history, the demands of faith ran afoul of the dictates of the secular state.

The extent to which mainland slaves adopted the religion of their new country remains one of the most hotly debated topics in American historiography. Scholars debate not only the extent of religious acculturation, but in which century it took place, whether this adoption allowed for West African religious traditions to survive, and whether the fusion of African and Euro-American religions hindered or helped support patterns of resistance to slavery. In the process, however, Old Testament thought is often merged with New Testament teachings, as if the Bible's two parts received equal attention from Southern whites and blacks and contained similar responses to servitude and retribution. Although it is true that most monographs that deal with slave religion touch upon the Old Testament, typically in a brief reference to the fondness most slaves demonstrated for the Exodus story, too few modern writers have observed that the injunctions of the Israelites allowed for a revolutionary tradition quite different from that found in the New Testament—or taught by white ministers in South Carolina.[2]

The Sunday parades that surprised and amused Clara Von Gerstner were less common on the plantations across the Cooper River. At the dawn of the nineteenth century, very few slaves in rural South Carolina exhibited much familiarity with the religious doctrines of their masters. Despite their own pious professions of faith, many planters feared that the Christianization of their laborers would produce egalitarian-minded, and hence unruly bondpeople.

---

2. Michael Mullin, *Africa in America: Slave Acculturation and Resistance in the American South and the British Caribbean, 1736–1831* (Urbana, 1992), 229, curiously suggests that religion was not "a dominant feature of Vesey's teaching and outlook." Instead, Vesey regarded religion as a tool and its places of worship as convenient" for organizing his conspiracy. Frey, *Water From the Rock,* 321, is far closer to the truth in suggesting that despite "a spate of books and articles on the Vesey plot, the close connection that existed between slave revolts and independent African churches has not been fully explored." Indeed, this chapter is informed by influential studies by Frey, Margaret Washington, Norrece T. Jones, and Graham R. Hodges.

In extreme cases, proslavery theorists rejected the proposition that Africans possessed souls; more commonly, white masters worried that canny slaves who obtained religious training might next demand commensurate political rights as Christians. Because many masters agreed with Joseph Ottolenghe when he complained that "a slave is ten times worse when a Christian, than in his State of Paganism," the few who permitted religious instruction on their estates did so only after warning their workers that baptism would not result in liberation. But even when heavily censored by white masters, a religion of universal brotherhood posed obvious problems in a slave society. Anyone who wanted to acquaint enslaved Africans with the *entire* Bible, lamented Whitemarsh Seabrook, a Sea Island planter and a member of the state Senate, was fit for "a room in the Lunatic Asylum."[3]

Seabrook need not have worried. Many of the Africans forcibly imported into the state prior to 1808 showed as little interest in learning about the religion of their captors as had the *kamina* on St. Thomas. Isolated on remote plantations strewn along the Atlantic Coast, the vast majority of Africans continued to practice the faith of their ancestors. Although few enough planters prior to the 1830s wished to convert their laborers, for those who did, African religiosity proved stubbornly resistant to Christianization. Old world traditions were ancient enough that African minds were hardly the uncommitted "heathen" slates whites believed them to be. Besides, wary captives suspected the deity of the whites "to be a cheat," and as one bold Carolina bondman explained it to the Reverend John D. Long, they believed "the preachers and the slaveholders to be in a conspiracy against them." If given Sunday as a day of rest, rural blacks used the time, sighed Henry Bibb, an unusually pious slave, to "gamble, fight, get drunk, and break the Sabbath."[4]

Precisely because of that profane indifference, well-intentioned

3. Genovese, *Roll, Jordan, Roll,* 192; Alan Gallay, *The Formation of a Planter Elite: Jonathan Bryan and the Southern Colonial Frontier* (Athens, 1989), 41–42; Kay and Cary, *Slavery in North Carolina,* 194; Cornelius, *When I Can Read My Title Clear,* 40–41.

4. Margaret Washington, *"A Peculiar People": Slave Religion and Community-Culture Among the Gullahs* (New York, 1988), 3; Kay and Cary, *Slavery in North Carolina,* 178–90; Jones, *Born a Child of Freedom,* 139; Kolchin, *American Slavery,* 146.

white ministers sought to convince the master class that the conversion of their laboring force would support, rather than undermine, the social order of slavery. Truly alarmed by the "little attention [Africans] paid to the sabbath, or religeon,"[5] and devoutly believing that unchurched Africans were lost souls, white missionaries argued that Christianity, if properly sanitized, could render slaves docile and obedient. As a creed that emphasized paying unto Caesar what was Caesar's, "Christianity," Frederick Dalcho insisted, "robs no man of his rights" under the law. Slaves might be taught to pray for eventual deliverance in heaven, rather than to attempt to seize it while on earth. Although slaves should not be allowed to hear preachers "of their own colour," Dalcho warned, white ministers could lecture black congregations on "their duties and obligations," supported by "instructive" examples prudently "*selected* from the Bible," especially "from the New Testament."[6]

In Charleston, where whites and blacks resided in far greater proximity than along the seacoast, the diligent efforts of white missionaries showed some success. Baptists and Methodist ministers in particular gained adherents by ignoring the counsel of men like Dalcho and enlisting black exhorters to venture into urban alleys and rural quarters. Their emotional style, their emphasis on universal salvation, and their early—if altogether too brief—opposition to unfree labor, combined with their theological flexibility, which allowed for the retention of African religious traditions, brought hundreds of city slaves into predominantly white Charleston churches. Desperate to save "heathen" souls for Christ, Methodist ministers and their black "assistants" shepherded their flocks with a light touch. Too-clear evidence of African "paganisms," such as the practice of polygamy, might be admonished, but loose structures of organization made strict enforcement of church dogma difficult. Black congregants found within Methodism the flexibility necessary to

5. Lucius Verus Bierce, *Travels in the Southland, 1822–1823: The Journals of Lucius Verus Bierce,* ed. George W. Knepper (Columbus, Ohio, 1966), 73.

6. Kolchin, *American Slavery,* 148; [Frederick Dalcho], *Practical Considerations Founded on the Scriptures Relative to the Slave Population of South Carolina* (Charleston, 1823), 21, 32.

practice their traditional religions even while adopting aspects of their new country's dominant faith.[7]

Largely because Methodism proved so attractive to the city's enslaved population, Charleston browns regarded Charleston's evangelical faiths as churches devoutly to be avoided. As part of their ongoing campaign to prove their fealty to white society, urban mulattoes kept as safe a distance from Methodist benches as they did from the African community. Most members of Charleston's free colored aristocracy flocked into Episcopal churches. Like all men of "high position in society," observed Francis Asbury, browns preferred the Episcopal Church, which enjoyed the "prestige of worldly wealth and honor." The venerable St. Philip's Protestant Episcopal Church, built in 1712 near the corner of Church and Queen Streets, attracted many of the city's wealthiest merchants and prosperous mulattoes; among their number was Joseph Vesey, the mixed race son of the old sea captain. According to one proud mulatto congregant, the parish register of St. Philip's read "like the social directory of the Brown Fellowship Society."[8]

Befitting his uncomfortable status as a member of neither the Brown Fellowship Society nor the slave community, Denmark Vesey initially avoided both Episcopalian and Methodist congregations. In mid-April 1817, Vesey was one of "three people of Colour" admitted "to Communion for the first time" at the Second Presbyterian Church. Built on Wragg Square on the corner of Charlotte and Elizabeth Streets, the church was one of the newer congregations in the city and had been dedicated only six years before the name "Danmark Vesey" first graced its session records. The predominantly white Calvinist congregation attracted few black Charlestonians. Perhaps the old captain introduced his former slave to the

7. Genovese, *Roll, Jordan, Roll,* 234–35; Hodges, *Slavery and Freedom,* 77, suggests that "Methodists did not respect African spirituality as much as fail to recognize it."

8. Holt, *Black Over White,* 64–65; Stephanie McCurry, *Masters of Small Worlds: Yeoman Households, Gender Relations, and the Political Culture of the Antebellum South Carolina Low Country* (New York, 1995), 139; Register, 1810–1857, St. Philip's Protestant Episcopal Church, Charleston, SCL, p. 260; Johnson and Roark, *Black Masters,* 227.

congregation before his latest marriage, which was conducted by the Methodist minister William Brazier. The fact that Vesey was admitted to communion, but unlike the other two "people of Colour," was not baptized at the same service, indicated that the April morning was not Vesey's initial contact with a Christian church.[9]

One can only assume, however, that while Vesey initially found great comfort in his new-found Christian faith, he also found much, at least in how it was presented in white churches, that drove him to look elsewhere for spiritual sustenance. White Southerners, steeped in traditions of Biblical orthodoxy, took great solace in the New Testament and its treatment of human bondage. The fact that Jesus, as far as the extant gospels indicated, failed to denounce the slavery practiced in Roman Judea, appeared to provide divine sanction for the peculiar institution. In "all the special instructions of our Saviour," thundered Charles Cotesworth Pinckney, "not one word condemns the practice." Slavery was not only "most unquestionably permitted," added a South Carolina editor, "perhaps we should speak more correctly to say [it was actually] encouraged" by the early Christians. Noting St. Paul's instruction to an abused slave to return to his master, South Carolina theologian Charles C. Jones found ample support for his view that the New Testament pronounced it "contrary to God's will *to runaway* [or] to *harbor* a runaway."[10]

Undoubtedly, some of these pronouncements were designed to assuage the embattled consciences of white Christians. Carolina planters as a class demonstrated little enough guilt over their ownership of other humans, but more than a few white theologians demonstrated some uneasiness over the unwaged exploitation of their black brothers in Christ. David Ramsay, a South Carolina physician and a devout Presbyterian, was almost certainly addressing his own soul rather than his Massachusetts correspondent when he pleaded that "[e]xperience proves that they who have been born & grow up

9. [No author], *An Architectural Guide to Charleston,* 82; Record of Sessions, Second Presbyterian Church, 1809–1837, Charleston County, SCL.

10. Kolchin, *American Slavery,* 192; Charles Cotesworth Pinckney, *An Address Delivered in Charleston Before the Agricultural Society of South Carolina* (Charleston, 1829), 8; Columbia *Southern Times,* April 8, 1830; Charles C. Jones, *A Catechism for Colored Persons* (Charleston, 1834), 95.

in slavery are incapable of the blessings of freedom." And Charlestonian Frederick Dalcho surely did not expect to persuade Northern "advocates of manumission" when he insisted that as "the descendants of Ham"—the cursed second son of Noah—blacks had "lost their freedom through the abominable wickedness of their progenitor."[11]

Undoubtedly also, many white Carolinians embraced this comforting, proslavery brand of Christianity in hopes that their slaves would do the same. Servants properly inculcated with the doctrine that God chose them, or perhaps condemned them, to serve their spiritual betters might prove easier to control. Charleston pulpits echoed with lectures to enslaved Africans on being content with their lowly station in life. Bishop Christopher P. Gadsden, the new rector of St. Philip's Episcopal Church, enjoined the few blacks who entered his doors to "fear God, obey the civil authority, [and] be subject unto their own masters." Echoing the common refrain that Africans were the "descendants of Ham [from the land of] Canaan," polemicist Dalcho instructed the black community that "according to the most ancient prophecies" their destiny was to remain "slaves to Christians," even following conversion. With that in mind, the industrious Charles C. Jones penned *A Catechism for Colored Persons*, which answered possible black queries in simple prose with pertinent Biblical references. When asked if it was wrong in the eyes of God to flee one's master, Jones reminded his black readers of the Eighth Commandment and the warning not to steal, even one's own body. "Also, that whenever we know that any persons are going to steal" themselves, that is, to run away, Jones admonished, "we are immediately to tell on them."[12]

11. Robert M. Calhoon, *Evangelicals and Conservatives in the Early South, 1740–1861* (Columbia, 1988), 128–29; [Dalcho], *Practical Considerations Founded on the Scriptures*, 8.

12. Fraser, *Charleston*, 204–5; [Dalcho], *Practical Considerations Founded on the Scriptures*, 18–20; Jones, *Catechism for Colored Persons*, 82. None of this is to deny, of course, that in other contexts evangelical Christianity often did, and still does, lead to social activism. The body of scholarship on the connection between the great awakening and militant abolitionism is enormous, but see especially John R. McKivigan, *The War Against Proslavery Religion: Abolitionism and the Northern*

The attempts of pamphleteers like Jones to peddle their vision of a proslavery God to black congregants was hindered by the fact that most Carolina ministers were hardly disinterested teachers. During the two decades that Vesey was a slave in Charleston, forty percent of the preachers or licentiates in the state owned one or more slaves; small wonder that many Africans regarded Christianity as a swindle concocted by planters and politicians. Yet enough American-born bondpeople listened to the theories of white ministers to produce a sense of inferiority or resignation in some quarters of the slave community, a feeling of submissiveness necessary for the survival of the master class. Richard Furman, a Baptist clergyman and the "Senior Vice-President" of the Charleston Bible Society, assured Governor Thomas Bennett that white ministers "establish Rules of a [subservient] Character, & enforce them by Considerations which far transcend all" that the "Punishment of Man made Laws can inflict." A minority of black voices endorsed Furman's sentiments. "De marstar had to put de fear of God in them sometimes," remembered one former slave in later years, "and de Bible don't object to it."[13]

For Denmark Vesey, such teachings produced only a sense of revulsion. A man given to haranguing white strangers in taverns about the injustice of slavery was not much given to feelings of inferiority, spiritual or otherwise. Even the trappings of his chosen faith served to remind him of his second class status, as segregated seating for people of color was standard practice in Charleston churches. Vesey might approach the front of the chapel for commu-

Churches, 1830–1865 (Ithaca, 1984), and Jama Lazerow, *Religion and the Working Class in Antebellum America* (Washington, D.C., 1995). However, Mitchell Snay, *Gospel of Disunion: Religion and Separatism in the Antebellum South* (New York, 1993), 28–30, warns that "the northern clergy and churches [often] proved unreceptive to the abolitionist message [as the] more conservative evangelical clergymen argued that abolitionism . . . threatened to undermine public order."

13. Genovese, *Roll, Jordan, Roll,* 203; Eugene D. Genovese, *The World the Slaveholders Made: Two Essays in Interpretation* (New York, 1969), 6–7; Charleston *Courier,* July 3, 1822; Richard Furman to Governor Thomas Bennett, no date, Richard Furman Papers, USC; George Rawick, ed., *The American Slave: A Composite Autobiography* (Westport, Conn., 1972), 2:207.

nion or baptism, but he spent the remainder of his Sunday mornings banished to the upstairs galleries. The sermons of the Reverend John Adger, minister of the Second Presbyterian Church, provided little comfort to those listening from above. Adger was moderate in his teachings by comparison to Jones and Dalcho, yet he too regarded Africans and their offspring as "a race distinct from" Euro-Americans. When he patronized black congregants by insisting that shackled laborers "are not more truly ours than we are theirs," Vesey must have turned away in disgust.[14]

Given these weekly humiliations at the hands of men who purported to represent a religion of universal brotherhood, many Afro-Christians, and especially many Afro-Methodists, who by the end of the War of 1812 outnumbered white Methodists ten to one in Charleston, began to resist white theological control. Literate blacks like Vesey knew of Richard Allen and his African Methodist Episcopal Church in Philadelphia. Born into slavery in Delaware in 1760, Allen converted to Christianity at the age of seventeen upon hearing an itinerant Methodist preach the gospels; his master, himself influenced by Methodism, allowed Allen to purchase his freedom. Like many young black men from the border South, Allen moved to Philadelphia, where he joined St. George's Methodist Church. But in 1792, Allen experienced the sort of humiliation blacks in Vesey's city witnessed each Sunday. When church elders yanked Absalom Jones to his feet in the middle of prayer and instructed him to retreat to segregated pews upstairs, Allen led an exodus from the church. Together they formed the African Methodist Episcopal Church. "Notwithstanding we had been so violently persecuted," Allen insisted, he wished to keep his "independent" church within the larger Methodist fold. No "sect or denomination," Allen believed, "suit[ed] the capacity of colored people as well as the Methodist."[15]

For Charleston's slave and free black population, Allen's church

14. Jordan, *White Over Black*, 418; Frey, *Water From the Rock*, 268; Fraser, *Charleston*, 204.

15. Blassingame, *Slave Community*, 86–87; Vincent Harding, *There Is a River: The Black Struggle for Freedom in America* (New York, 1981), 67; Nash, *Forging Freedom*, 95–96, 118–33; James T. Campbell, *Songs of Zion: The African Methodist Episcopal Church in the United States and South Africa* (New York, 1995), 10–11.

served as a model of black self-reliance and resiliency in a hostile white world, as well as a purer application of brotherly love. In early 1816, Morris Brown, a free black three years Vesey's junior, and Henry Drayton, a former Carolina slave, journeyed north to confer with Allen about the formation of a branch of the Philadelphia church in Charleston. Both Brown, a pious former bootmaker who served twelve months in prison for using his earnings to help slaves purchase their freedom, and Drayton were ordained for pastorates. They may even have been in Philadelphia when delegations from several mid-Atlantic cities met with Allen to confederate their congregations into a united church. This act of self-determination marked the final act of emancipation from the religious jurisdiction of white clergymen.[16]

Not surprisingly, white clergymen were as nervous about their loss of theological control as white authorities were about the practice of slaves hiring their time about the city. Brown and Drayton returned south in early 1817 only to discover that Anthony Senter, an influential Methodist leader, was attempting to reassert authority over the black Methodist majority and the disbursement of their collection plates and revenues. In a show of force, white trustees voted to construct a hearse house atop a small black cemetery adjoining the Bethel Methodist Church. In response, 4,376 slaves and free blacks quit the church in protest and began construction of an independent African church. The "Whites wanted nothing," the Reverend Drayton laughed, "but a good spanking with a sword."[17]

Built on Anson Street near the corner of Boundary, Charleston's African Methodist congregation grew so quickly that the city's black community soon began work on a second church on Cow Alley (now Philadelphia Street) in the predominantly black Hampstead neighborhood along the town's northern edge. The African Church, as both white and black Charlestonians dubbed the congregations, drew its leadership from free black artisans like Vesey. Of the

16. Wright, *African-Americans in the Early Republic*, 156–57; Harding, *There Is a River*, 67; C. Peter Ripley, ed., *The Black Abolitionist Papers: The United States, 1830–1860* (Chapel Hill, 1992), 3:134 note 3, 196 note 14.

17. Hinks, *To Awaken My Afflicted Brethren*, 27; Kennedy and Parker, eds., *Official Report*, 22, 76; Testimony of Monday Gell, July 16, 1822, RGA, GM, SCDAH.

twenty-six freemen who boldly affixed their signatures to the petition sent to the state legislature in 1818 for the incorporation of the African Methodist Church, at least ten were artisans. The two churches housed the largest black Methodist congregations in the South, and Charleston's membership was second only in size to the parent body in Philadelphia. As Vesey does not appear in the records of the Second Presbyterian Church after Easter 1817, he presumably became an early, perhaps even a founding, member of the Cow Alley Church. Monday Gell and Peter Poyas promptly joined, and as Gell himself put it, Sandy Vesey became a "zealous [member of] the African Church."[18]

Like Allen's Philadelphia church, Brown's emerging Charleston African Methodist congregations implicitly challenged not merely white religious domination, but white social and political control as well. The black community's struggle to create autonomous sacred institutions by seceding from white governance was, in the context of a slave society, a decidedly radical act. In the process of managing their own churches, slaves and free blacks defied established theories of African intellectual inferiority. As individuals, even the shrewdest slave marketeer could amass little property, but collectively, enslaved congregants purchased burial grounds, raised and disbursed charity funds for care of the aged or indigent, and maintained church buildings. Because both white ministers and secular authorities regarded the African churches as dangerous bastions of slave autonomy, Charleston's city government made it a practice to routinely disrupt these services of "Gullah tribe Mechanic's and draymen."[19]

Despite the persistent fears that an African Methodist leader

18. Harding, *There Is a River,* 67; Powers, *Black Charlestonians,* 19; Martha Proctor Richardson to James Screven, September 16, 1822, Arnold and Screven Papers, Southern Historical Collection, University of North Carolina (hereafter SHC, UNC).

19. Harris, "Charleston's Free Afro-American Elite," 292. Genovese, *Roll, Jordan, Roll,* 272–73, is especially good on the difficult position of black preachers in the slave states. During the organizing of his conspiracy, Vesey warned his followers not to tell "Morris Brown, Harry Drayton, and Charles Corr" of the plot "for fear they would betray us to the whites." See second confession of Monday Gell, July 13, 1822, in Kennedy and Parker, eds., *Official Report,* 98.

would emerge as a latter-day Moses, Morris Brown's eloquent sermons ultimately failed to deliver a theology of liberation. For all of
their facility in fusing the powerful creation stories of their ancestral home with the egalitarian teachings of their adopted land,
Southern AME clergymen rarely spoke of a promised land on this
earth. The Reverend Brown was a pragmatist who believed that his
first responsibility was to protect his black flock and preserve their
sense of hope for the future. White authorities daily threatened to
close his church, which is to say they threatened to close the focus
of black cultural and social life in Charleston. Such concerns forced
Brown and Drayton to surrender the principle of political leadership in hopes of keeping their church doors open. Although most
slave congregants appreciated his precarious position, some of the
more radical members of his church, including the increasingly bellicose Vesey, regarded him as a good man deserving of respect, but
not a safe man worthy of trust. It little helped matters that Malcolm
Brown, Morris Brown's oldest son and one of the six church trustees,
was the sole black member of the accommodationist Brown Fellowship Society.[20]

The decentralized organizational structure of American Methodism, however, together with the unwieldy size of Charleston's
growing African congregations, allowed for the introduction of a far
more radical message. Sunday, of course, was the black community's day of services, rest, and visitations. But during the working
week, lay clergy conducted nightly "class meetings" "in some retired
building" or private home. White authorities routinely sat in the
rear pews during Brown's formal sermons, but typically no "white
person attended" the nocturnal sessions. Each class had "a coloured
preacher, or leader," who was chosen by the church hierarchy. If
Vesey regarded Brown and Drayton as hopelessly accommodating to
white authority, they either failed to recognize his disdain or simply
felt the aging carpenter too important to be ignored. Like his old
comrade Peter Poyas, Vesey became a class leader as early as 1818,

---

20. Campbell, *Songs of Zion,* 35; Frey, *Water From the Rock,* 322; Hinks, *To
Awaken My Afflicted Brethren,* 26; William Colcock's Confession, July 12, 1822,
RGA, GM, SCDAH.

and for "four years," according to one admiring Charleston freeman, "preach[ed] his gospel of liberty and hate."[21]

If the Reverend Brown's Sunday sermons included a creative melding of African and Christian elements, Vesey's twilight teachings were far different. Historians traditionally suggest that the class leader "promoted the use of radical Christianity" to encourage resistance to white authority and "invoked Christian sanction" to support his secular pronouncements on black equality.[22] But former slave Archibald Grimké was far closer to the mark when he remembered that Vesey found "in the stern and Nemesis-like God of the Old Testament" a suitable vision "for a day of vengeance and retribution."[23] Embittered by the continuing bondage of his children and his first wife, and disgusted with the proslavery ministers of South Carolina, Vesey turned his back on the New Testament and what he regarded as its false promise of universal brotherhood. Having seceded from the white Presbyterian church and the white society of which it was a part, Vesey seceded a second time, from Christianity itself. In his numerous religious pronouncements, Vesey never once mentioned Jesus or a God that would have him forgive

21. Martha Proctor Richardson to James Screven, July 6, 1822, Arnold and Screven Papers, SHC, UNC; Hartford *Connecticut Courant*, August 6, 1822; Testimony of Harth's Robert at trial of Peter Poyas, June 21, 1822, in Hamilton, *An Account*, 33; Narrative, in Kennedy and Parker, eds., *Official Report*, 22–23; Grimké, *Right on the Scaffold*, 11.

22. Sterling Stuckey, *Slave Culture*, 48–49, and Genovese, *Roll, Jordan, Roll*, 593, who perhaps agree on little else, both suggest that Vesey used "radical Christianity" to justify his revolt. Two other important studies that come to similar conclusions are Powers, *Black Charlestonians*, 30, and Ball, *Slaves in the Family*, 267, who does however observe that the old carpenter "favored passages in the Bible concern[ing] the enslavement of the Jews."

23. Grimké, *Right on the Scaffold*, 12. Washington, *A Peculiar People*, 263–64, observes that Vesey's conscious association with the children of Israel "inspired some of the Charleston rebels of 1822." Most Carolina slave theology, however, "centered on the experiences of Jesus rather than the Jews." The "militant nationalism" of the ancient Israelites was a prominent ideology of slaves convicted of standing with Vesey, Washington suggests, "but was not a major orientation in Gullah religion," a finding of critical implications in the ongoing debate regarding Christian conversion and physical nonresistance.

his enemies. He simply knew that the instinct of freedom was the righteous voice of *his* God.

Most slaves, as they gathered about the table in Vesey's rented Bull Street home, were drawn to the Book of Exodus and the story of Israel delivered. Themselves enslaved laborers in a barbaric land, Africans naturally identified with those who centuries before had toiled under burning sun in pharaoh's Egypt; black Carolinians prayed only that the sacred liberation of God's chosen people would be repeated in North America. More to the point, the figure of Moses, who possessed the mystical ability to transform inanimate objects into living creatures, corresponded easily to African practices of conjure.[24]

According to his disciples, however, Vesey focused not on the epic of Moses but rather on the Jewish Bible's edicts on slavery. As he studied the Book of Exodus, Vesey obviously found great comfort in its teaching. Mosaic law permitted both divorce and polygamy, as it did slavery, but with specific admonitions. "Denmark read at the meeting different Chapters from the Old Testament," recalled a slave named John, and "spoke and exhorted from the 16th Verse [of Exodus, Chapter 21] the words 'and He that Stealeth a man.'" These "ordinances" regarding unfree labor allowed the Israelites to buy and own slaves in perpetuity, but only if the slaves were non-believers. "When you buy a Hebrew slave," the Israelite lawgiver had cautioned, "he shall serve six years, and in the seventh he shall go out free, for nothing." And whoever steals a man, Moses had warned, "shall be put to death." In the theology of Vesey's class, African Methodists were the new Israelites. St. Paul and his planter defenders could say what they wished, but Jehovah demanded the death of those who owned the chosen people.[25]

When not at his workbench, Vesey devoted every available moment to exploring the mysteries of the Old Testament. He became

24. Johnson and Roark, *Black Masters,* 38; Albert J. Raboteau, *Slave Religion: The "Invisible Institution" in the Antebellum South* (New York, 1979), 311; Theophius H. Smith, *Conjuring Cultures: Biblical Formations of Black America* (New York, 1994), 40.

25. Confession of Enslow's John, no date, William and Benjamin Hammet Papers, DUL; Exodus 21:1–4.

the master, as white magistrates later conceded, of "all those parts of the Scriptures" that dealt with servitude, and he could "readily quote them, to prove that slavery was contrary to the laws of God." If Africans, or at least those blacks who joined the Methodist ranks, remained captives beyond their allotted six years, they "were absolutely enjoined" by God's law to "attempt their emancipation, however shocking and bloody might be the consequences." Vesey's favorite texts became "Zechariah, Chapter 14th, verses 1, 2 and 3," which foretold of the sack of Jerusalem, and Joshua, Chapter 6, verse 21: "Then they utterly destroyed all in the city, both men and women, young and old [with] the edge of the sword."[26]

For the slaves and free blacks in Vesey's class, word that the most ancient books of the Bible condemned their bondage reminded them anew of the treachery of the white clergy who had hidden this knowledge from them. Bacchus demanded to know why South Carolina whites "did not preach up this thing (meaning the passages on liberty &c) to them before." All "the Ministers [should] be killed except a few," Vesey replied brusquely. He reminded his pupils of the "19th Chap[ter of] Isaiah": "And I will stir up Egyptian and Egyptian, and they will fight [and] I will confound their plans." For a man who took great interest in the bitterly divisive Missouri debates, it required little imagination to find a modern counterpart for the Egyptians.[27]

In his determination to spread his empowering version of the Gospel and to reveal the typically-censored passages of the Old Testament, the old carpenter used every opportunity to "prove," as his friend William Paul observed, "that Slavery and bondage is against the Bible." Vesey told all who would listen that white ministers were a fraud, that they "made a Catechism *different* for the Negroes" in an attempt to hide Jehovah's will from his chosen people. His tendency to preach to all comers grew so overpowering that even "his general conversation[s]" at carpentry sites and taverns, reported Ben-

---

26. Narrative, in Kennedy and Parker, eds., *Official Report*, 17–18; Zechariah 14:1–3.

27. Confession of Hammet's Bacchus, no date, William and Benjamin Hammet Papers, DUL.

jamin Ford, a white boy of sixteen years, "was about religion, which he would apply to slavery." Taught to believe that the heavens approved of unfree labor, Ford evidently challenged Vesey's teachings. But unmindful of the crowd gathering around them, Vesey, like the Puritan radicals who battled the majesty of King Charles I, fell back on the example of Eden. At the "creation of the world . . . all men had equal rights, blacks as well as whites."[28]

Before long, Vesey's disciples echoed his teachings—as well as his bravado. Jacob Glen, a young slave carpenter and a member of the African Church, fell into a debate with Reverend Drayton on the justice of seizing their freedom in *this* life. When the black minister counseled patience, Glen angrily "quoted Scripture to prove he would not be condemned for raising against the Whites." Rolla Bennett, the domestic servant of Governor Thomas Bennett, also began to speak about the coming wrath of Jehovah. When Joe LaRoche reminded Rolla that the God of the New Testament "says we must not kill," Rolla "laughed" in his face and called him "a coward."[29]

To be sure, not every member of the AME congregations followed the eloquent Vesey down the path of revolutionary theology. Of the twenty-six freemen who petitioned the General Assembly for the right to incorporate their church, not a single one was later implicated in Vesey's conspiracy. Many parishioners never strayed from the Christian doctrine of loving one's neighbor, even if that neighbor was their owner. Typical of these Afro-Christians was George Wilson, an enslaved blacksmith owned by Major John Wilson. Like Vesey, Wilson "could read and write" and served as a "class leader in the [African] Methodist Church." A "dark mulatto of large frame," George lived away from his master's Broad Street home and was allowed the privilege of hiring his services about the city and "paying to his owner a reasonable amount of wages." As a convert to Christianity, George struggled to love his master as he loved his God.

28. Examination of William Paul, June 19, 1822, RGA, GM, SCDAH; Mary Lamboll Beach to Elizabeth Gilchrist, July 5, 1822, Beach Letters, SCHS; Examination of Benjamin Ford, June 26, 1822, RGA, GM, SCDAH.

29. Examination of Charles Drayton, July 17, 1822, RGA, GM, SCDAH; Testimony of Joe LaRoche at trial of Rolla Bennett, June 19, 1822, in Kennedy and Parker, eds., *Official Report*, 62.

Like Brown and Drayton, he refused to listen to angry talk of Jehovah's bloody justice.[30]

But many congregants listened. One of Vesey's disciples may well have been young David Walker, a freeman who moved from his birthplace in North Carolina to Charleston around 1817. Several passages in Walker's uncompromising 1829 pamphlet, *An Appeal to the Colored Citizens of the World,* not only hint at a familiarity with events in the Cow Alley church but echo the teachings of the old carpenter. When Walker sailed north for Boston in 1821, Vesey's message of divinely-inspired revolution sailed with him in a warning to those modern scholars who tend to exclude slave rebels from the roster of leading abolitionists. Few congregants, however, were free to leave the city; those held behind by shackles instead cast their lot with Vesey and the sword. As Abraham Poyas put it: "Fear not, the Lord God that delivered Daniel is able to deliver us." Of the seventy-two slaves and freemen found guilty of conspiracy in 1822, exactly half, or thirty-six, were or had been members of the African church.[31]

Modern scholars have found many points of convergence between Christianity and West African theology, yet it is possible that the Old Testament provided an even better fit with African religious traditions. It was not merely that the saga of the enslaved children of Israel reminded black Charlestonians of their own unhappy condition, although it surely was that in part. Vesey's habit of reading aloud "two Chapters from the prophet Tobit," who described the trials of the Jewish people in the early diaspora, indicated that he

30. AME Petition, [1818], General Assembly Papers, Petitions, no. 1893, pp. 4–9, SCDAH; W. Hasell Wilson to Reverend Robert Wilson, no date, CLS; Pharo, ed., *Reminiscences of Wilson,* 6.

31. Peter P. Hinks, "'There Is a Great Work for You To Do': The Evangelical Strategy of David Walker's *Appeal* and His Early Years in the Carolina Low Country," in Randall Miller and John McKivigan, eds., *The Moment of Decision: Biographical Essays on American Character and Regional Identity* (Westport, Conn., 1995), 104–6; Hinks, *To Awaken My Afflicted Brethren,* 38; Abraham Poyas to Peter Poyas, no date, in Kennedy and Parker, eds., *Official Report,* 84; Examinations, RGA, GM, SCDAH. (The court became so convinced of the connection between the African church and Vesey's conspiracy that they routinely asked the accused if they were members.)

found parallels between Tobit's injunctions to hold true to the covenant and the difficulties of Africans in *their* diaspora. (Vesey's emphasis on Tobit also indicated that he had abandoned his Presbyterian Bible, for Protestant Bibles typically omitted the fourteen books of apocrypha.) But Vesey's fondness for the Hebrew Bible was more than a coincidental identification with the tale of the exodus from Egypt. African cosmology held that natural places could hold magical power, and certain objects, especially holy ones, could alter nature itself. Protestant theologians frowned on such notions, which they associated with "popery" or barbarian superstition, but the Hebrew Bible was filled not merely with miracles but with magic—and therefore power: blazing bushes that did not burn, walking staffs that turned into serpents that terrified the master class, and holy men who could part the great water while Jehovah's chosen people escaped their captivity.[32]

Strengthening Vesey's belief in a divine ability quite literally to manipulate the natural world was his decade-long association with another member of the African church, Jack Pritchard. Known as "Gullah Jack, [or] sometimes Cooter Jack" to his fellow congregants, Pritchard was an East African priest and woodworker. Zephaniah Kingsley, a seasoned slave trader and Florida planter who purchased Pritchard as "a prisoner of war at Zinguebar" in late 1805, later wrote that "Jack the Conjurer was a priest in his own country [of] M'Choolay Morcema." The port was adjacent to the island of Zanzibar, where Swahili and Arab traders sold men and women from a broad region of central and eastern Africa to American and European traders. Kingsley remembered that Jack boarded his ship, the *Gustavia,* with his "conjuring implements" carried "in a bag." Upon arriving in Charleston in April 1806, Jack was purchased by Paul Pritchard, a ship carpenter who operated a shop at Gadsden's Wharf.[33]

32. See, for example, Boles, *Black Southerners,* 158; Sobel, *World They Made Together,* 74; Blassingame, *Slave Community,* 72; Joyner, *Down by the Riverside,* 142–43; Examination of William Paul, June 19, 1822, RGA, GM, SCDAH.

33. Examination of Y, unnamed slave of George Cross, no date, RGA, GM, SCDAH; Zephaniah Kingsley, *A Treatise on the Patriarchal, or Co-operative System of Society* (New York, 1970 reprint of 1829 edition), 13; Daniel Schafer to author,

Paul Pritchard resided at 44 Hasell Street. Despite the fact that Jack openly "practised [his mystical] arts," Pritchard came to regard the African carpenter as a skillful and obedient slave. At length, Pritchard permitted Jack to live away from Hasell Street, and perhaps also to hire his own time about the city. Jack rented a house on Meeting Street, "next to Monday Gell's," who also lived apart from his master. Whites saw him as nothing more than an industrious "little man with large black whiskers," but to the black AME community, Gullah Jack was an African priest of great power and magic.[34]

Where Vesey used his towering height and dominating personality to gain disciples, Jack's fellow African congregants instinctively regarded the diminutive man as a natural leader. African priests typically obtained their powers from some unnatural circumstance of birth, such as entering the world with an amniotic caul over one eye. But in rare cases, powerful sorcerers might pass their arcane abilities on to their children, who in time would take their place as village leaders. Members of the Cow Alley church understood Jack to be a "conjurer by [both] profession and by lineal heritage," and their respect—and fear—grew accordingly. Like all charismatic leaders, Jack recognized that he possessed the gift of authority, and he labored to accentuate that gift by adopting, or perhaps maintaining, a menacing appearance. Charleston whites discouraged their slaves from wearing their hair in a bushy and "uncivilized" manner, as they had in Africa, and Paul Pritchard threatened to shave Jack's whiskers "as a punishment when he misbehaved." But Jack defiantly grew his "large pair of whiskers" ever longer. Like Vesey's elegant apparel, Jack's appearance at once impressed his fellows and defied the conventions of local authorities.[35]

August 2, November 15, 1996. (Professor Schafer is writing a biography of Kingsley and kindly shared his research with me.) On Zinguebar and Zanzibar, see Mannix and Cowley, *Black Cargoes,* 241–43, and George L. Sulivan, *Dhow Chasing in Zanzibar Waters* (London, 1873), 74.

34. Hamilton, *An Account,* 23; *Directory and Stranger's Guide, 1819,* 77; Examination of Vanderhorst's George, no date, RGA, GM, SCDAH.

35. Charles Joyner, "'If You Ain't Got Education:' Slave Language and Slave Thought in Antebellum Charleston," in Michael O'Brien and David Moltke-Hansen,

Many historians suggest that Vesey, as he began to consider a modern exodus from Charleston, consciously used Jack Pritchard to reach the African plantation constituency, while he himself used the AME Church to reach the more assimilated urban creole population.[36] But in fact no such dichotomy existed. African magic and European Christianity may have uneasily coexisted on the Carolina countryside, but Old Testament tales melded easily with Africa's sacred legends in Charleston's African churches. Gullah Jack was, after all, a member of Vesey's African Church, as was his neighbor Monday Gell, an Ibo. Neither man appeared to find any contradiction between the religious teachings of their childhood, and what they heard in Cow Alley. It was not that the old carpenter cynically used his church to recruit revolutionaries, but rather that his fusion of Old Testament law and African ritual transformed his timid disciples into revolutionaries.[37]

---

eds., *Intellectual Life in Antebellum Charleston* (Knoxville, 1986), 274; Higginson, *Black Rebellion,* 230–31; Testimony of Paul Pritchard at trial of Jack Pritchard, July 9, 1822, in Parker and Kennedy, eds., *Official Report,* 105; Shane White and Graham White, "Slave Hair and African American Culture in the Eighteenth and Nineteenth Centuries," *JSH* 61 (February 1995): 58.

36. Five scholars who suggest that Vesey "had the best of both religious worlds, the doctrinal sanction of Scripture and practical protection of conjure," are Raboteau, *Slave Religion,* 163 (quoted above); Vincent Harding, "Religion and Resistance Among Antebellum Negroes," in August Meier and Elliot Rudwick, eds., *The Making of Black America: Essays in Negro Life and History* (New York, 1969) 1:186; Freehling, *Prelude to Civil War,* 55; Philip S. Foner, *History of Black Americans: From the Emergence of the Cotton Kingdom to the Eve of the Compromise of 1850* (Westport, 1983), 144; and Smith, *Conjuring Cultures,* 159, who observes that Vesey practiced "radical Christianity" while Jack relied on African "conjurational practices." Kolchin, *American Slavery,* 147–48, says only that slave magic and slave religion coexisted, "but appropriated different spheres."

37. Genovese, in *From Rebellion to Revolution,* 46, and in *Roll, Jordan, Roll,* 37, correctly, in my view, argues that Vesey "did not play a double game" but instead formulated a flexible religious appeal based on . . . both African and classical Christian ideals." This chapter suggests, however, that Vesey did so by abandoning the Christian books and fusing African religion with Judaic teachings. Many of Vesey's disciples may not, of course, have understood that he was deviating from the teachings of the Charleston AME leadership, but as E. P. Thompson reminds

For all that, it is nonetheless possible that Vesey's revolutionary theology might never have translated into revolutionary activity were it not for the behavior of Charleston authorities. Under two South Carolina statutes of 1800 and 1803, blacks were permitted to gather for religious worship, but only after the "rising of the sun" and before "the going down of the same." Moreover, state law demanded that a "majority of [the congregation] shall be white persons."[38] Perhaps hoping that the Christianization of the city's black labor force would have a stabilizing effect, a series of intendants (mayors) had chosen to ignore the African Church's—and their evening classes—blatant violation of these laws. But the intendant's inclination to look the other way suddenly changed in June 1818 when six bishops and ministers from the parent church in Philadelphia arrived in Charleston. Area whites trusted Brown, but envoys from Richard Allen's northern church were quite another matter. On Sunday, June 7, the city guard burst into the church and arrested 140 "free Negroes and Slaves," one of them presumably Denmark Vesey. Confined for the night, the Charleston and Philadelphia blacks were released the next morning "by the City Magistrates, who explained the law to them."[39]

Not to be dissuaded, the "Black Priests" appeared before the City Council and requested a dispensation to "allow them to hold their meetings in the way they wished." Believing Allen's Bethel "Missionaries" to be "fire-brands of discord and destruction," the Council flatly refused. City authorities were willing to bend the law of 1803 so that daylight meetings could be held if but a "single white person" was present to monitor the sermons, but beyond that the Council would not go; the supervision of Charleston's black major-

---

us that popular revolutions arise from the "conjunction between the grievances of the majority and the aspirations articulated by the [literate leadership] minority." See his *The Making of the English Working Class* (New York, 1963), 168.

38. "An Act Respecting Slaves, Free Negroes, Mulattoes, and Mestizoes," December 20, 1800, in Cooper and McCord, eds., *Statutes at Large*, 7:440–43; "An Act Regarding Religious Worship," 1803, in Brevard, ed., *An Alphabetical Digest,* 2:261.

39. Charleston *Courier,* June 9 and 11, 1818.

ity was "so essential a part of the policy of the state." The Philadelphia churchmen, however, proved determined to carry on. On the following Sunday, they organized a large service "in a [private] house in the suburbs of the city." Once again the city guard invaded the service and arrested the congregation. This time, the City Council sentenced the Philadelphia leadership to "one month's imprisonment, or to give security [and] leave the state." Eight unnamed Charleston churchmen were sentenced "to receive ten lashes" or to each pay a fine of five dollars.[40]

The armed assault on the African Church demoralized many congregants and forced Morris Brown to be even more cautious, unless he too wished to find himself at the receiving end of "a little sugar," as Charleston whites euphemistically called the Workhouse whipping post. But the desecration of sacred ground—a capital crime under Mosaic law—had a very different effect on the African priest. Gullah Jack told Monday Gell that he "wanted to begin" to organize against the whites, when the "African Church was taken up in 1818." Gell himself was much inclined to go "after the same thing."[41] Only Denmark Vesey, now approximately fifty-one-years-old and known to his friends as the "old man," was ready to give up. His friend George Creighton, a wealthy freeman, had grown weary of his endless, humiliating confrontations with Charleston whites, and planned to emigrate to Sierra Leone or Liberia, which in 1819 was purchased at gunpoint by the American Colonization Society with funds allocated by Congress.[42]

For most men, even if young and vigorous, the prospect of starting life anew in a foreign land was daunting at best. But Vesey's life had been little but a succession of migrations from one point in

40. Edwin C. Holland, *A Refutation of the Calumnies Circulated Against the Southern & Western States* (Charleston, 1822), 11; Charleston *Courier*, June 11, 1818.

41. Third confession of Bacchus, July 17, 1822, RGA, GM, SCDAH; Confession of Smart Anderson, July 1822, RGA, GM, SCDAH.

42. For the formation of the Society, see Douglas R. Egerton, "'Its Origin is Not a Little Curious:' A New Look at the American Colonization Society," *Journal of the Early Republic* 5 (Winter 1985): 463–80; see also Marie Tyler-McGraw, "Richmond Free Blacks and African Colonization," *Journal of American Studies* 21 (1987): 210–17, for black attitudes toward emigration.

Atlantic waters to another. St. Thomas, Saint Domingue, Norfolk, Charleston, perhaps even West Africa, had each been his home during various chapters in his long life. Sierra Leone could use both capital and carpenters. After some time and thought, however, Vesey decided to stay in Charleston. Perhaps the bold words of Jack Pritchard, perhaps the plight of his Robert, Sandy, Polydore and his other children, all of whom remained human property and so chained to Charleston, restored the revolutionary fire in the former slave. "[H]e had not a will" to "go with Creighton," he finally confided to Frank, another member of the African Church. "[H]e decided to stay, and see what he could do for his fellow creatures."[43]

Charleston whites, in later years, came close to making the connection between the temporary closure of the African Church and the first stirring of black revolt. But they never came close to recognizing as legitimate the radical theology forged in its basement. As a class leader, Vesey "grossly perverted Scripture," insisted one white Christian, who once bragged that he watched Jack Pritchard die. Richard Furman, the white clergyman, rightly insisted that slave restiveness could not be blamed on the Christianization of bondpersons. The "Chief himself [was a] Member of an irregular Association, which called itself the African Church." Despite the fact that Vesey's nocturnal teachings consisted of accurate quotations from the Old Testament, Intendant James Hamilton accused him of "pervert[ing the Bible] to his purpose." Perhaps, however, Anna Haynes Johnson, the daughter of the Supreme Court justice, came closest to the truth when she observed that "nothing but the merciful interposition of our God has saved us." In saying this, she appeared to understand that her God was not Vesey's.[44]

Perhaps recognizing the dangerous words of Jehovah, city authorities continued to harass the black congregations. In 1820, several "Negroes was taken up" for holding a late-night service on Anson Street, and on January 15, 1821, Councilman John J. Lafar warned

43. Examination of Ferguson's Frank, June 27, 1822, RGA, GM, SCDAH.

44. John B. Adger, *My Life and Times* (Richmond, 1899), 54; Richard Furman to Governor Thomas Bennett, no date, Richard Furman Papers, USC; Hamilton, *An Account*, 29–30; Anna Haynes Johnson to Elizabeth Haywood, July 18, 1822, Haywood Papers, SHC, UNC.

Morris Brown that the city would not tolerate class leaders conducting instructional "schools for slaves," as "the education of such persons [was] forbidden by law." The "African Church was the people," Monday Gell hotly replied. He had considered divine insurrection in 1818, he swore, "and now they had begun again to try it."[45]

Try it again they would. By early 1821, if not before, the enslaved Africans who listened to Vesey's preaching and sat about his Bull Street home as he read from his Bible, came to regard the militant lessons of the Israelites as sacred writ consciously hidden from them by the white clergy. Literally *all* of Vesey's numerous religious pronouncements were drawn from the Old Testament, and in a very real sense, Vesey and his disciples turned their back on the New Testament God of love. Attracted instead to Jehovah, the ancient God of divine wrath and justice, Denmark Vesey, together with Peter Poyas and Africans Monday Gell and Jack Pritchard, fashioned a theology of liberation that fused the demanding faith of the Israelites with the sacred values of Africa.[46]

Although there is little reason to doubt that the deeply-devout class leader believed in what he taught, Vesey found in the Hebrew Bible, and his nightly class meetings, the means to produce a profound sense of racial identity among his adherents, which would form the framework for his modern exodus from pharaoh's land. Vesey "said we were deprived of our rights and privileges by the white people," Jesse Blackwood remembered, "and that our Church was shut up, so that we could not use it, and that it was high time for us to seek our rights." In short, Vesey used his classes as a forum

45. Thomas W. Higginson, *Black Rebellion* (New York, 1969 reprint of 1889 edition), 241–42; Confession of Hammet's Bacchus, no date, William and Benjamin Hammet Papers, DUL.

46. Jones, *Born a Child of Freedom,* 146–47, suggests that it "is no more valid to assert that Vesey, a class leader in a Charleston church, was divinely inspired to wage rebellion than to claim that the slave [George Wilson] who held the identical church rank betrayed the plot because he felt God decried such upheavals." But Wilson, reading deeply in the New Testament, learned to love his fellow man, even if that man was his master. Vesey, reading equally deeply of the Hebrew Bible, learned a very different kind of lesson.

to create the level of psychological autonomy that had to exist before his enslaved disciples could do what he had been doing since
1800: challenging white authority. Under his guidance, the Cow
Alley Church became a place where traditionally cowed and intimidated men could gather to collectively achieve that level of independence necessary for them to rise up as one for their freedom. All
Vesey required was a plan.[47]

47. Second confession of Jesse Blackwood, June 27, 1822, in Kennedy and
Parker, eds., *Official Report,* 82. This analysis follows Lawrence Goodwyn, *The
Populist Moment: A Short History of the Agrarian Revolt in America* (New York,
1978), x–xix.

Chapter Six

---○---

Exodus
1821–1822

A VERY FAINT LIGHT twinkled through the winter morning from the window of the small rented house at 20 Bull Street. The night watch, if they noticed at all, thought nothing of the early hour; the old builder and his young wife enjoyed the reputation of exceptional industry. But as Christmas of 1821 approached, Denmark Vesey, reading his Bible by the light of a candle, came at last to a history-making resolution. Rather than abandon his children and sail with Susan for Sierra Leone, he would lead his sons and friends and disciples on a modern-day exodus out of Charleston. Vesey had long since rejected the teachings of the carpenter from Nazareth; he instead prepared to begin yet another new life as an African Moses and guide his followers into the promised land of Haiti.[1]

Vesey's emphasis on a mass exodus, together with his determination to flee the United States, made him as unusual in the early nineteenth century as it would have made him commonplace during the first part of the previous century. Too many historians have

---

1. Grimké, *Right on the Scaffold,* 13; Narrative, in Kennedy and Parker, eds., *Official Report,* 23–24.

constructed a generic slave rebel for the pages of their textbooks; black radicals like Vesey are often divorced from the mainstream of the abolitionist movement (despite his association with the young David Walker), even as they are thoughtlessly merged with the personalities and goals of other rebels like Gabriel or Nat Turner. But where most of those who battled for freedom during the age of revolution fought to join political society on equal terms—and both Gabriel and Toussaint Louverture fit this pattern—Vesey simply sought to escape it. Like the Africans who attempted to flee the plantations along the Stono River in 1739 for freedom in Spanish Florida, Vesey was too shrewd to believe that he could put an end to slavery in South Carolina. But he could escape Charleston, and he could take a large number of slaves with him.[2]

As Vesey pondered the possibility of a mass escape, he had to face the grim prospect of failure and death. But there was little to dissuade him from his course. At the age of fifty-four he was very old for his day, already twenty years beyond the average life expectancy for black men in the Old South. (In 1820 there were only 38,000 black men above the age of fifty in the entire country.) At best, he had but a few good years left. If he perished trying to lead his people out of the land of pharaoh, he at least would be spared the frightening prospect of an impoverished dotage in a slave society. But if failure was possible, it was not probable. So unshakable was Vesey's faith that he was convinced that the "Lord will assist them as he did the Israelites from their Bondage," not perhaps, through miraculous intervention as much as by divine guidance.[3]

2. Eugene D. Genovese, *From Rebellion to Revolution: Afro-American Slave Revolts in the Making of the Modern World* (Baton Rouge, 1979), xix–xx, argues that after the age of revolution in general, and the Haitian revolution in particular, "slaves increasingly aimed not at secession from the dominant society but at joining it on equal terms," which makes Vesey's exodus all the more unusual. On Gabriel and Stono see, respectively, Douglas R. Egerton, *Gabriel's Rebellion: The Virginia Slave Conspiracies of 1800 & 1802* (Chapel Hill, 1993) and Wood, *Black Majority*, chapter 12.

3. Jack Ericson Eblen, "New Estimates of the Vital Rates of the United States Black Population During the Nineteenth Century," *Demography* 11 (May 1974): 304, 309; Johnson and Roark, *Black Masters*, 37; Mary Lamboll Beach to Elizabeth Gilchrist, July 5, 1822, Beach Letters, SCHS.

Hindsight is often the enemy of understanding. Secure in the knowledge that Vesey failed to lead his black Israelites to freedom, scholars have concluded that his plan therefore *must* have been unworkable. But Vesey neither survived the killing fields of Saint Domingue nor endured four decades in Charleston by being a fool. As a revolutionary leader, Vesey had the responsibility of seeing to it that his adherents were not slaughtered in a futile effort. The fact that Vesey was prepared to die for his cause hardly implied that the man who had always been a devoted father wished to imperil the lives of his sons in an impossible venture. And his cause was not impossible. Vesey was aware that numbers were on his side. Charleston's annual *Directory and Stranger's Guide,* available in most any shop, told the story. In 1822, the city of Charleston was home to 24,780 people. Only 10,653 men and women were white. Even assuming that most of the 623 free men of color were mulattoes who preferred to remain members of pharaoh's regime, Vesey had a decided black majority at his disposal. No other Southern port was so demographically black.[4]

After twenty-one years a freeman, Vesey knew how white military authority functioned in the city, or rather, how it frequently failed to function. Under the law, the city guard marched nightly through the streets, checking errant slaves for passes and breaking up illegal waterfront gatherings of blacks and working class whites. The reality was altogether different. A small, weary group of night watchmen armed only with sheathed bayonets, wandered the main streets, cursing the ordinances that disturbed their slumber. Most guardsmen were shopkeepers who did business with slaves during the day and so were inclined to ignore their gambols after darkness fell. Somewhat more formidable was the state militia. But the state stored its arms in the arsenal on Meeting Street, a busy thoroughfare that was also home to slaves like Monday Gell. Without even a brick wall to enclose it, the arsenal was protected only by wooden

4. *Directory and Stranger's Guide, 1822,* Appendix 2. As to the feasibility of Vesey's plot, Denmark's earliest biographer wrote: "Before embarking on his perilous enterprise he must have carefully reckoned on . . . its successful achievement." See Grimké, *Right on the Scaffold,* 8.

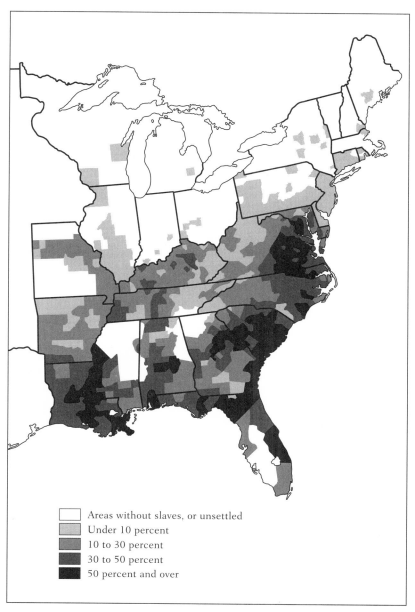

Percentage of Slaves in total population, 1830.

"doors not stronger than those of many dwelling houses." On James Island, just opposite Charleston, sat Fort Johnson, the repository of "a few implements of War" and roughly 140 barrels of partially damaged gunpowder. Befitting its dilapidated condition, only five men stood guard at its ancient doors. In early 1822, the federal Board of Engineers quietly pronounced "the defences" of Charleston "worse than useless." As Vesey strolled the city, discreetly inspecting its lack of security, he could not have failed to notice that the walls of Jericho had already tumbled down.[5]

If white precautions were at their nadir, black discontent in the city had reached its zenith. From December 1819, until late March 1820 a sectional war of words erupted in Washington City as Congress debated the admission of Missouri territory to the union as a slave state. Among those most determined to prohibit the further westward expansion of the peculiar institution was New York Senator Rufus King. An urbane Federalist in a time when that party had ceased to exist, and a bitter foe of the War of 1812 in a time of patriotic postwar nationalism, King was already despised in the South when he twice rose in February to denounce slavery as an affront to natural law. By the time of King's second speech, the Senate galleries were crowded with blacks who had come to hear the one-time presidential candidate announce that he felt degraded at having to sit in the same chamber as slaveholders. Reading the debates in Charleston—and they were widely covered in both newspaper and pamphlet—Vesey came to understand that America was two countries, and that the North, if not hospitable to African Americans, might prove a bit tardy in riding to the defense of the Southern

5. William W. Freehling, *Prelude to Civil War: The Nullification Movement in South Carolina, 1816–1836* (New York, 1966), 56–57; Kennedy and Parker, eds., *Official Report*, 34; Thomas Bennett to Secretary of War John C. Calhoun, July 15, 1822, Joel Poinsett to Calhoun, July 21, 1822, in W. Edwin Hemphill et al., eds., *The Papers of John C. Calhoun* vols. to date (Columbia, 1973), 7:210, 219. My analysis dissents from the view presented in Merton L. Dillon's eloquent *Slavery Attacked: Southern Slaves and Their Allies* (Baton Rouge, 1990), 133, which argues that Vesey's army "could have counted for little against the white militia and the large store of firearms cached by the United States government." But Vesey did not intend to tarry in Charleston long enough for white military power to present an effective counterassault.

planter class. "Mr. King was the black man's friend," Vesey told Jack Purcell, for he pronounced slavery "a great disgrace to the country."[6]

Amidst such rehearsals for civil war, a compromise was reached in far-distant Washington, and Missouri entered the union with slavery intact. But to Denmark Vesey was left the last words in this debate. For all of their timidity and hypocrisy, Northern politicians had at least criticized unfree labor and tried to restrict it to the Southern States. Learned man that he was, Vesey understood all too well that Congress never actually debated emancipation where slavery already existed, but he realized that the peculiar institution was now part of the national discourse. He realized, too, that selected passages from the debates might help him to recruit followers; under-armed insurgents would more readily join if they believed they enjoyed staunch friends in foreign places. Even as the passions in Washington dissipated, Vesey took to telling slaves he encountered on the streets that "Congress had actually declared them free," and that "they were held in bondage contrary to the laws of the land." No less than Rolla Bennett, the sophisticated house servant of Governor Bennett, heard Vesey insist that "we"—Denmark still identified himself as a member of the slave community—"are free but the white people here [in South Carolina] won't let us be so." The only solution, Vesey growled, was "to rise up and fight the whites."[7]

In defiant response to Northern attacks on the westward expansion of slavery, the South Carolina legislature began to reassert its authority over the state's black majority—and over any potential Rufus Kings hiding in their midst. On December 20, 1820, the Assembly passed "An Act to Restrain the Emancipation of Slaves." The law forbade masters from privately manumitting their slaves by deed or self-purchase. Henceforth, Carolina whites were forced to petition both houses of the state legislature to liberate even a single

6. Charles M. Wiltse, *John C. Calhoun: Nationalist, 1782–1828* (New York, 1944), 193; George Dangerfield, *The Era of Good Feelings* (New York, 1952), 223–26; Confession of Jack Purcell, in Hamilton, *An Account*, 42.

7. Grimké, *Right on the Scaffold*, 13; [Pinckney], *Reflections*, 8; Narrative, in Kennedy and Parker, eds., *Official Report*, 19; Testimony of Rolla Bennett, June 26, 1822, in Kennedy and Parker, eds., *Official Report*, 66–67.

bondperson. Slaves who had saved their meager earnings for decades in hopes of buying their own freedom now saw their dreams blasted. But it also made them more susceptible to Vesey's solution. Only one path to freedom remained for Charleston's African community: to band together with the black Moses and escape from Carolina's shores.[8]

Having surveyed the sorry condition of white military prepared-ness, and having considered the level of black frustration with the law of 1820, Vesey began discussing his tentative plan with his clos-est friends. At this early stage of planning, Vesey wished to keep the conspiracy as small as possible. Until the last minute, his army of God needed officers, not soldiers; there was always the danger that as word of the conspiracy spread, somebody might reveal the scheme to the whites. Vesey required lieutenants much like him-self, men already recognized as leaders by the slave community and who could quickly raise large numbers of recruits when the time to strike arrived. Having resolved to select only a few lieu-tenants—none of them mulattoes, and all of them members of the African Church—his choices were obvious: Peter Poyas, Rolla Ben-nett, Monday Gell, and Jack Pritchard. Even the city magistrates, who later sought to portray Vesey as a cruel and embittered man, were impressed by the logic and "sound judgement" of his selec-tions. According to Judge Lionel Kennedy, Rolla was courageous and displayed "uncommon self-possession." Poyas "was intrepid and resolute, true to his engagements, and cautious in observing secrecy," while Gell, an African-born Ibo, was literate, "discreet and intelligent."[9]

Just after Christmas, Vesey explained his plan to Rolla and Ned Bennett. The two men had long been his confidants; Governor Thomas Bennett owned an impressive home at 19 Lynch Street, where the boulevard intersected with Bull, less than two blocks

8. "An Act to Restrain the Emancipation of Slaves," December 20, 1820, in Cooper and McCord, eds., *Statutes at Large*, 7:459–60; Senese, "Free Negro and the South Carolina Courts," *SCHM* 68:142; [Bibb], *The Late Contemplated Insur-rection*, 5.

9. Genovese, *From Rebellion to Revolution*, 9; Grimké, *Right on the Scaffold*, 13–14; Narrative, in Kennedy and Parker, eds., *Official Report*, 24.

from Vesey's house. Rolla thought the governor a decent enough master, but decent or not he kept Africans as chattel; both of Bennett's slaves readily "acquiesce[d] in his schemes." Shortly thereafter Peter Poyas "also consented with equal promptness." The last to sign on was Monday Gell. Vesey arrived one afternoon in Gell's harness shop on Meeting Street and "asked [him] to join." Gell inquired how many others had enlisted, and Vesey "mentioned the names of Peter Poyas [and] Ned Bennett." At length Gell, who remembered what it was like to be free, also agreed. Vesey encouraged all of his lieutenants to enlist a small number of others, who would become members of each officer's "company or band."[10]

Although Charleston authorities expressed grudging admiration for Vesey's organizational skills, they failed to appreciate that in his choice of officers, the aged carpenter consciously selected men who could communicate with various African and African-American constituencies. Historians, perhaps unwisely, debate whether acculturated urban slaves or African rural bondmen were more prone to violent resistance. Vesey's choice of officers bridged such artificial distinctions. As a Carolina-bred shipwright who sold his time on the docks at South Bay Street, Poyas was popular among the skilled blacks who labored along the waterfront. Gell, an Ibo, knew the African men who worked the fields across the rivers but travelled to the city on Sunday to market their wares, as did Mingo Harth, a twenty-six-year-old Mandingo who joined the conspiracy in early spring. (As the conspiracy progressed, both Gell and Harth organized companies along national and ethnic lines.) But the one man whom Vesey was most determined to enlist in his cause was Jack Pritchard. As an Angolan-speaking priest, Jack was both respected and feared by the native Africans who toiled northeast of the Cooper River. Africans not only regarded Pritchard as "invulnerable," they believed he "could make others so by his charms."[11]

The Reformation had purged magic (at least among the edu-

10. *Directory and Stranger's Guide, 1822,* 25; Narrative, in Kennedy and Parker, eds., *Official Report,* 20, 24–25; Second confession of Monday Gell, July 23, 1822, RGA, GM, SCDAH.

11. Washington, *A Peculiar People,* 158; Stuckey, *Slave Culture,* 47; Hamilton, *An Account,* 23–24; Narrative, in Kennedy and Parker, eds., *Official Report,* 20, 24.

cated classes) from Protestant Christianity, but magic remained an integral part of African religion. In East Africa, Jack had been at once a woodworker, a priest, and a folk doctor. Zephaniah Kingsley, the slave trader who purchased Pritchard in Zinguabar, recalled that Jack boarded the ship carrying his bag of charms, herbs, and amulets; the mystical powers in his bag were used to heal, protect, and in rare cases, even kill. For human beings contemplating the frightening prospect of servile revolt against an inherently violent white minority, Pritchard and the leather bag hanging about his neck provided a powerful remedy to the all-too rational fears of young recruits. Vesey, who knew Jack both as a fellow carpenter and as a member of the African Church, understood that the priest's African disciples "firmly believed" that "he could neither be killed nor taken." Perhaps Vesey believed it himself; only the white magistrates, who devoutly accepted the litany of miracles chronicled in the New Testament, denounced African doctrine as a "strange [and] credulous superstition."[12]

Like Monday Gell, Jack Pritchard required little persuasion; he too could remember a life of freedom before being taken captive in 1805. But while Susan Vesey, and perhaps the other wives of his chief lieutenants, knew of the plot, the old carpenter declined to recruit women and discouraged his officers from doing so. There are several possible explanations for the exclusion of women, even from the lowest ranks of his army. Although some urban domestics and free black women hired out around the city, fewer women than men worked away from their masters' eye. To the extent that the final recruiting took place on street corners and along the waterfront, women simply had less opportunity to hear about the planned exodus. Given the possibility of bloody failure, it is equally plausible that Vesey wanted to spare black mothers who would have to care for their children after the execution of their husbands. But perhaps the most obvious explanation is the correct one. Both West Africa and South Carolina were profoundly patriarchal societies. Like King David, Vesey was building an army, and African legions did not

12. Raboteau, *Slave Religion*, 13–14; Genovese, *From Rebellion to Revolution*, 47; Narrative, in Kennedy and Parker, eds., *Official Report*, 21.

include women. "It is said they were true warriors," observed Martha Proctor Richardson, who was hardly surprised to discover that "not a single Woman knew a word of their plans."[13]

Sitting around his table one evening with his circle of five officers, Vesey spelled out his plan in detail. At midnight on the chosen evening, the exodus would begin. "House servants were to kill their Masters" as they slept, admitted one young soldier; Rolla Bennett's murder of the governor and mayor served to introduce chaos into the city's political structure. Almost as one, urban slaves would then move into the streets to take the "positions assigned to them." Having ridden across the Cooper on the previous afternoon, Gullah Jack would return at the head of his Angolan company, while Peter Poyas was to approach the militia arsenal while his men remained hidden in nearby alleys. Vesey instructed Poyas to secure the arms in the arsenal and the night watch's guard house opposite, and then ride the main boulevards to "prevent the Citizens from assembling" for a counter-attack.[14] Slaves moving south from the Neck—the northern suburbs—were to "fire the city in various places" and slaughter the confused and sleepy inhabitants as they stumbled out of their doors. Bringing their wives and children with them, the country slaves and their urban brethren would move toward the docks on the southeastern edge of the Cooper, "to be [secured] by Gullah Jack." As one Southern editor later conceded: "The plot seems to have been well devised, [and] its operation was extensive."[15]

Rolla Bennett's assignment was especially important. Following the death of the governor and Intendant Hamilton, who lived nearby at 28 Bull Street, Rolla and his men intended to secure Common's Bridge on the Ashley so that no whites from Saint Andrews parish to

13. Deborah Gray White, *Ar'n't I a Woman? Female Slaves in the Plantation South* (New York, 1985), 75–76; Martha Proctor Richardson to James Screven, August 7, 1822, Arnold and Screven Papers, SHC, UNC. Stuckey, *Slave Culture*, 69, comments that a "number of African secret societies excluded women."

14. Confession of Enslow's John, no date, William and Benjamin Hammet Papers, DUL; Grimké, *Right on the Scaffold*, 16–17; Narrative, in Kennedy and Parker, eds., *Official Report*, 36.

15. Martha Proctor Richardson to James Screven, July 6, 1822, Arnold and Screven Papers, SHC, UNC; *Niles' Register*, September 14, 1822.

the west could enter the city. At the same time, urban slaves from the Neck were to hold the Lines—the decaying northern fortifications built during the War of 1812—until the enslaved Africans in the countryside who had rendezvoused at Bulkley's farm two miles north of the city could make it into Charleston. The final company, under Vesey's command, planned to seize the guard house from the incompetent night watch.[16]

Vesey could not count on local militia incompetence to last forever; even with many whites absent from the city, the besieged black majority would inevitably fall victim to the combined wrath of state and federal military power. But historians who regard Vesey's plan as doomed to failure mistakenly assume that he planned to remain in the city and fight to the last man. Although city magistrates, for obvious reasons, later downplayed the importance of Haiti in Vesey's plans, for the aged carpenter the promised land lay to the east in the black republic. According to Rolla Bennett, who knew his old friend's mind better than anyone, the slave army would not linger in Charleston. "[A]s soon as they could get the money from the Banks, and the goods from the stores," Rolla insisted, "they should hoist sail for Saint Doming[ue]" and live in freedom amongst Toussaint's descendants. For all of his acculturation into Euro-American society, Vesey, as a native of St. Thomas, remained a man of the black Atlantic.[17]

Two years before, President Jean-Pierre Boyer placed advertisements in American newspapers inviting American freedpeople to

16. Narrative, in Kennedy and Parker, eds., *Official Report*, 36–37; Grimké, *Right on the Scaffold*, 17.

17. Narrative, in Kennedy and Parker, eds., *Official Report*, 27, 34–35; F. A. Michaux, *Travels to the West of the Allegheny Mountains*, in Thomas D. Clark, ed., *South Carolina: The Grand Tour: 1780–1865* (Columbia, 1985), 34; Second confession of Monday Gell, July 23, 1822, RGA, GM, SCDAH. On July 14 as a day of celebration in Massachusetts, see Hinks, *To Awaken My Afflicted Brethren*, 74 note 24. Vesey's choice of Bastille Day may not have been unusual. David Waldstreicher, *In the Midst of Perpetual Fetes: The Making of American Nationalism, 1760–1820* (Chapel Hill, 1997), 315, comments that "it is striking how often black revolutionaries planned slave revolts for the days of jubilee." Despite all of these precise plans, Wade, "Vesey Plot," 150, curiously suggests that "no cache of arms lay hidden about the city; no date for an uprising had been set."

Jean-Pierre Boyer, president of Haiti. Vesey and his followers planned to sail to Haiti after their revolt. *Courtesy of the Schomburg Center for Research in Black Culture.*

relocate to Haiti. The once prosperous French colony had yet to recover from the 1791 rising of the slaves, the costly war of independence, or the crippling 1806 American embargo on trade with the black republic. Promising free land and political opportunity to black settlers, Boyer hoped to recruit skilled labor to his shores, and he desperately needed just the sort of artisanal capacity Vesey's crowded armada might bring. The community of established nations already treated Haiti as an international pariah and a dangerous symbol of black liberty; the administration of James Monroe might take action if Haiti welcomed slave rebels. But Vesey expected to buy his way into exile. Boyer's embattled republic required capital fully as much as muscle, and white voices echoed Rolla in believing that Vesey planned to "pillage" the "Banks [with] which they were immediate[ly] to go off with to St. Doming[ue]." But what Langdon Cheves, the president of the Bank of the United States, regarded as "plunder" was for Vesey's men nothing less than back pay. For harness-maker Monday Gell, the cash in Charleston's vaults was not merely his passport to Haiti; it represented decades of un-recompensed labor.[18]

Given Boyer's possible reluctance to open his ports to hundreds of men and women the Euro-American community would regard as murderers and thieves, Vesey had to prepare Haiti for the eventual-ity of his arrival fully as much as he had to prepare his own captains. The plan called for his soldiers to "put as many" aboard as made it to the docks and sail for Haiti on Monday, July 15, only "one day after they had taken the place." To alert Boyer, Gell "wrote more than one letter" to Haitian authorities, which were smuggled out of Charleston by a black "steward of a Brig lying at Gibbes & Harpers wharf." But if Haiti signaled the promised land for Carolina blacks, it so terrified Charleston whites that Anna Haynes Johnson, the daughter of Supreme Court Justice William Johnson, later believed that Vesey's lieutenants intended to "carry *us* & the common negro's to St D[omingue, and] there to be sold as slaves."[19]

Having planned his detailed scheme for many months, perhaps even for years, since the temporary closing of the African Church in 1818, Vesey did not intend to hurry the day of exodus. His captains required time to recruit their companies; the swords and muskets that proudly hung above the mantlepiece in many a parlor had to be sharpened and cleaned. Pikes had to be manufactured for the ma-jority who had no training with modern weapons (although rifles were common enough in West Africa). Vesey suggested mid-summer. With the arrival of humid temperatures and the attending dangers of yellow fever, those who could afford to abandoned Charleston and

18. Confession of Rolla Bennett, June 25, 1822, in Kennedy and Parker, eds., *Official Report,* 68.

19. John Chester Miller, *The Wolf By the Ears: Thomas Jefferson and Slavery* (New York, 1977), 272; Brenda Gayle Plummer, *Haiti and the United States* (Athens, 1992), 29; Nash, *Forging Freedom,* 243; Mary Lamboll Beach to Elizabeth Gilchrist, July 5, 1822, Beach Letters, SCHS; John Potter to Langdon Cheves, July 10, 1822, Cheves Papers, SCHS.

headed north. Traveler F. A. Michaux arrived in the port city during one yellow fever alarm to discover a nearly deserted town: "[T]here was not a person who conceived his business of that importance to oblige him to go there while the [warm] season lasted." Accordingly, Vesey identified Sunday, July 14, "as the day of the rising." Country slaves routinely entered the city on Sunday to sell their wares, so the night watch would not think it strange to see large numbers of Africans converging on Charleston. More to the point, the date carried symbolic importance. As an avid reader of illicit antislavery pamphlets, Vesey may have known that July 14 was the day Massachusetts freemen celebrated their emancipation. But given the vast Dominguan presence in his city, he *had* to know that it was also Bastille Day, a moment celebrated by Atlantic radicals as a bloody assault on despotism in the name of human liberty.[20]

As Vesey and his officers began to recruit in Charleston during the late winter months of 1822, they maintained both a rigid hierarchy and a tight control over the flow of information. All orders emanated from the old carpenter, and he saw to it that his captains discussed their companies only in terms of the numbers of recruits. For reasons of security, even Rolla Bennett and Peter Poyas refused to reveal to other leaders "the names of those whom they had engaged and who constituted their company." This cautious method of organization meant that a potential traitor could only name the man who recruited him; soldiers in the cause, until the final moments, were wholly ignorant of both the conspiracy's leaders as well as other members of their own company. So prudent were Vesey's captains, that John and Bram, both of whom worked in Jonathan Lucas's mill, were unaware that either was "engaged in the plot until they met in jail."[21]

Vesey also was careful as to what sort of bondman he allowed

20. Confession of Smart Anderson, July 12, 1822, RGA, GM, SCDAH; Hamilton, *An Account,* 21; Confession of Enslow's John, no date, William and Benjamin Hammet Papers, DUL; Anna Haynes Johnson to Elizabeth Haywood, July 18, 1822, Haywood Papers, UNC.

21. Narrative, in Kennedy and Parker, eds., *Official Report,* 26–27; Martha Proctor Richardson to James Screven, August 7, 1822, Arnold and Screven Papers, SHC, UNC.

his officers to recruit into his army of God. Aside from his old friend
Rolla, few domestic servants ever caught word of the plan. Instead,
Vesey preferred men like Monday Gell, slaves who hired their time
away from their masters and so had achieved a level of psychological and economic autonomy. The list of those later jailed read
like a directory of the city's black artisans: carters, carpenters, cooks,
stevedores, potters, draymen, stone cutters, and mechanics. At his
numerous nocturnal meetings—typically held around midnight—
Vesey frequently reminded his disciples to avoid the sort of devout
slaves who happily accepted "old coats and such things from deir
masters, or they will betray our secrets."[22]

Not surprisingly, nervous recruits like Robert Harth inevitably
inquired as to how many other soldiers they could count on. Vesey's
officers tended to be evasive. "[W]e'll find them fast enough,"
replied Peter Poyas, "we expect men from Country and town." No
reliable figure exists of the number who eventually joined. The city
magistrates later speculated that as many as 9,000 slaves at least
heard of the plot, a not irrational guess given the many thousands of
slaves who worked the plantations between the Santee River in the
northeast and the Combahee River to the southwest. But Vesey
ultimately relied upon the knowledge that nobody could be neutral
in a slave revolt. "[H]e that is not with me is against me," Vesey
taught (in his sole known reference to the New Testament). Once
the fighting began, slaves would be presented with a *fait accompli,*
and Vesey guessed that those who had not previously heard of the
plot would join if success appeared likely. As was the case with John
Brown three decades hence, Vesey did not require thousands of soldiers prior to the night of July 14; indeed, it was foolhardy to spread
the word too widely. "Let us assemble a sufficient number to commence the work with spirit," Vesey remarked, "and we'll not want
men, [as] they'll fall in behind us fast enough."[23]

22. Israel Nesbit, in Rawick, ed., *American Slave,* 11:262. Peter Poyas used precisely the same words when recruiting soldiers. See Narrative, in Kennedy and
Parker, eds. *Official Report,* 26.

23. Confession of Harth's Robert, June 21, 1822, RGA, GM, SCDAH; Narrative, in Kennedy and Parker, eds., *Official Report,* 37. Johnson and Roark, who are
perhaps overly concerned with numbers, suggest that the "practicality of a slave insurrection was not Vesey's chief concern. The realists' arguments about matters of

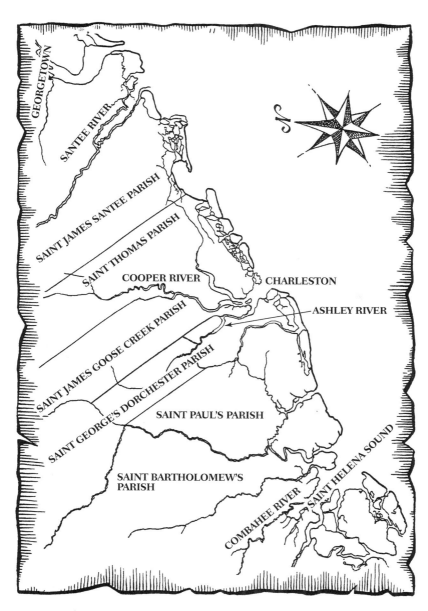

Map of the South Carolina coastline, 1821. *Map by the author.*

Those recruited into the plot during the winter of 1822 were directed to arm themselves from their masters' closets and mantle-pieces. But for those who were expected to join on the night of the rising, additional arms were necessary. To that end, Vesey approached Bacchus Hammet. Vesey was aware that the Charleston Neck militia company stored their muskets—estimated to be approximately 300 and bayonets—in the back room of Benjamin Hammet's King Street Road store, which stood just north of the Lines. Despite its location in the predominantly black Hampstead district, the unguarded store was secured by a single lock, to which Bacchus held a key. At length, Bacchus "agreed to deliver [the muskets] at the moment agreed upon."[24]

Equally cunning was Vesey's solution to the problem of how Peter Poyas could get close enough to the Meeting Street Arsenal without raising the alarm. Vesey had walked past the underguarded building often enough to know that it would be relatively easy to seize. But the success of his plan required utter silence for as long as possible; a sentinel's cry would bring alarmed whites into the streets before their slaves had the opportunity to quietly dispatch them as they slept. To disguise Poyas, Vesey commissioned a white barber to create "a number of wigs and false whiskers [from] the hair of white persons." With his skin lightened by powder and his downturned face hidden beneath beard and wig, Poyas, using the cover of night, could get close enough to murder the guards before one cried out. "[P]robably these precious few" so dressed, admitted businessman John Potter, "would have been enough" to capture the Arsenal.[25]

---

power and advantage meant little to this committed revolutionary." But city magistrates were deeply impressed by the practicality of his plan and prudent method of organization. See *Black Masters,* 40. But Marcus Rediker, in examining a similar context, found that a ship mutiny "could be put into effect with the support of only 20–30 percent of the crew so long as the majority of the seamen could be counted upon to remain neutral or to join once the seizure of power was underway." See *Between the Devil and the Deep Blue Sea,* 227–29.

24. Narrative, in Kennedy and Parker, eds., *Official Report,* 33, 39; John Potter to Langdon Cheves, July 16, 20, 1822, SCHS.

25. Narrative, in Kennedy and Parker, eds., *Official Report,* 39–40; Mary Lamboll Beach to Elizabeth Gilchrist, July 5, 1822, Beach Letters, SCHS; John Potter to Langdon Cheves, July 5, 1822, Cheves Papers, SCHS.

Neither was it particularly difficult to obtain the horses Poyas's company needed to sweep the main boulevards as the city's bond-people moved toward the docks. Most of the draymen and carters involved in the scheme either owned their own horses or enjoyed the use of their owners' animals; enslaved coachmen, like conspirators Isaac Harth and John Horry, were entrusted with the care of their masters' horses. John Gell's livery stables at 127 Church Street were to be emptied, and most of the "butchers boys could with ease provide themselves with horses." Far from being a disorganized and chaotic melee, Vesey's meticulously-timed plan, as one Charleston patrician later conceded, "denoted a fine Military *Tact* and admirable combination," while its leaders displayed "courage & sagacity."[26]

Even the most courageous armies required training. Although some African slaves on the countryside were familiar enough with rifles, most had no experience with either pistol or musket, and fewer still had handled guns in recent years. The Charleston streets were hardly conducive to black military drills; the central weakness of Vesey's exodus was that few of his soldiers were marksmen, whereas most Carolina whites were handy with firearms. Vesey consequently encouraged his officers to arm themselves with swords or long daggers, although he himself would carry a pistol. Swords in any case would make for quieter work as the city bells tolled midnight. By early spring, Poyas, Gell, Bacchus Hammet, and John Horry all possessed swords. Rolla obtained a crudely made dagger, which he kept hidden in a trunk in his room. For those untrained slaves who would join only on July 14, Vesey employed several enslaved blacksmiths to forge "pike heads and bayonets with sockets, to be fixed at the ends of long poles." Several recruits bragged that they had "2 or 300 Bayonets," which was surely an exaggeration. But authorities later discovered a bundle of twelve pikes, each "about nine or ten feet long," concealed at Bulkley's farm north of town.[27]

26. Narrative, in Kennedy and Parker, eds., *Official Report,* 37–38; Martha Proctor Richardson to James Screven, July 6, 1822, Arnold and Screven Papers, SHC, UNC. John K. Thornton, "African Dimensions of the Stono Rebellion," *American Historical Review* 96 (October 1991): 1111, demonstrates that the South Carolina rebels of 1739 demonstrated an awareness of military tactics. They "marched under banners like the unit flags that African armies flew in their campaigns."

27. Narrative, in Kennedy and Parker, eds., *Official Report,* 31–32; Confession of

Securing pikes and muskets enough was Vesey's greatest difficulty, and he knew it. Considerably easier was the recruitment of willing young men. Masters on rural plantations sought to isolate their laborers from the outside world, typically without much success, but few urban slaveholders even tried to limit contact between their servants and neighboring bondpeople. Given the close proximity of urban housing, each city block contained several hundred people, and whispered rumors across back walls were impossible to monitor. With Vesey and Pritchard employed about the city, it is hardly surprising that so many other carpenters and painters became involved in the plot. Peter Poyas, whose naval carpentry kept him near the docks on South Bay Street, enlisted young Paris Ball, a stevedore who hired his time from his mistress, Ann Simons Ball. Other recruiters, aware of the pressing need for security, used family connections to spread the word and raise their companies. Rolla enlisted his brother-in-law Sambo, who lived on a coastal rice plantation owned by Mrs. La Roche (who also owned Rolla's wife Amaretta). To Sambo, Rolla entrusted the job of organizing the Africans who worked on Johns Island.[28]

Most of all, Vesey and his lieutenants recruited out of the African Church. In converting disciples into warriors, Vesey was essentially continuing to preach the same "inflammatory and insurrectionary doctrines"—as the city magistrates put it—that he had long taught to the Hampstead congregation. God had created Africans the equal of the European, and now Jehovah called upon his children to take up the sword to uphold that truth. As a class teacher, Vesey was not only respected by the church membership, but he knew each of them well; he knew whom to trust and whom to avoid. As Archibald Grimké later wrote, Vesey's nightly classes provided him "with a singularly safe medium for conducting his underground agitation."[29]

Hammet's Bacchus, no date, William and Benjamin Hammet Papers, DUL; Confession of Enslow's John, no date, William and Benjamin Hammet Papers, DUL.

28. Wade, *Slavery in the Cities*, 56–57; Ball, *Slaves in the Family*, 266; Testimony of Joe LaRoche at trial of Rolla Bennett, June 19, 1822, in Kennedy and Parker, eds., *Official Report*, 64.

29. Narrative, in Kennedy and Parker, eds., *Official Report*, 23; Grimké, *Right on the Scaffold*, 11.

On occasion Vesey and the other class leaders conducted their lessons in the church. More commonly, to avoid the prying eyes of the night watch, church leaders held the meetings in their homes. Despite the small size of Vesey's Bull Street home, as many as thirty disciples often crowded into his parlor, sitting on the floor and spilling into the adjoining bedroom. Rolla recalled a typical class. Vesey "was the first to rise up & speak & he read to us from the Bible, how the children of Israel were delivered out of Egypt from bondage." The saga of Moses naturally allowed Vesey to introduce his modern-day exodus to the uninitiated. Mingo Harth, a native Mandingo, rose to add that "all of those belonging to the African Church are engaged [from] the Country to the Town." Mingo assured the stunned initiates that God was on their side. "[T]here is a little man," he said of Gullah Jack, "who can't be killed, shot or caught." Vesey nodded approvingly, then read on. "[I]n the Bible," Vesey preached, "God commanded, that all should be cut off, both men, women and children, [and] it was no sin for us to do so, for the Lord had commanded us to do it."[30]

Convinced, however, that the same God who instructed him did not speak to the accommodationist AME leadership, Vesey "expressly cautioned" his disciples not to breathe a word of the plan to Morris Brown, Harry Drayton, or Charles Corr. Reverend Brown's chief concerns included saving souls and maintaining his church as a vital center of black community life. Brown respected Vesey enough to appoint him a class leader, but the compliment was not returned. If the price of protecting his church meant abandoning the rebels to city authorities, Monday Gell for one had few doubts that Brown "would betray us to the whites." Robert Robertson, a church member and a soldier in Pritchard's company, heard rumors that Jack had "gone to Father Morris to ask whether he would sanction the insurrection," although it is improbable that Pritchard disobeyed Vesey's clear instructions on this point. Still, since a decided majority of the revolutionists were congregants in his church, Brown

30. Examination of Rolla Bennett, June 25, RGA, GM, SCDAH (This was Rolla's court examination, and not his jail confession to Reverend Hall given that night, which appears only in the *Official Report*); Confession of William Paul, June 19, 1822, RGA, GM, SCDAH; Confession of Rolla Bennett, June 25, 1822, in Kennedy and Parker, eds., *Official Report*, 67–68.

must have been aware that *something* of great importance was being discussed behind his back.[31]

Beyond their common concern for Charleston's enslaved community, Brown and Vesey shared few opinions on how best to deal with Southern racism. Brown remained a devout Christian, where Vesey had long ago lost patience with a theology that counseled him to love his oppressor. Brown tried to appease white authority through his moderation, whereas Vesey had grown ever more combative and accepting of violence. As his day of exodus approached, the belligerent former slave understood that black Charlestonians, long conditioned to passivity by the whip and the Workhouse, had to be made to confront the reality of impending revolution. He not only continued his personal campaign of loudly rebuking those who humbled themselves to whites by bowing to approaching strangers or stepping off the wooden sidewalk into the sandy street, he preached to all who might listen that "the master, with his white skin, was in the sight of God no whit better than his black slaves." For himself, he shouted, "he would not cringe like that to any man." So great was the purity of his racial outrage, that when Smart Anderson told him that it was a sin to "kill the women and children," Vesey retorted that Smart "had not a man's heart [and] that he was a friend to Buckra."[32]

Smart was horrified by the prospect of such slaughter, but Vesey refused to back away if such killing became necessary. After all, the Book of Exodus told of how pharaoh's refusal to allow the chosen people to leave Egypt led to the death of the first-born male of every household. Having survived in a brutal world that separated black sons from their fathers, and estranged spouse from spouse, Vesey could hardly be expected to grow soft or compassionate in his

31. Second confession of Monday Gell, July 23, 1822, RGA, GM, SCDAH; Examination of Perault at trial of Haig's Pompey, August 6, 1822, RGA, GM, SCDAH; Confession of Bulkley's Billy, July 13, 1822, RGA, GM, SCDAH; Narrative, in Kennedy and Parker, eds., *Official Report*, 44.

32. Grimké, *Right on the Scaffold*, 10; Confession of Smart Anderson, July 12, 1822, RGA, GM, SCDAH. Genovese, *From Rebellion to Revolution*, 10, observes that Vesey "expected to force his people to choose not between revolution and safety but between revolution and counter-revolutionary violence."

old age. If he indeed nursed for many years "the bitter wrongs of himself and [his] race" and burned with the "mad spirit of revenge," as former slave Grimké later charged, then Vesey simply revealed himself to be all too human. More than a few slaves heard Vesey remark that all of pharaoh's race, young and old, had to perish: "[I]f you kill the *Lice,* you must kill the *Nits.*"[33]

Vesey's harsh sermons were not lost on his lieutenants. During the early spring, Rolla encouraged his old friend Joe LaRoche "to join with him in slaying the whites." LaRoche was aghast. "God says we must not kill," he insisted, only to hear Rolla laugh and call him a coward. LaRoche asked whether Rolla could really murder the governor as he slept. "My Army," Rolla chuckled, "will first fix my old Buck, and then [kill] Intendant" James Hamilton.[34]

Nor were white noncombatants likely to be the only to fall victim as Vesey's desperate armada sailed out of Charleston harbor. Because the slave South routinely offered rewards to those who turned on their fellows as a way of dominating the enslaved labor force, there was always the danger of treachery from within the conspiracy. The cost of collaboration with whites thus had to be equal to the potential cost of engaging in—and failing at—armed rebellion. Rolla promised to "watch for [turn coats] night and day and kill them certainly," and whether he actually meant it or not, Vesey also threatened "to kill every man who did not wish to join." Failure to employ coercion against their own followers was a mortal weakness; Vesey so successfully acted the role of a benevolent tyrant that his disciples treated him as the sons of Israel had treated their ruling patriarchs, with terrified affection.[35]

Certainly the most willing to join the exodus to Haiti were those least distressed by the prospect of bloodshed: the slaves hauled into

33. Grimké, *Right on the Scaffold,* 12; John Potter to Langdon Cheves, July 20, 1822, SCHS; Confession of Enslow's John, no date, William and Benjamin Hammet Papers, DUL.

34. Confession of Joe LaRoche, June 19, 1822, RGA, GM, SCDAH; Confession of Rolla Bennett, June 25, 1822, in Kennedy and Parker, eds., *Official Report,* 68.

35. Genovese, *From Rebellion to Revolution,* 10–11; Confession of Hammet's Bacchus, July 12, 1822, RGA, GM, SCDAH; Confession of Joe LaRoche, June 19, 1822, RGA, GM, SCDAH.

Charleston in the early 1790s by refugees fleeing servile rebellion in Saint Domingue. As men who had not merely read of Toussaint but actually witnessed his slave armies drive their masters into the sea, many "French negroes" readily agreed to return to Haiti now that it was free. Few of their number shuddered at Vesey's injunction "not to spare one white skin, for this was the plan they pursued in St. Doming[ue]." Louis Remoussin gave Vesey his consent, as did Patrick Datty, a cook who lived at 94 Wentworth Street. House-painter William Colcock even understood that several of the "black frenchmen [were] very skilful in making swords and spears, such as they used in Africa."[36]

Whatever their differences, whether they were rural or urban, creole or African, Vesey's soldiers were united by their relative youth. Of the seventy-two men found guilty of insurrection, newspaper accounts or court records listed approximate ages for twenty-five of them. Not counting Vesey, who was then fifty-five, the average age of the conspirators was 29.8 years. Vesey was far and away the oldest convicted rebel for whom there is a known age. Africans, even more so than Europeans, venerated the wisdom of the elderly; for young slaves like Jesse Blackwood, Vesey was the "chief man," but his disciples were young men for the most part, and dangerous beyond their years.[37]

Their youth perhaps explains why so many bondmen were prepared to join a conspiracy that was more of a mass migration than a conventional slave rebellion. Some of Vesey's followers had yet to marry, but all were old enough to have been sold away from their mothers' homes. Many, in short, had little to lose but their lives. Vesey conspired not to abolish the peculiar institution in South Carolina, but to leave it behind, and inevitably, thousands of coastal slaves would be left behind as well. Mayor Hamilton later criticized

36. John Potter to Langdon Cheves, July 16, 1822, Cheves Papers, SCHS; Second confession of Jesse Blackwood, June 27, 1822, in Kennedy and Parker, eds., *Official Report*, 68; Confession of William Colcock, July 12, 1822, RGA, GM, SCDAH.

37. Ages were drawn from newspaper accounts and court records. I was able to establish the age for just more than one-third of the seventy-two slaves and free blacks found guilty of insurrection. Jesse Blackwood's reference to Vesey as his "chief" is taken from his confession, in Kennedy and Parker, eds., *Official Report*, 81.

Vesey for bringing white wrath down upon those unfortunates who would inevitably fail to reach the docks in time for the armada's embarkation.[38] But it ill-became proslavery pamphleteers or genteel ladies who defended unwaged labor to reproach the old abolitionist for failing to accomplish the impossible. Vesey could not end slavery in the United States; he could simply liberate a few men and women in a small corner of it.

Typical of the city slaves who agreed to fight was Bacchus Hammet, the slave of merchant Benjamin Hammet of King Street Road. By the late spring, Vesey and his officers held nocturnal meetings on an almost nightly basis. Bondmen from both "the country and town attended" to discuss the fine points of the plan and to collect coins for arms and ammunition. On May 2, Perault Strohecker, a blacksmith who lived away from his master, invited Bacchus to accompany him to Vesey's home. In the parlor sat Gell, Rolla Bennett, Sandy Vesey, Smart Anderson, and several others. On the table lay "a large Book," which Bacchus recognized as "the Bible." Vesey pulled Bacchus into a side room and warned him that they "were going to have a war and fight the white people" and that those who did not join "must be regarded as an enemy and put to death." Bacchus told Vesey that he wanted no part of it, and the scowling giant said he understood. But Vesey had one question. "Who made his master?" "God," Bacchus responded. "Who made you—God—And then aren't you as good as your master, if God made him & you, aren't you as free?" Faced with a potent combination of physical intimidation, logic, religion, and the prospect of freedom, Bacchus shook Vesey's hand.[39]

To guarantee that Bacchus's participation would not vanish after the exhilaration and danger of the moment, Vesey instructed him to raise his "right hand" as they all repeated their oath: "We will not tell on one another, we will not tell any body, We will not tell if taken by the Whites, nor will we tell if we are to be put to death." Vesey then asked about the key to his master's store, where the

38. Hamilton, *An Account,* 29.

39. Narrative, in Kennedy and Parker, eds., *Official Report,* 20; Confession of Hammet's Bacchus, no date, William and Benjamin Hammet Papers, DUL.

Neck militia kept their rifles, and he inquired also about powder. Later that week, when Benjamin Hammet was elsewhere occupied, Bacchus smuggled his master's pistol, an old cavalry sword, and a barrel of powder into the back alley and the waiting arms of Ned Bennett. Ned and Perault transported the barrel to Monday Gell's house, "where Gullah Jack came and got it."[40]

At the same time that Vesey held nightly meetings at his home, his captains began to organize the Africans who worked the countryside around Charleston. City magistrates later gave up trying to discover how far word of the conspiracy had spread, but trial testimony indicated that slaves as far north as Winyaw Bay in the Georgetown District were aware of the plot; to the south, bondmen near Saint Helena Sound agreed to fight, as had slaves up the Ashley River well beyond Bacon's Bridge. To aid the rural insurgents as they marched toward town, Vesey ordered muskets and bayonets hidden in Duquercron's store on King Street Road, where the thoroughfare meandered north toward Blake's Lands. Peter Poyas especially journeyed "into the country often" to maintain "communications in all the [sea] Islands" and to keep the far northeastern contingent "well informed in Georgetown."[41]

Not content to leave such critical arrangements to even his most trusted confederates, Vesey himself, perhaps accompanied by Jack Pritchard, hired a horse and rode southwest toward the Combahee River. By the late spring, Vesey began declining carpentry work "and employed himself exclusively in enlisting men." Yet even at this late date his essential organizational structure remained unchanged. Vesey searched not for soldiers but instead added "to his staff two principal and several minor recruiting agents," Lot Forrester, Frank Ferguson, and William Garner, a drayman whose already-free brother had important contacts as far inland as Columbia.[42]

Vesey's efforts were not in vain. In Saint John's Parish, "four en-

40. Confession of Hammet's Bacchus, no date, William and Benjamin Hammet Papers, DUL.

41. Narrative, in Kennedy and Parker, eds., *Official Report*, 27, 33–34; Confession of Enslow's John, no date, William and Benjamin Hammet Papers, DUL.

42. Grimké, *Right on the Scaffold*, 15; Narrative, in Kennedy and Parker, eds., *Official Report*, 20–21.

tire plantations of negroes" signed on as part of Ferguson's company, while "a great many" slaves—a number reputed to be several thousand—from James Island promised to cross the Ashley on the appointed night. Newspapers even alleged that ten bondmen "belonging to as many of the most respectable families" in Beaufort (beyond Saint Helena Sound) were involved in the "Insurrection of the Blacks."[43]

Both alarmed whites and resourceful recruiters tended to inflate the figures of those actually involved, the first to justify their retribution, the latter to convince wavering inductees to enlist in a desperate cause. But certainly the potential for thousands of rural slaves to at least *hear* of the revolt was enormous. Planters typically apprenticed some of their young country slaves to senior craftsmen for training. To the extent that a good many of the revolutionists were Charleston craftsmen, impressionable young country slaves first heard of the plan from skilled carpenters like Jack Pritchard. The rural slaves who produced a small agricultural surplus in their provision garden often traveled miles into the city to market their wares, sometimes catching a ride on the same wagons and coastal vessels that ferried word of the plot. Each Sunday, an "immense number of canoes" carried thousands of country people "to the Charleston market." For Sunday, July 14, Frank Ferguson instructed his company to arrive in Charleston with "their hoes, hatchets, axes, and spades, which might be used as offensive weapons, or as instruments to break open doors."[44]

Roughly three miles north of the city proper, where Meeting Street Road curved by pastures and barns, stood Bulkley's Farm, which became the nucleus of the rural conspiracy. Near to a fork in Town Creek, slaves on both sides of the Cooper could easily approach the farm by water and so avoid both the city watch and rural

43. Narrative, in Kennedy and Parker, eds., *Official Report*, 28–31; Confession of Joe La Roche, June 19, 1822, RGA, GM, SCDAH; Richmond *Enquirer*, September 27, 1822.

44. Joyner, *Down By the Riverside*, 71; Larry E. Hudson, Jr., "'All That Cash:' Work and Status in the Slave Quarters," in Hudson, ed., *Working Toward Freedom*, 79; Wood, *Women's Work, Men's Work*, 87; Narrative, in Kennedy and Parker, eds., *Official Report*, 34, 38–39.

patrols. Although most of those who attended the weekly meetings came from nearby farms and plantations, urban leaders like Pritchard frequently rode north to maintain contact with rural slaves. Because absentee landlord Stephen Bulkley lived on King Street, discipline on the farm was nonexistent. Conspirators often arrived at midafternoon to "roast a fowl" as "evidence of union" and to sing psalms and pray "until day light." On one occasion, "the old man (meaning Vesey)" killed a large snake near the gate to the farm. "[T]hat's the way we would do them," he laughed.[45]

Given the sizable African presence on the countryside, Gullah Jack remained one of, if not *the,* leading recruiter outside of Charleston, and he attended every important meeting at Bulkley's Farm. At one meeting, Jack bragged that he had been up the Ashley as far as Dorchester, where "6,600 persons had agreed to join." More commonly, Pritchard used the farm to inspire his company through his creative melding of Old Testament theology and African spirituality, which journalists later derided as an uneasy blend of "religion and superstition." During one ceremony, Jack performed a ritual over a half-cooked fowl and then tore it into small portions, saying: "[D]o so we pull the Buckra to pieces."[46]

If Vesey was the mastermind of the conspiracy, the African priest became its heart and soul. So great was his influence, that both African and creole alike prepared for battle by eating nothing besides "parched corn and ground nuts." But not until the night of the rising would the diminutive "Gullah man" pass out his most valuable charms. Those who carried "this crab claw" in their mouths "can't be wounded." But for whites, Jack's most terrifying ability was his power to persuade. Harry Haig later testified that Pritchard gave him "a bottle with poison to put into [his] Master's pump, & into as many [wells] as he could about town." For a society who dined on food prepared by bond cooks, the realization that Africans possessed a

45. *Directory and Stranger's Guide, 1819,* 29; Confession of Bulkley's Billy, July 13, 1822, RGA, GM, SCDAH; John Potter to Langdon Cheves, July 15, 1822, Cheves Papers, SCHS; Confession of Smart Anderson, July 12, 1822, RGA, GM, SCDAH.

46. Confession of Ferguson's Frank, June 1822, RGA, GM, SCDAH; Hartford *Connecticut Courant,* August 6, 1822.

knowledge of poisons was a horrifying thought. "Good God," wailed businessman John Potter, "what have we come to!"[47]

As May drew to a close, all was in readiness. Following work one evening, Monday Gell returned home to find "Vesey's son-in-law" (probably Charlotte's husband) waiting at his door. At a final conference with Poyas, Bacchus, Ned Bennett, Pritchard, and Frank Ferguson, Vesey and Gell attended to the remaining details. Ferguson reported on his progress on the countryside and suggested he station his company in "the woods" about "three miles from town until Sunday night." Each man contributed "seven pence a piece" so that one of their recruiters could "pay his wages to his master" before he rode again "into the Country." The conspirators embraced and melted into the shadowy night.[48]

47. Examination of Y (unnamed slave of George Cross), no date, RGA, GM, SCDAH; Examination of Perault at trial of Haig's Pompey, August 6, 1822, RGA, GM, SCDAH; Confession of Harry Haig, July 10, 1822, RGA, GM, SCDAH; John Potter to Langdon Cheves, July 16, 1822, Cheves Papers, SCHS. So terrified were Charleston whites of poison that magistrates Kennedy and Parker omitted Haig's reference to it in their published report. In a strange case of editorial honesty, they replaced the quotation with twenty-six asterisks to indicate that a sentence had been left out. See *Official Report*, 107. Poison, of course, was a powerful weapon for the powerless. On its use by slaves, see Philip J. Schwarz, *Twice Condemned: Slaves and the Criminal Laws of Virginia, 1705–1865* (Baton Rouge, 1988), 92–113, and Robert L. Paquette, *Sugar Is Made With Blood: The Conspiracy of La Escalera and the Conflict Between Empires Over Slavery in Cuba* (Middletown, Conn., 1988), 222–23.

48. Second confession of Monday Gell, July 23, 1822, RGA, GM, SCDAH; Confession of Hammet's Bacchus, July 12, 1822, RGA, GM, SCDAH.

Chapter Seven

⸻○⸻

Lamentations
May–June 1822

MAY OF 1822 FOUND the South Carolina lowcountry in a state of steamy commotion. The uncommonly early arrival of hot, damp air obliged many genteel ladies and their daughters to begin packing their trunks for the upcountry. On west Bull Street, black artisans bustled about at all hours, but no carpentry jobs were accepted. Vesey declined all requests for his building skills as he made final preparations for July 14. All was in readiness, down to the final detail. As Governor Bennett's niece wrote during that feverish, angry July: "I never heard in my life more deep laid plots or plots more likely to succeed."[1]

But even as Vesey and his lieutenants attended to last details on Saturday, May 22, their dreams of a successful exodus began to fade. Ten blocks away at the Market Wharf, William Paul, one of Vesey's minor recruiters, committed a fatal blunder. As he strolled to the fish market, William came upon Peter, "a brown man belonging to Colonel [John C.] Prioleau." They gossiped of idle things

1. Anna Haynes Johnson to Elizabeth Haywood, July 18, 1822, Haywood Papers, SHC, UNC.

154

until Peter called William's "attention to a pennant on a Vessel's mast" slowly emerging from the forest of sails in the harbor. As the ship grew larger they could see that it was the *Sally* out of Cap Haitien (as Cap François had been christened after the Revolution). William scarcely knew Peter, a fifty-five-year-old mulatto cook, but despite the fact that Peter was precisely the sort of loyal domestic that Vesey counseled his followers to avoid, William unwisely saw the mention of Haiti as an opening to discuss the escape into the Caribbean. Peter curtly told William that he "did not understand such talk, and stopped the conversation." William began to warn Peter to silence, but it was too late. The crowd at the dock favored his disappearance, and Peter was soon out of sight.[2]

The idea of slaying his master and abandoning Charleston for freedom in the Caribbean frightened Peter, who had grown fleshy and old in the indulgent service of the Prioleau family. But as his master was out of town, Peter hastened to the Logan Street home of his friend William Penceel. Like Peter, Penceel was of mixed ancestry, but unlike the mulatto cook, Penceel was both free and prosperous enough to join the Brown Fellowship Society. For more than a decade, Penceel had made it his practice to purchase slave boys as apprentices in his tin plate business, which meant that a mass exodus out of the city endangered his livelihood fully as much as it did Thomas Bennett's. Penceel urged Peter to waste no time in telling his owners what he had heard at the docks.[3]

Upon returning to the Prioleau residence at 50 Meeting Street, however, Peter waited five long days before again speaking of the

2. Lofton, *Insurrection in South Carolina*, 146; Confession of William Paul, June 19, 1822, RGA, GM, SCDAH; Higginson, *Black Rebellion*, 216. Richard Wade, "The Vesey Plot: A Reconsideration," *JSH* 30 (May 1964): 143, 148, and *Slavery in the Cities*, 240–41, 229, suggests that the conspiracy was "probably never more than loose talk by aggrieved and embittered men" but misidentifies Peter as "Devany Prioleau" despite the fact that he later observes that the state paid "Col. Prioleau's man Peter for secret services rendered." Freehling, *Reintegration of American History*, 44–46, discusses Wade's use of evidence.

3. Hartford *Connecticut Courant*, August 6, 1822; Koger, *Black Slaveowners*, 179; [Bibb], *The Late Contemplated Insurrection*, 5. Wade, "Vesey Plot," 143, fuses William Penceel and George Wilson into a single individual named "George Pencil."

plot. Perhaps he thought the tale too awful for his mistress to hear; perhaps instead he feared the retribution that William Paul shouted after him as he hurried away from the wharf. It was not until the afternoon of Thursday, May 30, that John Prioleau returned home. As a factor—a private banker who marketed plantation harvests in exchange for manufactured goods—Prioleau was often upriver on business, but no sooner was he in his door than his "favorite slave" begged a private interview. Peter stuttered out the appalling news and identified William Paul as his contact. Prioleau dashed a quick note to Intendant Hamilton then headed for John Paul's Broad Street grocery, where he had "the whole of their male servants committed to the Guard-House."[4]

Just after three o'clock, Peter knocked on the Bull Street door of Charleston's intendant, as the city styled its mayor. Then aged thirty-six, James Hamilton had followed the traditional Southern route to power. Born in Charleston, Hamilton briefly studied law under the respected Daniel Huger before admission to the bar in 1810. A brief stint as a cotton planter, together with his marriage to rice heiress Elizabeth Heyward, established his agrarian credentials enough to allow a return to the law in partnership with James Louis Petigru. (Although he continued to list his profession as "planter" in the city directory.) Two terms in the state Assembly led to his election as intendant earlier that year; now Peter stood "trembling" in his study, the letter from Colonel Prioleau loose in his hand. Hamilton glanced at the missive, then made Peter repeat his story. Even before Prioleau arrived, Hamilton sent word for the City Council to meet that evening at five o'clock. A clerk also hurried the news to Governor Bennett's nearby mansion.[5]

Two hours later, the City Council—formally known as the Charleston Corporation—convened in the intendant's stuffy office. Peter nervously repeated his story yet again. The Council found it hard to imagine that any such massive plan had been hatched with-

4. *Directory and Stranger's Guide, 1822*, 68, 70; Martha Proctor Richardson to James Screven, July 6, 1822, Arnold and Screven Papers, SHC, UNC; Hamilton, *An Account*, 3–4.

5. Hamilton, *An Account*, 3, 7; Anna Haynes Johnson to Elizabeth Haywood, June 28, 1822, Haywood Papers, SHC, UNC.

out their notice, and they attached "little credence" to Peter's improbable story. Even so, as a precaution they decided to examine William Paul, whom Colonel Prioleau had already marched off to the guardhouse. Since his arrest, William had readied himself for this moment. But upon entering the oppressively hot room, William glanced at the stone faces impassively watching him—and he came undone. After a good deal of equivocating, William finally admitted that he had spoken to Peter at the fish market. He flatly denied, however, that he ever mentioned an impending war "between blacks and Whites." William's inept performance was even harder to credit than Peter's absurd story of an immense conspiracy, and the Council voted to subject William to solitary confinement in "the black-hole of the Work-House" in hopes that a visit to the city's most infamous structure might loosen his tongue.[6]

As the great door clanged shut behind him, a terrified William began to ponder his options. The Council clearly doubted his denials, and at any moment the authorities might begin the questioning anew, this time with the aid of devices that would have impressed even the cruelest Medieval inquisitor. If he revealed what he knew, the state would surely reward him with his liberty. Western slave societies had long perfected the art of compensating those who informed on their brethren. But he was deep enough into the conspiracy to know the penalty for those who turned their coats; William later told Charles Drayton that he "would run a great risk of his life if he went out" of jail a free man. But the prospect of torture at the hands of skilled practitioners was a more immediate concern, and when Captain William P. Dove barged into his cell later that night, William reluctantly agreed to tell what little he knew. He gave up two names: Mingo Harth, in whose company he served, and Peter Poyas.[7]

On Friday morning, the city guard arrested both men and hauled them before Hamilton and the City Council. But unlike William

6. *Directory and Stranger's Guide, 1822,* 68; Charleston *Courier,* August 23, 1822; Richmond *Enquirer,* August 30, 1822; Hamilton, *An Account,* 4–5.

7. Confession of Paul's Edwin, June 1822, RGA, GM, SCDAH; Hamilton, *An Account,* 5–6.

Paul, who had time to collect his wits yet utterly failed to do so, both Poyas and Harth were as poised as they had been surprised by the guardsmen. When confronted with the allegations, Poyas burst out laughing and denounced William Paul for a young fool. "These fellows behaved with so much composure and coolness," an embarrassed Hamilton later admitted, that the wardens and Council "were completely deceived." Hamilton recommended that the two men be discharged but quietly watched by "spies" of "their own colour." William Paul continued in solitary confinement.[8]

The City Council nonetheless remained convinced that something was amiss. One week passed. Each morning, a committee paraded into William's unlit cell and demanded that the terrified slave provide them with more names. On the morning of Saturday, June 8, Warden Thomas Napier bluntly warned William that "he would soon be led forth to the scaffold, for summary execution." Nearly sick with fear and hunger, William blurted out that while he knew little of the plot, he understood it to be "very extensive, embracing an indiscriminate massacre of the whites." He had never been told the name of the leader but believed him to be a Gullah man "who carried about him a charm which rendered him invulnerable." When Napier looked doubtful, William added that Poyas had assured him that Ned Bennett was a leading conspirator. A skeptical Napier carried that information back to an equally incredulous Council.[9]

Not only could the frustrated intendant not confirm any of William's wild allegations, what evidence he did uncover pointed instead to the complete absence of any vast plot. When Ned Bennett heard that he had been implicated, without waiting for a summons he boldly strolled down Bull Street and hammered on the mayor's door, a particularly courageous gesture given Hamilton's reputation for violence. (The intendant fought fourteen duels, each time carefully wounding the men who dared insult his honor.) Like Poyas, Ned wore a natural "air of enormous innocence." So "surprisingly cool and indifferent" was Ned that Intendant Hamilton was again completely deceived. Besides, the notion that the gover-

8. Narrative, in Kennedy and Parker, eds., *Official Report,* 52; Hamilton, *An Account,* 6; Grimké, *Right on the Scaffold,* 18.
9. Richmond *Enquirer,* August 30, 1822; Hamilton, *An Account,* 6–7.

nor's domestics wished to slay their master was absurd. As a smug Governor Bennett assured Hamilton, he worked his bondmen "day & night [so] *they* had not *time* for *one* even of them to be engaged in it." Why would they wish to see him dead?[10]

As soon as he left the mayor's study, however, Ned hastened down the block to Vesey's home. Although William Paul was but a minor recruiter in the affair, he knew at least the names of most of the chief officers, including Denmark, and there was always the danger that one of the soldiers he implicated might break and confirm his story. Further delay meant danger. "[I]t was all over," Vesey told Monday Gell, unless they could take the city before another conspirator spoke to authorities. It was now late in the evening of June 8. Vesey suggested that they move their escape up to Sunday "the 16th of June." That gave them one week's time to get the word into the countryside.[11] But at that very moment, only eight doors away at 28 Bull Street, Intendant Hamilton sat brooding in his study, as "indefatigable in ferreting out the Leaders" as his black neighbor was in planning the mayor's death.[12]

Hamilton was about to get the information he desired. The next morning was Sunday, June 9, and Charleston's black community flocked to the African churches. Just as services ended, Joe LaRoche approached George Wilson and whispered that Rolla Bennett wished to see him. That evening, Wilson and LaRoche entered the governor's mansion through the back door. Rolla "complained of his hard living" and then told Wilson of the plan and urged him to join. George begged Bennett "to let it alone" and wept as he heard Rolla reply: "Tis now gone too far to stop it." If Wilson refused to accompany them to Haiti, Rolla warned, it was best for him "to go out of town on Sunday night, as he did not wish him to be hurt."[13]

10. Hamilton, *An Account,* 7; Grimké, *Right on the Scaffold,* 20; Mary Lamboll Beach to Elizabeth Gilchrist, July 5, 1822, Beach Letters, SCHS.

11. Narrative, in Kennedy and Parker, eds., *Official Report,* 36; Grimké, *Right on the Scaffold,* 17–18; Second confession of Monday Gell, July 23, 1822, RGA, GM, SCDAH.

12. *Directory and Stranger's Guide, 1822,* 46; John S. Cogdell to Langdon Cheves, July 6, 1822, Cheves Papers, SCHS.

13. Confession of George Wilson, June 20, 1822, RGA, GM, SCDAH; Confession of Joe LaRoche, June 19, 1822, RGA, GM, SCDAH; Testimony of Joe

Rolla's disclosure was as foolhardy as it was compassionate. Bennett had known George Wilson, "a heavily built dark mulatto" blacksmith, almost as long as he had known his neighbor Denmark. Although much attached to his master, Major John Wilson, George hired out his skills and even lived away from his owner's Broad Street home. As industrious as he was pious, George enjoyed a solid reputation among both blacks and whites. Despite his mixed ancestry, George became a founding member of the African Church, where as a class leader he taught others to read and write. Rolla admired George's Christian soul, even as he shared few of his opinions regarding the master class. Rolla could not have seriously envisioned George joining the conspiracy; he simply respected George enough to wish him safely out of the way.[14]

Rolla's words presented George with the same impossible choice that William Paul's information had bestowed upon Peter Prioleau. Africans believed that traitors were doomed to eternal wandering in the afterlife, which meant that an informer's soul could neither return to its native land nor communicate with the spirits of revered ancestors. But George was Christianized enough to share his master's disdain for African theology. Indeed, the simple, stoic Wilson never expressed any fears for his safety in this world or the next; he never said anything about Rolla's possible vengeance. He liked Rolla and even admired Vesey. Yet he loved his master with all his heart, as the New Testament and white clergymen encouraged him to do. As one disgusted conspirator later told his grandson, Wilson's loyalty "to his master was so deep under de skin [that] it was even stronger than de long dream of freedom."[15]

As they slowly ambled back toward the heart of the city, Wilson and LaRoche discussed their choices. George was inclined to tell his master, but he wanted a few days to think it over. Joining was never an option, but flight remained a possibility. Joe promised his com-

LaRoche at trial of Rolla Bennett, June 19, 1822, in Kennedy and Parker, eds., *Official Report*, 62–63.

14. Theodore D. Jervey, *Robert Y. Hayne and His Times* (New York, 1909), 131; Pharo, ed., *Reminiscences of Wilson*, 6.

15. Stuckey, *Slave Culture*, 6; Israel Nesbit, in Rawick, ed., *American Slave*, 11:262.

panion that he would tell his "master every thing" if George did, but Wilson, utterly despondent with grief, only muttered that he would consider the matter until Friday. After five sleepless nights, George reached a difficult decision. Early in the afternoon on June 14, he walked to his master's home at 106 Broad Street and turned on his old friend Rolla Bennett.[16]

At eight o'clock that evening, Major John Wilson burst into James Hamilton's study with the warning that Governor Bennett's slaves were leading an insurrection. But what was grim news to the major was confirmation to the intendant. Because the City Council had maintained absolute silence regarding William Paul's confession, Hamilton observed that "the [two] witnesses could have had no possible communication." The two accounts were similar enough in detail, and both William Paul and George Wilson implicated Bennett servants. Hamilton rushed the latest information to the governor, who instructed the commanding officers of the city's militia regiments to be at the intendant's home by ten o'clock that night.[17]

Long into the night, George repeated his story to Hamilton and a still-incredulous Governor Bennett. With each telling, George emphasized "with great confidence" that the rising would take place in only two days "on the ensuing Sunday night." Bennett refused to believe that Rolla, whom he held in the very highest favor, was involved. But both prudence and politics dictated at least the appearance of bold action. Just before midnight, he ordered the arrest of ten slaves. Among them were Poyas, Mingo Harth, and virtually his entire domestic household, including Rolla and Ned.[18]

If the governor was naive enough to think that his unpaid, overworked human property loved him as he loved them, the artful

16. Confession of George Wilson, June 20, 1822, RGA, GM, SCDAH; Testimony of George Wilson at trial of Rolla Bennett, June 19, 1822, in Kennedy and Parker, eds., *Official Report*, 64–65; Pharo, ed., *Reminiscences of Wilson*, 6; W. Hasell Wilson to Robert Wilson, no date, CLS.

17. Hamilton, *An Account*, 7–9; Charleston *Courier*, August 23, 1822, later wrote that George Wilson told his master on the night of "Thursday the 13th June." The intendant, however, was very precise as to day and time, and Governor Bennett did not issue orders to the militia until Saturday, June 15.

18. Richmond *Enquirer*, August 30, 1822; John Potter to Langdon Cheves, July 15, 1822, Cheves Papers, SCHS; Charleston *Courier*, August 23, 1822; Hamilton, *An Account*, 9.

Rolla was willing to support that gullibility in the name of survival. When arraigned, Rolla played the time-honored role of dutiful but dim-witted servant. He pretended "not to understand the charges against him" and politely asked that the accusations be explained in simpler terms. Hamilton repeated the charges, to which Rolla expressed "astonishment and surprise." That was enough for Governor Bennett, who again assured the intendant that it was foolishness to "believe that his own Negroes were implicated."[19]

As yet, Denmark Vesey's name had gone unmentioned. But living as he did directly between Bennett and Hamilton, the shrewd old carpenter had only to step onto his porch to witness the frantic activity at both ends of Bull Street. Early the next morning, Saturday, June 15, Vesey instructed young Jesse Blackwood to ride into the countryside in preparation for the attack. Blackwood found city guardsmen swarming along each main road and was forced to turn back. When Blackwood reported back to Vesey, "the Old Chief became very sorrowful." For all his great faith, for all his careful planning, his exodus to Haiti was not to happen. Any hopes of successful escape from Charleston harbor, as Colonel Wilson's son rightly observed, depended upon "secresy" and surprise and white military ineptitude. The flashes of sabre along Bull Street informed Vesey that it was finished.[20]

For all that, Vesey had never been one to easily give in to panic. Since that October day back in 1781 when he first stepped ashore in Saint Domingue, Vesey had learned to survive by his wits and iron determination. Even as they watched militiamen march by his window, Vesey and Gell methodically set fire to any incriminating letters and documents in their possession. Magistrate Lionel Kennedy later insisted that Vesey also burned "books relating to this transaction," by which Kennedy probably meant the collection of antislavery pamphlets that Vesey had amassed over the decades. At about

19. Narrative, in Kennedy and Parker, eds., *Official Report*, 45–46; John Potter to Langdon Cheves, June 29, 1822, Cheves Papers, SCHS.

20. Grimké, *Right on the Scaffold*, 20–21; W. Hasell Wilson to Robert Wilson, no date, CLS.

the same time, Jack Pritchard buried his small cache of gunpowder and weapons, probably near Bulkley's farm.[21]

Only then did Vesey prepare to go into hiding. Mayor Hamilton later wrote that Vesey was captured "in the house of one of his wives." Presumably he decided to conceal himself with Beck, his first wife (who also lived just a few doors from Hamilton's mansion). His own home on Bull Street would be the first place authorities would search. Susan remained behind. Although she had known about the conspiracy, she had never been actively involved, and the white patriarchs who governed the city were hardly inclined to put a woman on trial for complicity in a man's war. Sometime before dawn on Sunday, June 16, Vesey said his farewells to Susan and quietly slipped out the door. She was only twenty-seven.[22]

Despite the frenetic activity on the part of both white authorities and black conspirators, Hamilton rather absurdly decided to publicly say as little as possible about the impending rebellion, as if inhabitants of the city could neither hear the terrified gossip nor see the military preparations all about them. Local newspaper editors behaved as if nothing was awry. More than two weeks passed between Rolla's arrest and the first terse reference to the conspiracy in the June 29 edition of the *Charleston Mercury*. As one astonished North Carolina journal observed, "not a whisper of all this was echoed in the Charleston papers." But despite all attempts to keep the arrests "a profound secret," by Saturday afternoon the city was alive with rumors "of a very extensive conspiracy." Even the *Courier* later admitted that the prospect of servile rebellion was "generally known to our fellow-citizens [by] Sunday, producing a night of sleepless anxiety."[23]

21. Narrative, in Kennedy and Parker, eds., *Official Report*, 26; Confession of Hammet's Bacchus, no date, William and Benjamin Hammet Papers, DUL.

22. Hamilton, *An Account*, 17. Because William Paul testified that Beck lived "near the Intendant's" home, she obviously did not live with her daughter Sarah (Denmark's step-daughter) in 1822, as Sarah was owned by John Paul, who lived six blocks away at 47 Broad Street. See his testimony at trial of Denmark Vesey, June 22, 1822, in Kennedy and Parker, eds., *Official Report*, 85.

23. Gary Philip Zola, *Isaac Harby of Charleston, 1788–1828: Jewish Reformer and Intellectual* (Tuscaloosa, 1994), 95; Charleston *Mercury*, June 29, 1822; Salisbury

Due perhaps to the fact that their bondpeople continued to wear the impenetrable mask of obedience, white Charlestonians initially paid "little attention" to the rumors. So confident were Carolina paternalists in the docility of their black children that they simply could not fathom a murderous plot involving thousands of slaves. But as the weekend wore on, the story "kept gaining ground by whispers and hints" until it was widely known "that a secret conspiracy was going on." Martha Proctor Richardson noticed the genteel ladies of the city to be "in aweful commotion," and Charles Blackner Vignoles informed a correspondent of the "great ferment occasioned" by the tales. Planter Vignoles comforted himself, however, with the belief that the scheme "does not appear to have extended among the negroes in the Country[side]."[24]

Sunday morning broke clear but hot. As if by common consent, the black community remained indoors, and few ventured out for services in the African churches. Taking no chances, Governor Bennett and Intendant Hamilton—who had earned the rank of major in the War of 1812—ordered the militia to patrol the city streets starting in mid-afternoon. "The Military force out that day was so overpowering," wrote Mary Lamboll Beach, to render all but the most "*desperate* attempts" impossible. In hopes of finding his company awaiting his arrival at Bulkley's farm, Jack Pritchard walked north on King Street Road only to find the Charleston Neck patrol "out quite strong." The patrol discovered twelve pikes concealed at the farm but were dismayed by indications that other weapons had been "removed, destroyed, or effectively concealed." The clatter of musket and sword was not lost on the conspirators, and so "vigilant" were the patrols that evening, Magistrate Lionel Kennedy observed, that even the most intrepid rebels "did not dare to show themselves."[25]

Western Carolinian, July 16, 1822; Martha Proctor Richardson to James Screven, August 7, 1822, Arnold and Screven Papers, SHC, UNC; Charleston *Courier,* August 23, 1822.

24. Richmond *Enquirer,* July 30, 1822; Martha Proctor Richardson to James Screven, July 6, 1822, Arnold and Screven Papers, SHC, UNC; K. H. Vignoles, ed., "Charles Blackner Vignoles in South Carolina and Florida, 1817–1823," *SCHM* 85 (April 1984): 103.

25. Mary Lamboll Beach to Elizabeth Gilchrist, July 5, 1822, Beach Letters,

Even the sight of enlarged patrols, however, could not soothe the rattled nerves of white Charlestonians, and memories of Saint Domingue murdered sleep in the lowcountry that Sunday night. Outside the city, members of the Ball family armed themselves with rifles and sat vigil by their windows, while their overseers lit enormous bonfires near the gates to their plantations. In Colonel Wilson's Broad Street home, "no one not even the children ventured to retire." Every passing patrol, W. Hasell Wilson remembered, "and every slight noise, excited attention." But at long last daylight turned their fading candles pale, and with the morning came "a general feeling of relief, [although] the anxiety and suspense were not dissipated for some time."[26]

Having survived the long night, white Carolinians transformed Monday into a day of prayer and thanksgiving. Eliza Ball, who had been raised on the same Windsor plantation as Peter Poyas, fell to her knees in supplication. "Oh heavenly Father," she prayed, "how great has been thy mercy to us, [in] protecting and saving us & our city from fire & murder which threatened us." Masters who had kept a sharp eye on their servants the night before now assured themselves that they had nothing to fear. "[M]any I hope were not implicated," John Potter told Langdon Cheves, and "I have no reason to suppose any of my house servants were guilty." And citizens who had jumped at every shadow suddenly scoffed at their own fears. "I do not think that the object could have been accomplished to any save a very limited extent," one gentlewoman confided to James Screven.[27]

Bravado aside, the master class had come within a sword's blade of disaster, and they knew it. Two days before, the white minority had every confidence in the security of their world, but now every smiling domestic was a potential assassin. John Potter was hardly

SCHS; Confession of Hammet's Bacchus, no date, William and Benjamin Hammet Papers, DUL; Narrative, in Kennedy and Parker, eds., *Official Report,* 32, 36.

26. Ball, *Slaves in the Family,* 268; W. Hasell Wilson to Robert Wilson, no date, CLS.

27. Ball, *Slaves in the Family,* 268; John Potter to Langdon Cheves, July 20, 1822, Cheves Papers, SCHS; Martha Proctor Richardson to James Screven, September 16, 1822, Arnold and Screven Papers, SHC, UNC.

alone when he spoke of how the unending night "awakened unpleasant feelings" in his household. Potter tried to maintain a brave
front before his family, "who have been more alarmed than I have
ever seen before." But the (incorrect) rumors that slave cooks
planned to take *"care of the meals"* with poison reminded every
slaveholder of the danger lurking within their own doors. For those
along the coast, where blacks outnumbered whites by more than
two to one, sanity required the sincere belief that Africans were
happy in their captivity. June 16 reduced those beliefs to ashes.
"There is a look of horror in every countenance," confessed Anna
Haynes Johnson, who added that if she had her way she "would not
stay in this city another day."[28]

The fiction that planters were burdened by their peculiar institution was an old one, as was the ubiquitous complaint that they
would happily liberate their lazy, ungrateful bondpeople had not the
British saddled them with unfree labor. Left unsaid in these endless
protests, was the question of who might plow the fields and scrub
the floors if slavery were to vanish. But the conspiracy forced white
society to confront the hard fact that slavery (which many pretended to abhor) and slaves (whom many professed to love) were
one and the same thing. Had she not been so frightened during that
"night of Terror," Mary Lamboll Beach "could have smiled" when
her companion Mary Jones angrily announced that she could never
"bear the sight of a *Negro* again" and planned to relocate to New
England. Two days before Jones had bragged about her devoted servants, but now she had "a *hatred* of them *all*."[29]

The imperatives of property and work, however, meant that
for all of their grousing, Carolina slaveholders had no intention of
emancipating their black labor force and wading into the rice and

28. John Potter to Langdon Cheves, July 5, 1822, Cheves Papers, SCHS; Anna
Haynes Johnson to Elizabeth Haywood, July 27, 1822, Haywood Papers, SHC, UNC.

29. Mary Lamboll Beach to Elizabeth Gilchrist, July 5, 1822, Beach Letters,
SCHS. Diarist Mary Chestnut, who often wrote about slavery with honesty and insight, made a similar comment during a different time of crisis when she lashed
out at Northern troops: "How I wish they had the Negroes—we the cotton. They
may have all the credit of their philanthropy if we had peace & this black incubus
removed." See C. Vann Woodward and Elisabeth Muhlenfeld, eds., *The Private
Mary Chestnut: The Unpublished Civil War Diaries* (New York, 1984), 203.

cotton fields themselves. Paternalists claimed that they ruled with benevolence rather than coercion (the treadmill in the city Work-house notwithstanding), and so white Charlestonians had to find another explanation for recent events. John Adger pinned the blame on the alleged greed of the rebels. They desired but "blood and booty, and that [they] might get off with a load of specie" to Haiti. More typical was John Moultrie, who attributed the presumed aber-ration of dissatisfied slaves to the influence of Yankee abolitionists and the Missouri debates. "[I]n these times of emancipation free-dom and liberality," Moultrie warned his brother-in-law Isaac Ball, "the Southern States will be in constant apprehensions [of] insur-rection." The daughter of Supreme Court Justice William Johnson agreed that outside influences were involved. Without a hint of irony, Anna Haynes Johnson, born and bred in a slave society, told a cousin that she was astounded "to have found" such "villain[s] breathing the pure air of free born America."[30]

The master race was united on one point. Regardless of what might explain this allegedly atypical behavior on the part of seem-ingly content slaves, the gentry harbored no doubts about the inten-tions of the rebel leadership toward white women. The sexual ex-ploitation of slave women by predatory masters was frequent enough that most visitors to the South, as well as a good number of Carolina diarists, commented on the practice. Perhaps guilty planters as-sumed that given the chance, vengeful bondmen might violate their wives in retaliation. Others, in the tradition of all victimizers, justified rape by projecting their own sexual desires onto their female prey. African women, they laughed, were lusty savages who enjoyed their master's nightly visits to the quarters. But whatever the excuse, fears of rape at the hands of black men grew loudest during times of slave unrest. Far more comforting it was to believe that what African Americans truly desired was not liberty or the right to wages and property, but instead sexual relations with aristocratic women.[31]

---

30. Adger, *My Life and Times,* 55; Ball, *Slaves in the Family,* 268; Anna Haynes Johnson to Elizabeth Haywood, June 28, 1822, Haywood Papers, SHC, UNC.

31. White, *Ar'n't I A Woman,* 42–46; Jordan, *White Over Black,* 150–54. Diana Miller Sommerville, "The Rape Myth in the Old South Reconsidered," *JSH* 61 (August 1995): 490, makes the startling claim that there "is no evidence . . . to sug-

Such allegations litter the documentary record. The rebels wanted nothing more than to abandon their own spouses so that they could take superior white "ladies for their wives," editorialized one Southern newspaper. Another horrified correspondent, John Potter, insisted he had evidence for his assertion that "the females were to be reserved *for worse than death*." According to Joe LaRoche, Rolla Bennett was crudely frank in his intentions. When asked by Joe "what was to be done with the [white] women and children," Rolla replied that "when we have done with the fellows, we know what is to be done with the wenches." It is possible, of course, that LaRoche remembered the conversation correctly. Conquering armies rarely behave with gallantry toward their enemies, especially if the vanquished differ in religion or race. But Joe, who lost his wife Amaretta to Rolla some years before, probably told the court what they expected to hear. Vesey's escape was a mass exodus of families, and the notion that the notoriously hot-tempered Amaretta could have stood idly by while her husband ravished female prisoners was nonsense served up for the magistrates.[32]

The bizarre story quickly evolved into a number of permutations. Anna Haynes Johnson understood that not only "we poor devils were to have been reserved to fill their—Harams—horrible," but that Vesey's army intended to "indiscriminately" murder "the [white] Men & Black Women." John Potter heard the allegations

---

gest that white southerners were apprehensive or anxious about their slaves raping white women." In fact, there is a wealth of evidence, which, Jordan suggested, became more noticeable during insurrection scares. See, for example, Egerton, *Gabriel's Rebellion*, 77–78, for such fears in 1800, and Michael Craton, "Slave Revolts and the End of Slavery," in Northrup, ed., *Atlantic Slave Trade*, 206–7, in which an 1816 black Barbadian flag showing an African-American man on terms of equality with a white male was widely reported to instead depict "the [sexual] Union of a Black Man with a white female," revealing, Craton writes, "the planters' Freudian fears." Martha Hodes, *White Women, Black Men: Illicit Sex in the 19th Century South* (New Haven, 1997), 63, discusses rape allegations in Virginia and North Carolina in the wake of Nat Turner's revolt.

32. Richmond *Enquirer*, July 30, 1822; John Potter to Langdon Cheves, July 10, 1822, Cheves Papers, SCHS; Testimony of Joe LaRoche at trial of Rolla Bennett, June 19, 1822, in Kennedy and Parker, eds., *Official Report*, 63.

somewhat differently. In his version, Rolla Bennett planned to carry off "Miss B. the Governor's daughter," and "that the white males were all to be Cut off—!!" The theory that Rolla's regiment, desperately fighting its way to the ships waiting at dock, might pause and methodically castrate white males evidently struck Potter as completely plausible. In point of fact, to the extent that wholesale liberation served to eliminate the authority white men held over their female slaves, Vesey's exodus, if successful, would have diminished rather than increased interracial sexual liaisons in the Carolina low-country.[33]

But even as Charleston whites elaborated upon Rolla Bennett's alleged sexual desires, most of the other rebel leaders remained at large. Vesey had gone into hiding by Sunday morning, but Jack Pritchard remained determined to do *something,* perhaps even to storm the Workhouse and free Ned and Rolla. One of attorney George Cross's slaves encountered Jack, who worried "that Whites were looking for him and [that] he was afraid of being taken." Two white men had already inquired about him at Paul Pritchard's carpentry shop near Gadsden's Wharf. Cross's man was surprised by Jack's fear and wondered about his magic. But Jack replied "that his charms would not protect him against the treachery of his own colour." Pritchard wisely avoided returning to his rented Meeting Street home, but an unruffled Monday Gell continued to work in his neighboring harness-making shop. Frank Ferguson nervously looked in, only to find the African back at his labors. Gell wondered if Frank knew "that Bennett's and Poyas' people" had been arrested. "[T]was a great pity," Gell added, shaking his head sadly.[34]

When a few days passed and Gullah Jack remained free, some of his former boldness returned. On Tuesday, Pritchard returned home, where he found a small band of resolute soldiers awaiting

---

33. Anna Haynes Johnson to Elizabeth Haywood, June 28, 1822, Haywood Papers, SHC, UNC; John Potter to Langdon Cheves, June 29, 1822, Cheves Papers, SCHS. This point was first made by Leon Litwack, *Been in the Storm So Long: The Aftermath of Slavery* (New York, 1980), 266.

34. Confession of Cross's unnamed slave, July 1822, RGA, GM, SCDAH (The court withheld the slave's name for his own safety); Confession of Ferguson's Frank, June 1822, RGA, GM, SCDAH.

him. Vesey was nowhere to be found, so "Jack stood at the front of all" and announced that he was the new "head man." Any chance of a safe escape had evaporated, but if only to allay their own fears, those in attendance "agreed to die together." Certainly the most determined to fight on were those who had witnessed the bloodshed in Saint Domingue. The black "frenchmen" resolved that if those in captivity "were hung, they were ready to rise and defend them."[35]

But without Vesey to orchestrate the effort, Pritchard's plans remained as chaotic as they were desperate. One slave wanted to wait until after July 4, by which time the patrols might be reduced in size and frequency, but Charles Drayton shouted him down, saying that "in the meantime [Rolla and Poyas] will be hanged." Jack suggested instead that he attempt to return to the countryside and rally his African company to "attempt the rescue of those" in the Workhouse. When they heard the clatter of horses in the street, he warned "you must come out and help us to get the Arms of the Neck Company." No one spoke of escape to Haiti. The suicidal "General plan" was to slaughter those they could and somehow drive the rest of "the white people" out of the city long enough to fortify it.[36]

Persuading more than a handful of conspirators to engage in such folly was impossible. But the knowledge that Rolla and Poyas were sure to swing only fueled the simmering anger and frustration of the black community, especially toward those who gave the leaders up to James Hamilton. Five days after Rolla's arrest, Joe LaRoche heard that "the friends of those in prison [were] trying about the streets" to discover "who has given information." Rolla and William Paul certainly knew who had betrayed them. But they had no way to get word to their supporters. "If my name was known," Joe whimpered, "I would certainly be killed."[37]

For his part, Governor Thomas Bennett was equally determined that LaRoche and Peter Prioleau should live to testify. Only hours

35. Confession of Vanderhorst's George, June 1822, RGA, GM, SCDAH; Confession of William Colcock, July 12, 1822, RGA, GM, SCDAH.
36. Confession of Cross's unnamed slave, July 1822, RGA, GM, SCDAH; Confession of Biddle's Harry, August 6, 1822, RGA, GM, SCDAH; Confession of Hammet's Bacchus, no date, William and Benjamin Hammet Papers, DUL.
37. Confession of Joe LaRoche, June 19, 1822, RGA, GM, SCDAH.

after hearing George Wilson denounce his beloved Rolla, the governor sat at his desk and penned a series of general orders. As commander in chief of the state militia, Bennett called up four companies from Colonel Croft's 16th Regiment, including the Washington Light Infantry and the Charleston Neck Rangers. Colonel Cobia's cavalry was mustered, as were the flamboyant Republican Artillery and the somewhat more sober Federalist Artillery, whose partisan designations divulged the essential disorganization behind their impressive sounding titles. Functioning on a different political level, Intendant Hamilton detached four non-commissioned officers of the City Guard as police officers to search for concealed caches of weapons. Although Bennett prayed the worst was over when the sun rose over a tranquil city on Monday morning, the weary guardsmen continued to serve extra duty, and each evening detachments from the volunteer militia companies reenforced the night watch.[38]

Governor Bennett also turned to the federal government for assistance. Evidently, South Carolina's notorious fear of national authority vanished during periods of slave unrest. States' rights theories were useful when defending the peculiar institution from the growing menace of antislavery politicians like Rufus King, but troublesome in moments of internal crisis; the same ideology of limited government that established maximum liberty for white men hindered the South's ability to combat thousands of armed slaves. An embarrassed Bennett informed Secretary of War John C. Calhoun of the "State of alarm" and admitted his inability to defend his city against a determined black majority. The governor complained that only five soldiers guarded Fort Johnson and its "few implements of war." A show of federal force, Bennett insisted, "would tend not only to tranquilize the public mind, but produce the happiest effects upon that class of persons who have caused the present excitement."[39]

Although a native of Abbeville District, South Carolina, Secre-

---

38. Thomas Bennett, General Order, June 15, 1822, RGA, GM, SCDAH; Hamilton, *An Account,* 12; W. Hasell Wilson to Robert Wilson, no date, CLS.

39. Wiltse, *Calhoun,* 1:256; Thomas Bennett to John C. Calhoun, July 15, 1822, and Thomas Bennett to John C. Calhoun, July 30, 1822, both in Hemphill, ed., *Papers of Calhoun,* 7:210, 227.

tary Calhoun was not yet the proponent of extreme states' rights and nullification he was later to become. If he harbored few doubts about the basic correctness of his plantation world, at this early stage of his political career he had no reservation as to the propriety of using federal authority to crush slave resistance. (Calhoun's wife Floride was rather more ambivalent about slavery due to the fact that Africans on the family plantation tried to poison her father when she was a child.) Calhoun notified Bennett that he ordered "one Company" of artillery to sail north from St. Augustine, Florida, in hopes that "will be sufficient to remove the uneasiness in the publick mind." Calhoun also promised that hereafter the harbor garrisons would be fully staffed "as soon as the recruits are made."[40]

The forty-year-old Secretary of War was the very model of efficiency. Calhoun suspected that Bennett was not up to the task at hand, but his own future career required maintaining cordial relations with powerful state officials. As he was contemplating a run at the White House in 1824, Calhoun advised Major John Bankhead to "consult with the Governor" in all matters pertaining to "the disturbances at Charleston." To the relief of the citizenry, the company of federal troops under Captain Matthew Paine at last sailed into the harbor on August 15 and landed at Fort Moultrie.[41]

For the conspirators yet at large, Governor Bennett's request for federal troops was an obituary itself. If Jack Pritchard's rapidly-dwindling African company stood little chance against an enhanced state militia, they had even less hope of defeating well-drilled professional soldiers. All talk of rescuing Rolla and Peter Poyas vanished as the remaining rebels went into hiding. On Tuesday, June 18, Mayor Hamilton approached two prominent members of the Charleston bar, Lionel Kennedy and Thomas Parker, and asked

40. Irving H. Bartlett, *John C. Calhoun: A Biography* (New York, 1993), 218–19, 281; Charleston *Courier,* July 30, 1822; John C. Calhoun to Thomas Bennett, July 22, 1822, and John C. Calhoun to Abram Eustis, July 22, 1822, in Hemphill, ed., *Papers of Calhoun,* 7:220, 220–21.

41. Richmond *Enquirer,* August 23, 1822; Washington *National Intelligencer,* August 24, 1822; Charleston *Courier,* August 16, 1822; Hartford *Connecticut Courant,* July 16, 1822; John C. Calhoun to James Bankhead, July 22, 1822, in Hemphill, ed., *Papers of Calhoun,* 7:219.

them to oversee an ad-hoc "Court of Magistrates and Freeholders [to be] assembled" in the Workhouse. Most of the suspects had been incarcerated for nearly a week, and Hamilton hoped that coercion might produce evidence enough to start the trials "of those criminals" by the following afternoon. The attorneys agreed and recommended that they be joined in their inquiry by Hamilton's brother-in-law, planter Nathaniel Heyward, customs collector J. Robert Pringle, planter James Legare, attorney Robert J. Turnbull, and retired Colonel William Drayton.[42]

To better prepare their case, Lionel Kennedy instructed the warden to obtain new information from those already under arrest. The turnkey used promises of pardon, threats, and finally floggings to induce testimony. Among those tortured was Peter Poyas, who remained chained to the floor of his cell when not tied to the whipping post. One of his cellmates, perhaps Mingo Harth, began to weaken under the beatings and begged for mercy. Poyas was lying on his stomach and with much difficulty raised himself up on one elbow. "Die like a man," he gasped.[43]

But somebody *did* weaken. On Thursday, June 20, "one of the convicts" identified Vesey as the "instigator and chief of this plot." The fact that the court now possessed the leader's name set off a frenzied, two-day-long search of the city. The city guard prowled the docks near departing ships, while militia companies erected pickets and examined the papers of every freeman riding out of town. On Saturday night, during a howling tempest, guardsmen under the command of Frederick Wesner and Captain William P. Dove burst into the "house of one of his wives," probably Beck, and arrested the old abolitionist. Most likely, Vesey was betrayed by William Paul, who later testified that he had "often heard [Denmark] speak of the rising" at Beck's house.[44]

42. Introduction, in Kennedy and Parker, eds., *Official Report,* iv–v; Richmond *Enquirer,* August 6, 1822; Hartford *Connecticut Courant,* August 6, 1822; Hamilton, *An Account,* 12; Charleston *Courier,* August 23, 1822.

43. Lofton, *Insurrection in South Carolina,* 154.

44. Charleston *Courier,* August 23, 1822; Hamilton, *An Account,* 17; Testimony of William Paul at trial of Denmark Vesey, June 26, 1822, in Kennedy and Parker, eds., *Official Report,* 85.

With the passing of each day, coerced confessions and fresh testimony brought more arrests. On Thursday, June 27, authorities arrested a resigned Monday Gell as he labored in his harness shop near the center of town. By shaving off his impressive whiskers, Jack Pritchard eluded the guardsmen until July 5, when he became the last of the rebel leadership to be captured. Upon being apprehended, Jack vehemently denied that he was "a Doctor or Conjurer," although "the map" of where his sideburns had been was "plainly discernable on his face." The guardsmen dragged the African priest before his owner, Paul Pritchard, who identified him as the man known as "Gullah Jack." By then the hangings had started, and Jack knew that he was going to die.[45]

45. Grimké, *Right on the Scaffold*, 21; Testimony of Paul Pritchard at trial of Jack Pritchard, July 9, 1822, in Kennedy and Parker, eds., *Official Report*, 105.

Chapter Eight

Judges
June–August 1822

THE DISTANT SOUND that Jack Pritchard heard as he was led off to the Workhouse was not merely the hammering of carpenters as they repaired the dilapidated gallows. It was the clatter of planter discomfort. "The negroes of the Southern states of this country," the editor of the Columbia *Southern Times* once maintained, "are better off and better contented, than the labourers of many other civilized countries." But if the editor truly believed his own words, the events of 1822 presented him with a predicament. Carolina masters assumed far more than the contentment of their bondpeople. They based their paternal ideals on the notion that their childlike wards could not survive without their guidance and care. Yet thousands of allegedly-loving children had plotted patricide, which meant that infantile property had to be put to trial. But in the process, Magistrates Kennedy and Parker were forced to confront the accused as adults who consciously chose to defy the law, and not as naughty children or inanimate property. By characterizing Vesey's soldiers as children and defining them as things but hanging them as men, the

Charleston court revealed the fundamentally irrational nature of Southern slave law.[1]

In preparation for the first day of trial, Kennedy and Parker scanned the comprehensive Negro Act of 1740. The sections pertaining to insurrections were as succinct as they were brutal. Fearing that free blacks involved with bondmen might escape punishment under the old Roman code (upon which much American slave law was based) that servants could not testify against freedmen like Vesey, colonial legislators had clarified the point. "The evidence of any free Indian or slave [was] allowed and admitted in all cases, against free negroes." In 1805, an amendment to the act defined the crime of rebellion in such broad terms that few accused could escape the wrath of the courts: Any person, free or bond, "who shall, in any manner or to any extent, excite, counsel, advise, induce, aid, comfort or assist any slave or slaves to raise or attempt to raise an insurrection" was guilty of "treason against the state." As evidence, the amendment allowed for "confession in open court" or the testimony of two or more witnesses. For those adjudged guilty there was but one punishment: to "suffer death."[2]

Lionel Kennedy hastened to assure the public that he planned to conduct the most equitable of courts. In addition to the safeguards established by statute, the magistrates "laid down for their own government" two additional rules. No bondman would be tried except in the presence of his owner, and slaves might be represented by legal counsel if the master so wished. Second, slaves had the right to confront their accusers, "except where testimony was given under a solemn pledge that the names of the witnesses should not be divulged." In addition, Mayor Hamilton presented the court with a calendar containing the "names of all the criminals" then in custody, together with the charges against them and the witnesses prepared to testify. Hamilton also encouraged the court to take as

1. Columbia *Southern Times*, April 12, 1830; Freehling, *Reintegration of American History*, 38–39; Thomas Morris, *Southern Slavery and the Law* (Chapel Hill, 1996), 272–73.

2. "Negro Act," 1740, in Brevard, ed., *Alphabetical Digest*, 2:232, 202. On Roman slave law and its influence on American slave codes, see Alan Watson, *Slave Law in the Americas* (Athens, 1989), chapter 2.

many depositions as possible before proceeding to trial, "in order to ascertain how far a conspiracy had really been formed." By adopting guidelines that surpassed the draconian laws of 1740 and 1805 in protecting the rights of the accused, the magistrates sought to maintain the charade of benevolence so critical to their paternalistic pretensions, or at least to convince white Charlestonians of their magnanimity. "They *convict* none on a *single* testimony," gushed Mary Lamboll Beach.[3]

Although the magistrates presumed that most of the men brought before them would be slaves, they promised to protect the rights of free blacks as well. Masters had the prerogative of requesting an attorney for their bondmen, but this could also be "requested by [the] prisoners themselves, if free." Kennedy not only promised that his court was willing to hear any "statements or defenses" the accused might wish to make, he guaranteed defendants the privilege of "examin[ing] any witness they thought proper" and vowed not to decide capital cases on "hearsay communications." Finally, Hamilton thought it wise to close the proceedings to the general public. The intendant feared that a courtroom swarming with vengeful planters might intimidate the magistrates into hanging every slave brought through their doors. (His public explanation, however, was to avoid exciting white Charlestonians with rumor and "exaggerated representations" of slave testimony.)[4]

Hamilton may well have convinced himself of the objective nature of his proceedings. Certainly his smooth promises convinced many white Carolinians. But the Charleston trials of 1822, like all slave trials, never resembled the proceedings accorded white defendants. For all the guarantees of counsel and cross-examination, a

3. Introduction, in Kennedy and Parker, eds., *Official Report*, vi–v; Mary Lamboll Beach to Elizabeth Gilchrist, July 5, 1822, Beach Letters, SCHS. Although I have never said anything in print to support so bizarre a reading, because Thomas C. Parramore once charged that I regarded Virginia slave court "procedure[s] as a triumph of judicial decorum," I should say here that I do not regard Vesey's men as morally guilty of any crime. See his "Aborted Takeoff: A Critique of 'Fly Across the River,'" *North Carolina Historical Review* 68 (April 1991): 115.

4. Introduction, in Kennedy and Parker, eds., *Official Report*, vi–vii; Hamilton, *An Account*, 12.

capital case involving a bondperson was never an impartial hearing of
a citizen by his peers. At bottom, slave codes defined Africans and
their progeny as property, and even when magistrates like Kennedy
and Parker reluctantly acknowledged the human agency inherent in
servile insurrections, they treated the accused as a creature of inferior rights, little different from an errant cow or runaway wagon.
White abolitionist Thomas Higginson later charged that the Charleston court routinely deviated from the settled rules of evidence established in English common law, and certainly it was true that
most western nations had abandoned the practice of obtaining testimony through torture. Even Lionel Kennedy conceded that his
ad-hoc court was organized "under a statute of a peculiar and local
character" that was devised for "a different class of [unfree] persons" only. If his court indeed "depart[ed] in many essential fea-
tures, from the principles of common law," such detours were justified by the idiosyncratic demands of white minority rule.[5]

Among the few native Charlestonians who regarded the closed
trials as a travesty of justice was Supreme Court Justice William
Johnson, a Jefferson-appointee and Thomas Bennett's brother-in-
law. The jurist, in fact, regarded the entire Negro Act as an archaic
vestige of colonial mismanagement. Under the law, enslaved defendants were tried by two magistrates (or justices of the peace), who
then selected three to five "freeholders" (voters) to serve with them.
This meant that judges at capital trials might be wholly ignorant of
the law, as were the two planters—Heyward and Legare—who sat
on Kennedy's court. The right to counsel was equally fraudulent; as
white court-appointed attorneys shared the racialist assumptions of
the magistrates, the slave's lawyer was as likely to believe him guilty
as not. Worst of all, Johnson observed, Carolina law denied black
defendants the right to challenge rulings or appeal to higher courts.
No matter how flawed their verdict, the court's provincial decisions
were final.[6]

Influenced by his kinsman's critique, as well as by his own stub-

    5. Stampp, *Peculiar Institution*, 226–27; Higginson, *Black Rebellion*, 251–52;
Introduction, in Kennedy and Parker, eds., *Official Report*, v–vi.
    6. Morgan, *William Johnson*, 129.

born insistence that his beloved Rolla was guilty of nothing more than unwise associations, Governor Bennett approached state Attorney General Robert Y. Hayne with his concerns. Bennett queried Hayne as to the propriety of the court meeting behind "closed doors and without [always] confronting the witnesses with the accused." But Hayne had no patience for such permissive nonsense and swatted Bennett's protests aside. "[N]othing can be clearer than that *slaves* are not entitled to *these rights*," an annoyed Hayne lectured. "Magna Charta and Habeas Corpus and indeed all the provisions of our constitution in favour of Liberty, are intended for *freemen* only." Not yet thirty-two, Hayne had already married two of the tidewater's richest heiresses (his first wife died in 1819), and as the master of hundreds of laborers, the attorney general worried that if "a slave could profess these privileges, he would [better] his condition." It was not even necessary that a bondperson be formally indicted. "[H]e has no right of challenge and the witnesses are not even sworn in [at] his Trial."[7]

Free blacks fared little better under Carolina law. Although former servants like Denmark Vesey were no longer human property, neither were they, most likely, citizens of the United States. (Until the ratification of the Fourteenth Amendment in 1868, the Constitution was silent on the question of federal citizenship.) The Negro Act, as its name implied, drew few distinctions between slaves and freedmen. South Carolina did not permit slaves to testify against whites, but in a legal double-standard, bondmen could furnish testimony against free blacks. So too was Vesey denied the right of trial by his free black peers. African Americans could not sit on juries, and in any case no jury ever heard Vesey's statement of innocence; Kennedy's court was an irregular tribunal of magistrates and freeholders. A peculiar institution indeed![8]

For the captured rebels awaiting trial in the Workhouse, the alleged safeguards guaranteed them were a mystery. From the moment

7. Robert Y. Hayne to Thomas Bennett, July 1 and 3, 1822, RGA, GM, SCDAH.
8. Daniel J. Flanigan, "Criminal Procedure in Slave Trials in the Antebellum South," *JSH* 40 (November 1974): 556; Senese, "Free Negro and the South Carolina Courts," 150; Morgan, *William Johnson*, 129–30.

of their seizure to their appearance in court, the accused sat in solitary darkness, either chained to the stone floor, or held in isolation at the neighboring jail at 21 Magazine Street. Ever since Peter Poyas's stern warning of silence to his cellmate, the intendant tried to confine the prisoners to "different rooms." When slaves were needed to testify against their fellows, the magistrates ordered them held in a chamber "adjoining that in which the Court was sitting." No attorney bothered to discuss the case with his client in advance of a court appearance. When Kennedy was ready to hear the next case, he directed the prisoner be yanked from his unlit "dungeon" and brought directly into his courtroom, which was established deep within the Workhouse. The rebels, black abolitionist Henry Bibb complained, stood before the bench "without a friend to support him in this dreadful emergency." As they followed the dark hallway into court, terrified defendants heard only the sound of guardsmen marching around the building, barking at black women wandering by to stay at least two blocks away from the proceedings.[9]

If the magistrates showed any solicitude toward those tangled in their web, it was for the dozens of masters who stood to lose their human property to the gallows. Kennedy's assurance that no slave should appear before him unaccompanied by his owner was designed to assuage the financial concerns of whites, not to protect the nonexistent rights of blacks. Whether a defendant obtained counsel was likewise up to the master, not to the slave. As most of the accused were the sort of skilled, literate artisans who would be hard to replace, owners had good cause to worry. Almost a century before, colonial legislators, fearing that planters cared more about their capital investment than for the public safety, promised that justices of the peace "shall apprise and value the said negroes to be put to death." But penurious magistrates recognized the limited tax base of the agrarian South and rarely compensated masters for the full value of their condemned property. Worse yet, the Negro Act excepted those slaves "guilty of murder" or "taken in actual rebellion."[10]

9. Note, in Kennedy and Parker, eds., *Official Report*, 68; Greene, *Charleston*, 68; [Bibb], *Late Contemplated Insurrection*, 6; Higginson, *Black Rebellion*, 250, 265.

10. Higginson, *Black Rebellion*, 252–53; Stampp, *Peculiar Institution*, 198–99; Negro Act, 1740, in Brevard, ed., *Alphabetical Digest*, 2:233.

The legal doctrine that the defendants were merely things to be assessed or machines to grow rice and cotton, perhaps more than any other aspect of Southern law, revealed the critical difference in how blacks and whites regarded Carolina courts. With their rituals and regulations and safeguards, the magistrates who sat in judgment in the Workhouse visualized themselves as executors of what Kennedy called "divine law," as if the law and the legislators who drafted it formed two separate establishments. Far from being a vindictive ruling race, they were but impartial administrators who carried the burden of hundreds of years of western jurisprudence. But for the Africans who had never consented to the sale of their bodies or the appropriation of their labor, the courts that condemned them for the crime of wishing to be free were a farce, and the magistrates nothing more than a well-dressed mob. The freeholders were "gentlemen slaveholders," sneered Henry Bibb, acting "upon the plan of Judge Lynch."[11]

Farce or not, state and federal military power supplied the magistrates with whatever authority they required over the black majority, and on the afternoon of Wednesday, June 19, the trials began. The first name to be called was that of Rolla, "the slave of His Excellency, Governor Bennett." Two guards prodded the dejected young man forward. Before him sat Magistrates Kennedy and Parker, flanked by freeholders Drayton, Heyward, Pringle, Legare, and Turnbull. A lone scribe sat perched behind a high desk, quill pen poised above a sheaf of foolscap. But neither jury box nor prosecutor's table graced this idyllic scene. Perhaps the only face Rolla recognized was that of Thomas Bennett, who stood smiling beside Jacob Axson, a superb, high-priced Charleston attorney.[12]

Kennedy explained the charges to Rolla, who stared in disbelief as Joe LaRoche entered the courtroom. No clerk stepped forward to swear Joe's veracity upon an opened Bible, but it mattered little; Joe knew what the court expected him to say. Facing the table at the front of the small room, LaRoche insisted that Rolla had first asked

11. Douglas Hay, "Property, Authority, and the Criminal Law," in Douglas Hay, ed., *Albion's Fatal Tree: Crime and Society in Eighteenth Century England* (New York, 1975), 29; [Bibb], *Late Contemplated Insurrection*, 6.

12. Trial of Rolla Bennett, June 19, 1822, in Kennedy and Parker, eds., *Official Report*, 61.

him to join the conspiracy three weeks ago, before pressing the issue on June 8. Determined to play the obedient servant, Joe assured
the court he had never considered joining. "I told him it could not
be done," he swore, and "that our parents for generations back had
been slaves, and we had better be contented."[13]

If the sight of one of his closest friends pretending contentment
was not painful enough, Rolla next watched George Wilson enter
the chamber. Rolla had confided in George in hopes of sparing his
life, and now George repaid the favor by helping the tribunal to take
Rolla's. Wilson repeated the story he had told so many times before.
Like LaRoche, he too professed to love his white neighbors, but his
halting, tearful testimony was easier to credit than Joe's transpar-
ently self-serving performance. Major John Wilson spoke next, but
his endorsement of George's "very best character" was quite unnecessary as far as the satisfied magistrates were concerned.[14]

Two more witnesses spoke, both of whom identified Rolla as one
of Vesey's chief officers. Then it was Axson's turn. The fact that Bennett chose to retain one of the most expensive litigators in the city
was public testimony to the governor's unshakable confidence in his
domestic (as well as the source of not a little mirth on the bench).
Axson was not accustomed to slave trials, but he had not earned his
silk for nothing. Realizing that George Wilson's credibility was impossible to destroy, Axson pounced on the inviting target of LaRoche.
Was it not true, Axson wondered, that Joe's lies were due to the fact
that Rolla's wife Amaretta had once been married to Joe? But Axson's
attempt to impeach Joe's integrity, Kennedy later wrote, "rather
strengthened it." LaRoche admitted that his separation three years
before led to "a quarrel" with Rolla, but since then they had "live[d]
like brothers." Besides, Joe insisted, "he was very glad to get rid of
her [as] she is a very blood thirsty character." Joe's owner rose to second that uncharitable assessment of the fiery Amaretta.[15]

13. Testimony of Joe LaRoche at trial of Rolla Bennett, June 19, 1822, in Kennedy and Parker, eds., *Official Report*, 61–63.

14. Testimony of George Wilson at trial of Rolla Bennett, June 19, 1822, in Kennedy and Parker, eds., *Official Report*, 64–65.

15. Freehling, *Reintegration of American History*, 48; Note, in Kennedy and

Axson knew he had blundered. But Rolla never expected any other outcome and was hardly surprised to hear the "Court *unanimously*" declare him guilty and warn him "to prepare for death." When asked if he had anything left to say, Rolla boldly "confessed his guilt [and] exhibited no fear."[16] Governor Bennett sat stunned. He would not believe that his cherished servant wished him dead, he whispered, "till he heard it from [Rolla's] *own* lips." Staring down at his master, Rolla sadly replied that "he would not have done the deed" himself; another rebel "had undertaken the office" for him.[17]

Even less penitent was coachman John Horry. According to one witness, John had obtained a sword, and as soon as the slaves took the streets, he planned to "go up stairs and kill his master and family." Like the disbelieving governor, planter Elias Horry found it impossible to fathom that his submissive coachman truly desired his death. When John was arrested at his master's Meeting Street townhouse, Horry promised the guardsmen that "he could answer for [John's] innocence—he would as soon suspect himself." But upon hearing the evidence, Horry turned on John, saying: "[T]ell me, are you guilty? For I cannot believe [it] unless I hear you say so." John nodded assent. "What were your intentions," Horry whimpered. Having spent an entire lifetime masking his emotions, John exploded: "[T]o kill you, rip open your belly & throw your guts in your face."[18]

Batteau was next. Despite a written request from a crestfallen Governor Bennett that Batteau's obvious guilt be considered "with a view to the mitigation of his punishment," the magistrates made quick work of the matter and sentenced him to swing. Even as the

---

Parker, eds., *Official Report*, 66–67; Testimony of Mr. LaRoche at trial of Rolla Bennett, June 22, 1822, RGA, GM, SCDAH.

16. Sentence of Rolla Bennett, in Kennedy and Parker, eds. *Official Report*, 46, 67.

17. Mary Lamboll Beach to Elizabeth Gilchrist, July 5, 1822, Beach Letters, SCHS; John Potter to Langdon Cheves, July 10, 1822, Cheves Papers, SCHS.

18. Trial of John Horry, July 1822, in Kennedy and Parker, eds., *Official Report*, 102–3; Martha Proctor Richardson to James Screven, August 7, 1822, Arnold and Screven Papers, SHC, UNC.

guards dragged Batteau from the chamber, a defiant Peter Poyas marched through the door. The whippings administered behind the sand-filled walls of the Workhouse had utterly failed to crush his spirit, and if anything, the irritated magistrates found Poyas even more insubordinate than John Horry. Resigned to his fate, Poyas stared at the ceiling as Robert Harth testified that Peter had tried to recruit him into the plot. Even William Paul's assertion that "all the African Church were engaged in it" failed to alter his serene "countenance and behavior." When sentenced to hang, Poyas said only: "I suppose you'll let me see my wife and family before I die," and that "not in a supplicating tone." Kennedy was furious and demanded to know whether Peter truly wished to see his master slain. Poyas "only replied to the question [with] a smile."[19]

The prospect of impending death upon the gallows typically weakened the resolve of even the most sanguine of revolutionaries. But Poyas never faltered. For the past week, the warden had attempted to house the accused in separate cells, but with the arrests increasingly daily, it became necessary to incarcerate Peter with three other rebels. Poyas' composure bolstered the courage of those awaiting trial, as did his frequent admonition: "Do not open your lips! Die silent, as you shall see me do." Poyas had given "his pledge of secrecy" to his recruits, and nothing could force him to break that promise. According to a frustrated Lionel Kennedy, of the 131 blacks arrested, "not one of them belonged to Peter's company."[20]

More trials followed, few of them lasting more than a single afternoon. Ned Bennett and Jesse Blackwood both received swift sentences of death. Finally, on Wednesday, June 26, Kennedy called out the name of "Denmark Vesey, a free black man." Mayor Hamilton and the magistrates had prepared their case by interviewing Joseph Vesey. The ancient mariner, now seventy-five-years-old and living at 82 Anson Street, gave no testimony in court, but the pre-

19. Narrative, in Kennedy and Parker, eds., *Official Report,* 46; Trial of Bennett's Batteau, June 20, 1822, in Kennedy and Parker, eds., *Official Report,* 69–71; Trial of Peter Poyas, June 21, 1822, in Kennedy and Parker, eds., *Official Report,* 71–76; Higginson, *Black Rebellion,* 256.

20. Narrative, in Kennedy and Parker, eds., *Official Report,* 25, 45.

cise details of Denmark's childhood that Hamilton later published
were known only to the old slave trader. As a free man, Vesey possessed the option of counsel, and his former landlord, George W.
Cross, served as his attorney, probably at the request of Susan Vesey
(who was not allowed in the courtroom).[21]

As a resident of Charleston for the past forty years, Vesey knew,
at least by name, most of the men he now faced. Hamilton he recognized from his neighborhood, as he did James Legare, whose family
and their eleven domestic slaves were also Bull Street residents. The
magistrates began by once again calling William Paul into the chamber. Still hoping to save his skin, William played the role of innocent
recruit whom others had unsuccessfully "trie[d] to induce" into the
plot. "Mingo Harth told me that Denmark Vesey was the chiefest
man," he insisted, "and more concerned [than] any[one] else." Despite their public promise not to permit hearsay evidence, no magistrates interrupted William as he reported that Mingo had heard
Vesey say that the escape was "his chief study [for] a considerable
time." Joe LaRoche spoke next, but all he could add was that Vesey
"was bitter toward the whites." Kennedy, however, was only saving
his most important witness for last. "Rolla was also re-examined,"
the clerk wrote, and Vesey's close friend of twenty years quietly told
the court that the old carpenter "was the leader in this plot." Astonished that the specter of death could compel Rolla to turn his coat,
Vesey "remained unmovable" throughout the testimony, his massive
arms "folded" across his chest and his "eyes fixed on the floor."[22]

By then it was late in the day, and the court recessed until the
following morning. Although the Negro Act required but two witnesses, Kennedy was taking no chances with the black Moses and

21. *Directory and Stranger's Guide, 1822*, 84; Trial of Bennett's Ned, June 22,
1822, in Kennedy and Parker, eds., *Official Report*, 77–79, Trial of Jesse Blackwood,
June 22, 1822, in Kennedy and Parker, eds., *Official Report*, 79–81; Trial of Denmark Vesey, June 26, 1822, in Kennedy and Parker, eds., *Official Report*, 85.

22. Michael O'Brien, *A Character of Hugh Legare* (Knoxville, 1985), 46; Testimony of Joe LaRoche, June 26, 1822, in Kennedy and Parker, eds., *Official Report*, 85–86; Testimony of Rolla Bennett, June 26, 1822, in Kennedy and Parker,
eds., *Official Report*, 66–68, 86; Narrative, in Kennedy and Parker, eds., *Official
Report*, 44–45.

summoned a fourth witness, Frank Ferguson. "I have heard him say that the Negroes' situation was so bad that he did not know how they could endure it," Frank stated. He "advised me to join and rise up for my freedom." Because the tribunal was not bound by the traditions of courtroom deportment, Kennedy interrupted Frank to put a question to Vesey himself. Given William Paul's assertion that the AME congregations were a hotbed of insurgent activity, Kennedy wondered "to what church he belonged." Vesey glanced up. "None," he responded, in "a very firm decisive tone." But the magistrates looked doubtful. As one Charlestonian put it, the court considered Vesey "the Champion [of] the African Church" and held the "opinion that *this* church commenced this awful business."[23]

The accused, who was already being mentally hanged by everyone there, next heard the French wigmaker testify that the old carpenter had commissioned him to create several "wigs and whiskers." With the greatest "effrontery and composure," Vesey denied that he had ever seen the wigmaker before, at which point Kennedy dramatically pulled from his pocket the light-colored wig fashioned for Vesey himself. Jolted by the sight, Vesey murmured "good God" before regaining his self-control. He remained silent for several minutes, but finally admitted that he knew the Frenchman.[24]

For all that, Vesey had not lived so long by giving in easily. Angry with his attorney's inept performance, Vesey requested the right to cross-examine the witnesses himself. According to Kennedy, he questioned LaRoche and Ferguson with the same "dictatorial, despotic" manner he had often used to intimidate less resolute bondmen into standing up to white authority. When his questions failed to force the witnesses to retract their testimony, Vesey sought to turn his harsh demeanor to his own benefit. In a speech of "considerable length," Vesey assured the court that it was but his pride and arrogant manners that earned "the great hatred" of LaRoche and

23. Examination of Ferguson's Frank, June 27, 1822, RGA, GM, SCDAH; Mary Lamboll Beach to Elizabeth Gilchrist, July 25, 1822, Beach Letters, SCHS.

24. John Potter to Langdon Cheves, July 5, 1822, Cheves Papers, SCHS; Narrative, in Kennedy and Parker, eds., *Official Report*, 40.

Ferguson. As a former slave of some small prosperity, Vesey suggested, he aroused jealousy in less ambitious bondmen. After all, why should he "join in such an attempt?"[25]

But the tribunal had predetermined to take Vesey's life. "[H]is allegations" of jealousy, Kennedy snorted, "were unsupported by proof." The court declared Vesey guilty and sentenced him to hang "on Tuesday next, the 2d July, between six and eight o'clock in the morning." But the outraged paternalists behind the bench could not resist denouncing the ungrateful freeman at length, and Kennedy read an obviously prepared statement into the record:

> [T]he Court were not only satisfied with your guilt, but that you were the author, and original instigator of this diabolical plot. Your professed design was to trample on all laws, human and divine, to riot in blood, outrage, rapine and conflagration, and to introduce anarchy and confusion in their most horrid forms. Your life has become, therefore, a just and necessary sacrifice, at the shrine of indulgent Justice. It is difficult to imagine what *infatuation* could have prompted you to attempt an enterprize so wild and visionary. You were a free man, were comparatively wealthy, and enjoyed every comfort compatible with your situation. . . .
> A moment's reflection must have convinced you, that the ruin of *your race*, would have been the probable result, and that years would have rolled away, before they could have recovered that confidence, which they once enjoyed in this community. The only reparation in your power, is a full disclosure of the truth. In addition to treason, you have committed the grossest impiety, in attempting to pervert the sacred words of God into a sanction for crimes of the blackest hue. It is evident, that you are totally insensible to the divine influence of that Gospel. . . . "Servants" (says Saint Paul) "obey in all things your masters." . . . Your "lamp of life" is nearly extinguished, your race is run, and you must shortly pass "from time to eternity." Let me then conjure you to devote the remnant of your existence in solemn preparation for the awful doom that awaits you. . . . You cannot have forgotten the history of the malefactor on the Cross, who, like yourself, was the wretched and

25. Narrative, in Kennedy and Parker, eds., *Official Report,* 45.

deluded victim of offended justice. . . . and yet there is reason to believe, that his spirit was received into the realm of bliss. May *you* imitate his example and may *your* last moments prove like his![26]

As Vesey heard his sentence read, a single tear "trickled down his cheek," not perhaps, from comprehending the eternal separation of the grave, but rather from disappointment at failing his sons and disciples. Standing before the bench, Vesey glared down at his executioners. "[T]he work of insurrection would go on," he whispered.[27]

That night, Vesey prowled the small, dank cell he shared with Poyas and Jesse Blackwood. He stopped upon hearing someone at the locks and bolts. Reverend Richard Furman entered the chamber, with Reverend Benjamin Palmer and a Mr. Boris trailing behind. In keeping with Judge Kennedy's hope that Vesey would die penitent, Furman suggested they pray together, a somewhat unnecessary proposal given the mournful "singing of Psalms" drifting in from the other cells. Vesey snapped that he "would hear *nothing* they had to say." Furman tried again, only to be interrupted by Vesey. It "was a Glorious cause he was to die in," Vesey replied, and "it was of no use to say any thing more." Outside the Workhouse, beyond the pickets, dozens of slaves kept a quiet vigil. Many believed that Vesey and his followers "*would* be delivered & if in *no* other way the Jail doors opened by a Supernatural Power."[28]

July began with the weather "unusually severe." Temperatures well above ninety drove Charlestonians indoors, and "[t]hunder squalls [were] frequent and violent," as if Jehovah himself was furious with events below. On the first night of July, militia companies roamed the streets and remained in a state of alert "until the next

26. Charleston *Courier,* June 29, 1822; Charleston *Mercury,* June 29, 1822; Sentence of Denmark Vesey, June 27, 1822, in Kennedy and Parker, eds., *Official Report,* 89, 172–73.

27. Narrative, in Kennedy and Parker, eds., *Official Report,* 45; Higginson, *Black Rebellion,* 265. (Higginson's account of Vesey's retort was at least third-hand. A free black carpenter who worked "in Vesey's shop" in 1822—who could not have been in the courtroom—told the story to David Lee Child, who repeated it to Higginson.)

28. Mary Lamboll Beach to Elizabeth Gilchrist, July 5, 1822, Beach Letters, SCHS.

morning." As dawn broke on July 2, Warden John Gordon marched Vesey, Rolla, Ned, Poyas, Batteau, and Jesse Blackwood out of their cells. The coffle shuffled slowly, each man hindered by heavy leg irons.[29]

Gordon loaded the six men into a "cart" for the two-mile ride to Blake's Lands, an open space surrounded by marshes just north of the Hampstead suburbs. Fearless to the last, Poyas "laughed when first brought out of the Jail & preserved this state of mind" even as the gallows loomed into view. Vesey was equally courageous. Northern supporters, Mary Lamboll Beach admitted, "will say perhaps he behaved with Magnanimity." But where Poyas was obstinately cheerful, "the old man" remained implacable. One white observer who stood close enough to brush against his sleeve, remarked that Vesey stared straight ahead, as if "collecting his thoughts for the scene before him."[30]

Despite the intense heat, large numbers of blacks and whites lined the streets as the cart paraded north on King Street. Even more so than in other parts of the republic, hangings in the Old South were public rituals, and people came from miles around to witness the event. For whites, the execution of African Americans not only provided closure to the terrors of May and June, they were a visible sign that security was fully restored. For black Carolinians, who were encouraged, even forced, to watch as their husbands and sons swung from the gallows, the terrible majesty of the event served as a reminder of the fate awaiting those who defied white minority rule. Presumably, a distraught Susan Vesey watched as her husband passed by; the young wife had not seen her husband since he fled their home on June 17.[31]

29. Charleston *Mercury*, June 26, July 3, 1822; Charleston *Courier*, July 3, 1822; Charleston *Southern Patriot*, June 29, 1822; Mary Lamboll Beach to Elizabeth Gilchrist, July 5, 1822, Beach Letters, SCHS.

30. Hamilton, *An Account*, 43; Mary Lamboll Beach to Elizabeth Gilchrist, July 5, 1822, Beach Letters, SCHS. (Beach, who was not present, put the place of execution "near the Lines," but Hamilton, who was, later wrote that the six men died a mile away "on Blake's lands, near Charleston.")

31. Peter Linebaugh, "The Tyburn Riot Against the Surgeons," in Hay, ed., *Albion's Fatal Tree*, 67; Edward L. Ayers, *Vengeance and Justice: Crime and Punish-*

In later years, John Adger remembered arriving at Blake's Lands to find "[i]mmense crowds of whites and blacks" surrounding the gallows. Only too late did authorities perceive the folly of allowing a small army of slaves so close to the rebels. One genteel lady "greatly feared they would [make] some address to excite further rebellion; but they did not attempt it." The six men hobbled up the steps, and stood in a row as the hangman dropped sacks over their heads and adjusted the nooses. The trap fell. According to Intendant Hamilton, they collectively "met their fate with the heroic fortitude of Martyrs."[32]

As the bodies gently swayed in the humid breeze, the hangman began the work of cutting them down for delivery to "the surgeons for dissection." For Africans and their descendants, the inability to properly bury their dead was a calculated offense. In accordance with old world traditions, funerals were rituals of great consequence, accompanied by ancient pageantry and solemn spectacle. Had they been allowed to do so—as they commonly were on the nearby plantations—enslaved women would have prepared a feast, both to honor their ancestors and to sustain the departed during the journey to the spirit world. As they had in Africa, blacks waited until darkness to begin the burial ceremony. After the repast and an all-night vigil, survivors left small gifts of food and drink upon the grave; oftentimes mourners smashed crockery on the headboard to symbolically free the spirit of the deceased.[33]

Virtually all Carolina blacks, whether Christianized or tradition-

ment in the Nineteenth-Century American South (New York, 1984), 136; Jones, Born a Child of Freedom, 91; Betty Wood, "'Until He Shall Be Dead, Dead, Dead': The Judicial Treatment of Slaves in Eighteenth-Century Georgia," Georgia Historical Quarterly 71 (Fall 1987): 395.

32. Adger, My Life and Times, 52; Mary Lamboll Beach to Elizabeth Gilchrist, July 5, 1822, Beach Letters, SCHS; Martha Proctor Richardson to James Screven, July 6, 1822, Arnold and Screven Papers, SHC, UNC. (Hamilton's remark about Vesey's "heroic fortitude" appeared in a letter to a Mr. Harris, who read it to Richardson.)

33. Charleston Mercury, July 27, 1822; Josephine A. Beoku-Betts, "'She Make Funny Flat Cate She Call Saraka': Gullah Women and Food Practices Under Slavery," in Hudson, ed., Working Toward Freedom, 220; Wood, Women's Work, Men's Work, 167; Stuckey, Slave Culture, 108–9.

alist, believed that their spirit lived on after the death of their body. Those who remained unconverted maintained that the spirit world —which was rarely depicted to be in the heavens above—was a bountiful place where their forefathers yet lived. But even those who entered the doors of Charleston churches held to the belief that funerals hastened the deceased toward the spirit world. By contrast, the failure to observe the historic rituals could doom the soul to wander forever in the desolate waste of the damned, unable to become a protecting ancestor for later generations to appeal to for assistance. As one former slave later explained: "Us doan want 'e spirrit lebe behin'."[34]

Lionel Kennedy hardly prided himself on his keen knowledge of African beliefs. But no resident of the lowcountry could fail to notice the elaborate funerary customs of the slave community. The magistrates' decision to deny Amaretta Bennett and Susan Vesey the right to bury their husbands was a deliberate act of cruelty that had nothing to do with the need to train white doctors. Since the reign of King George II, Anglo-American society had regarded mutilation by a surgeon's knife as a "peculiar Mark of Infamy [to] be added to [capital] Punishment." Indeed, Isaac Harby, the editor of the *City Gazette,* recommended that *all* the bodies of Vesey's followers be given up "to the surgeons." A sentence of death and dismemberment "would be regarded with much more terror than they now are, and consequently be much more effectual to the prevention of crimes."[35]

The surgeons were kept busy; seven days later, on July 9, the trials resumed. Jack Pritchard was next. Several men from his company, including George Vanderhorst and Harry Haig, a thirty-five-year-old carpenter, testified in hopes of avoiding the gallows. But Jack's great power had not diminished with his incarceration, and as

34. Sobel, *World They Made Together,* 174; Washington, *A Peculiar People,* 54–55; Frey, *Water From the Rock,* 301; Joyner, *Down By the Riverside,* 138.

35. Linebaugh, "Tyburn Riot Against the Surgeons," 73–77; Charleston *City Gazette,* July 20, 1822. Genovese, *Roll, Jordan, Roll,* 203, makes an apt comparison: "The Nazis knew what they were doing when they refused to bury concentration camp victims. . . . Respect for the dead signifies respect for the living—respect for the continuity of the human community and recognition of each man's place within it."

Vanderhorst identified Jack as "the head of the Gullah Company" the African priest glared at the witness with "malignant glance[s]." Even now, Vanderhorst was "afraid of Gullah Jack as a conjurer," and he begged the court to send him far "away from this place." He thought his life "in great danger from giving testimony." Kennedy made no promises, but scribbled instead that Pritchard's "wildness and vehemence of gesture" was evidence that he remained a "savage who had indeed been caught but not tamed." Harry Haig testified next, and he too admitted that "[u]ntil Jack was taken I felt as if I was bound up and had not the power to speak one word about it."[36]

The court had heard enough. As they had with Denmark Vesey, the magistrates regarded the moment of sentencing as an opportunity to impress upon the slave community the superiority of their brand of Christianity over rival faiths:

> In the prosecution of your wicked designs, you were not satisfied with resorting to natural and ordinary means, but endeavoured to enlist on your behalf, all the powers of darkness, and employed for that purpose the most disgusting mummery and superstition. You represented yourself as invulnerable; that you could neither be taken nor destroyed, and all who fought under your banners would be invincible. Your boasted charms have not protected yourself, and of course could not protect others. "Your alters and your Gods have sunk together in the dust." The airy spectres, conjured by you, have been chased away by the special light of truth, and you stand exposed, the miserable and deluded victim of offended justice. Your days are literally numbered. You will shortly be consigned to the cold and silent grave, and all the powers of darkness cannot rescue you from your approaching fate.[37]

Having been captured as recently as July 5, three days after Denmark's execution and mutilation, Jack knew what awaited him. Shorn

36. Trial of "Gullah Jack" Pritchard, July 9, 1822, in Kennedy and Parker, eds., *Official Report*, 103–5, 47; Confession of Harry Haig, July 10, 1822, RGA, GM, SCDAH.

37. Sentence of Jack Pritchard, July 9, 1822, in Kennedy and Parker, eds., *Official Report*, 179; *Niles' Register*, September 7, 1822; Richmond *Enquirer*, September 3, 1822.

of his whiskers and deprived of his bag of amulets, Jack was powerless. His courage vanished. He begged the court to live for "a fortnight longer," and when that was denied him, he begged for a single week. Pritchard was still pleading for a few days more when the magistrates ordered him dragged "from the Court Room to his cell."[38]

On the following afternoon, the court heard the case of Monday Gell, the last of Vesey's officers to be put to trial. Monday's master, John Gell, attended, and despite the considerable hash he had made of Rolla's defense, Jacob Axson returned to the chamber. By now the proceedings had become a lethal minuet, in which both magistrates and witnesses danced their parts; Frank Ferguson performed the part of loyal servant and placed Gell at numerous planning sessions "at Vesey's house," while the judges pretended to give Axson's eloquent defense due consideration before handing down a finding of guilty. Gell sat unimpressed. He "heard the testimony given against him," Kennedy recorded, "and received his sentence with the utmost firmness and composure."[39]

While Warden Napier prepared new cells, Gell and four other rebels wandered the "common ward." Charles Drayton, a cook owned by District Judge John Drayton, reproached Gell for getting them all hanged. Gell remained serene. It was all they "had a right to expect," he replied, given their failure to take the city. The bitter conversation ended only when the prison blacksmith arrived "to iron the convicts, and the turnkey to convey them to separate cells." But Drayton was not ready to die. That night he called for Warden Gordon and begged to see the intendant. At "sun-rise" Hamilton entered the cell, and Drayton, "depress[ed] and panic[ed]," said he was prepared to reveal all he knew of the conspiracy in exchange for escaping the gallows.[40]

Hamilton was ready to listen, but it was really Gell's information that he wanted. He ordered Monday placed in the same cell with Drayton, "and left for twenty-four hours alone." No record of

38. Narrative, in Kennedy and Parker, eds., *Official Report,* 47.

39. Trial of Monday Gell, July 10, 1822, in Kennedy and Parker, eds., *Official Report,* 90–91, 46.

40. Hamilton, *An Account,* 19–20.

their conversation exists. But it is as curious as it is tragic that Gell, who appeared so resigned to his fate, decided not only to confess but to give the court "a list of the forty-two names" of the men who served in his African company. In exchange, the magistrates requested Governor Bennett spare Gell and Drayton and "commute their sentence[s] to transportation beyond the limits of the United States." For Hamilton, the deal with Monday Gell was worth it. "[E]very one of" the men Gell named was "apprehended, and disposed of."[41]

Certainly the magistrates saw the wisdom in obtaining the collaboration of a key officer, even one they regarded "a villain of the deepest dye," and not merely for the information Gell could provide about his Ibo company. Equally important was the pretense of benevolent mercy. No slave society in which the masters were the minority—no matter how heavily armed they were—could long survive unless solitary bondmen frequently turned on their fellows. Every slave knew the rewards that awaited those who whispered secrets to their masters (which makes the silence of hundreds of Vesey's disciples all the more impressive). For people already broken down by their bondage, or terrified of the noose, the public image of graciously granted mercy often created the mental structure of paternalism so necessary for the maintenance of the lowcountry's social structure. As W. Hasell Wilson smirked, "there were enough of the weak hearted coming forward to testify in hopes of getting clear."[42]

With the arrests of "upwards of sixty [more] slaves" over the next four days, Kennedy thought it prudent to establish "certain rules of discrimination" before their court hanged a good portion of the city's laboring population. Kennedy suggested they adopt "two classes of offenses." For the leaders, those who "attended meetings at Denmark Vesey's" or at "Monday Gell's shop," there could be no clemency. Upon conviction they would "be punished with death." But those recruits who took no part in organizing the conspiracy

41. Hamilton, *An Account,* 20–21, 28; Charleston *Mercury,* July 12, July 19, July 27, 1822; Charleston *Courier,* August 23, 1822.

42. Richmond *Enquirer,* September 3, 1822; Hay, "Property, Authority, and the Criminal Law," 42; W. Hasell Wilson to Robert Wilson, no date, CLS.

might join Gell and Drayton in enslaved exile to a foreign land, "not to return under penalty of death."[43]

Kennedy's decision did nothing to alter the fate of Jack Pritchard, whose fear of the noose never translated into a desire to cooperate with the magistrates. Perhaps no confession could have saved the African priest; next to Denmark Vesey, white Charlestonians were most terrified of Gullah Jack and his poisons. On the morning of Friday, July 12, either the warden or the hangman, Constable Belknap, drove Pritchard and John Horry beyond the Lines, the crumbling walls thrown up during the War of 1812, toward Blake's Lands. John, who had publicly threatened to disembowel his master, hobbled bravely up the steps. But Jack had to be "dragged forth to the scaffold," and according to Hamilton, he "gave up his spirit without firmness or composure." For the slaves who watched the executions, the priest's death was the final, terrible evidence "that he could be killed."[44]

Despite the second round of hangings, the magistrates saw no end in sight. With each new arrest the court discovered "that the Conspiracy had spread wider and wider." As one nervous Charlestonian observed on July 10, "most of the coachmen & favourite servants in the City knew of it even if they had not participated in the intentions & plans proposed." On the day after Pritchard died, James Legare pled "feeble health and great exhaustion" and begged leave to quit the tribunal. To fill his chair, Kennedy and Parker settled upon Colonel Henry Deas, the president of the board of trustees of Charleston College and a former member of the South Carolina Senate. Kennedy knew what he was about. According to the Reverend William Wightman, "the cruelty of Colonel Deas to his slaves [was] proverbial in South Carolina."[45]

The court quickly resumed their labors. Within two weeks, the tribunal sentenced twenty-two more rebels to swing, respited ten

43. Narrative, in Kennedy and Parker, eds., *Official Report,* viii, 59.

44. Charleston *Courier,* July 10, July 13, 1822; Charleston *Mercury,* July 10, July 13, 1822; Hamilton, *An Account,* 24, 43; Narrative, in Kennedy and Parker, eds., *Official Report,* 47; Hartford *Connecticut Courant,* August 6, 1822.

45. John Potter to Langdon Cheves, July 10, 1822, Cheves Papers, SCHS; Hamilton, *An Account,* 23; Weld, *Slavery As It Is,* 175.

more in hopes of obtaining further information, and ordered three
men transported outside the United States. Among those sentenced
to die was Bacchus Hammet, who rivaled Peter Poyas in sheer disdain for the court. On the night before his execution, the Reverend
John Backman, the pastor of the German Church, visited the cell of
the condemned man. Bacchus refused to join Backman in a prayer,
saying: "He never had any goodness in him, and that Hell was his
portion." Backman urged Bacchus to try and recall if he "ever did a
good action," but Bacchus only laughed. "*[H]e was the Devil amongst
the women,* [and] he believed he would go to Hell."[46]

All that night, prayers and moans drifted on the wind from the
Workhouse. But as the sun rose on Friday, July 26, Charleston prepared for an orgy of violence; the magistrates had ordered the
twenty-two rebels to die together as a gruesome lesson to the slave
community. In addition to Bacchus, those sentenced to hang included Mingo Harth and Jane Thompson's Pharaoh, who had turned
"states-evidence on the promise of rewards."[47] Hamilton argued
against hanging the men in shifts, which meant that the rickety gallows on Blake's Lands would not suffice. Instead, the constable constructed a series of three low benches along the north side of the
Lines. By tossing nooses over the walls, the hangman could finish
the job in one dreadful moment. At dawn, the rebels were brought
"to the vault under the City Hall" before mounted guardsmen
herded the chained men "up Meeting Street." As he marched toward his death, Bacchus stunned observers by "laughing and bid-
ding his acquaintances in the streets 'good bye.'" Even as Belknap
fixed a noose around his throat and drew "the cap" over his head,
Bacchus "was seen to laugh."[48]

46. Trial of Bacchus Hammet, July, 1822, in Kennedy and Parker, eds., *Official
Report,* 140–42; Confession of Bacchus Hammet, no date, William and Benjamin
Hammet Papers, DUL.

47. Charleston *City Gazette,* July 27, 1822; Hartford *Connecticut Courant,* August 6, 1822; Hamilton, *An Account,* 43; Washington *National Intelligencer,* August 2,
1822; Charleston *Courier,* July 19, 1822; [Bibb], *Late Contemplated Insurrection,* 6.

48. Pharo, ed., *Reminiscences of Wilson,* 8; Adger, *My Life and Times,* 52–53;
Mary Lamboll Beach to Elizabeth Gilchrist, July 25, 1822, Beach Letters, SCHS;
Confession of Bacchus Hammet, no date, William and Benjamin Hammet Pa-
pers, DUL.

Even for a culture that regarded executions as a social event devoutly not to be missed, the hanging of twenty-two men attracted a surprisingly "immense crowd" of "white as well as black." According to Mary Lamboll Beach, the rebels all "behaved with great firmness." Just before nine, Belknap began to kick out the boards that supported the low benches, but as a distraught Beach admitted, "the business was managed very badly." The bondmen dropped only a few inches, and most began to strangle; by perishing on the gallows, Vesey at least died quickly of a broken neck. To put an end to the torment, Captain Dove of the City Guard dispatched those still alive with his "pistol," their bodies jerking as the balls hit them. No ball was required for Bacchus. As he swung back and forth "he lifted his feet, so that his knees might not touch the Board," and so asphyxiated himself. In the clamor and chaos, a "small black boy," presumably the son of one of the executed, was trampled by mounted guardsmen when "several horses pass[ed] over his body." At long last the final shot echoed off the Lines, and a "death like silence" fell over the city.[49]

The eerie stillness was a marked contrast with the fury and violence of the previous weeks, as if the mad bloodlust of the morning washed away Charleston's collective wrath. A few voices, aware of the growing "agitation and extreme feeling in the public mind" caused by the mass hangings, stubbornly defended the court. The "wretches" deserved to lose "their worthless lives," insisted John Potter, while the ever-militant Charleston *Mercury* demanded even more deaths for those slaves guilty of "villainy, hypocrisy, and ingratitude." Whether the final death toll was "two hundred or two thousand," the *Mercury* editorialized, "[j]ustice is not to be disarmed because she is called upon to strike among the multitude."[50]

But most Charlestonians, even hardened as they were to the harsh realities of survival in a slave society, thought that July 26

49. Confession of Bacchus Hammet, no date, William and Benjamin Hammet Papers, DUL; Mary Lamboll Beach to Elizabeth Gilchrist, July 25, 1822, Beach Letters, SCHS; [Bibb], *Late Contemplated Insurrection,* 8; Charleston *Southern Patriot,* July 26, 1822.

50. John Potter to Langdon Cheves, June 29, 1822, Cheves Papers, SCHS; Charleston *Mercury,* August 15, 1822.

should be the end of it. Anna Haynes Johnson was sickened by the "aweful tragidy" of the morning. "Gracious heaven to what will all this lead," she wondered. "Certainly it will throw our city back at least ten years." Martha Proctor Richardson agreed that her city had "undergone a dreadful state of things." But the best bellwether of public sentiment was Mary Lamboll Beach, who had staunchly supported the tribunal until then. "The day before I felt strangely firm about it," she confided to a friend, but "by evening my distress about the business returned."[51]

Tender sentiments alone, especially those expressed in the private correspondence of Carolina gentlewomen, could not stay the hand of the executioner, but pragmatic considerations might. Constable Belknap, who was widely blamed for bungling the executions on the Lines, fired back at the magistrates. The frequency of the hangings caused him enormous "personal inconvenience [and] deranged [his] private business." For the past several weeks, Belknap complained, he had spent "night and day, in assisting at the preparation of the Gallows, [and] the digging of the graves" after the surgeons were done dissecting the corpses. The City Corporation (council) also urged restraint. The city had already spent $2,284 on confining the accused in the Workhouse, "erecting a Gallows," and obtaining "carts to carry the criminals to the place of execution." Because the Negro Act did not require the state to reimburse masters for property hanged in the sin of insurrection, owners like Thomas Bennett, who was paid a paltry salary of $875 each year to serve as governor, lost skilled bondmen they could ill-afford to replace. James Louis Petigru, Hamilton's law partner, later reduced the destruction of life to simple economics when he chided a magistrate: "I am afraid you will hang half the country. You must take care and save negroes enough for the Rice crop."[52]

51. Anna Haynes Johnson to Elizabeth Haywood, July 27, 1822, Haywood Papers, SHC, UNC; Martha Proctor Richardson to James Screven, August 7, 1822, Arnold and Screven Papers, SHC, UNC; Mary Lamboll Beach to Elizabeth Gilchrist, July 25, 1822, Beach Letters, SCHS. (The last letter was misdated, as Lamboll speaks in the past tense of the "22 [who] were executed" on July 26.)

52. Wade, "Vesey Plot," 147–48; South Carolina Treasury Records, Journal C, 1814–1824, SCDAH; William Pease and Jane Pease, *James Louis Petigru: Southern Conservative, Southern Dissenter* (Athens, 1995), 30–31.

The tribunal had no intention of depleting their labor force, and on the afternoon of July 26, the "enlightened gentlemen and conscientious Christians" adjourned *sine die*. For those yet imprisoned in the Workhouse, Kennedy and Parker recommended pardon and transportation. "The terror of example we thought would be sufficiently operative by the number of criminals [already] sentenced to death," they told Governor Bennett. Among those to be spared were Monday Gell and Charles Drayton, who had cooperated "under the impression that they would ultimately have their lives spared." No better evidence existed for the authorities' fatigue than the fact that one of the rebels "respited" for transportation was Sandy Vesey, who had been sentenced to swing on Saturday, July 27.[53]

A small band of extremists was appalled. A notice under the heading of "Many Citizens" promptly appeared in the *Southern Patriot*. "Permit us to express an earnest hope," they wrote, "that no *consideration whatever* may at this momentous crisis" influence the tribunal "to retire." Determined not to allow even a vocal minority to impede his political career, Intendant Hamilton wearily appointed a new board led by former defense attorney Jacob Axson and Charles B. Furman. To obtain the necessary five freeholders, Hamilton evidently promised the court they need only put on one final week of show trials. Robert Hayne, Thomas Rhett Smith, Thomas Roper, John Gordon, and Joel R. Poinsett, who would gain lasting fame through his discovery of an exotic Mexican plant, finally agreed to serve.[54]

To justify their proceedings and appease those not yet satiated, the new tribunal served up five more lives. On Tuesday, July 30, a churlish Belknap carted four more rebels, including Jack McNeill and Caesar Smith, to the Lines for execution, before "deliver[ing] their bodies] to the surgeons for dissection."[55] The last to die was Vesey's old friend William Garner, a drayman who hired his time

53. Charleston *Mercury*, July 29, 1822; Kennedy and Parker to Thomas Bennett, July 24, 1822, RGA, GM, SCDAH; Trial of Sandy Vesey, July 1822, in Kennedy and Parker, eds., *Official Report*, 123–24; Charleston *Mercury*, July 26, 1822.

54. Charleston *Mercury*, August 3, 1822; Jervey, *Robert Hayne*, 132–33; Charleston *Southern Patriot*, July 1, August 2, 1822.

55. Charleston *Mercury*, July 31, 1822; Charleston *City Gazette*, 27, 1822; Hamilton, *An Account*, 43; Richmond *Enquirer*, August 6, 1822.

from his widowed owner Martha Garner. William had escaped to Columbia, where his free brother lived. Captured on July 23, Garner was returned to Charleston, where the court sentenced him to hang on August 9 before adjourning after nine days of "painful duty."[56]

The two courts, with the assistance of James Hamilton and the city guardsmen, had arrested 131 slaves and free blacks. Thirty of those apprehended were released without trial, although some served as witnesses. Of the 101 men who appeared before the tribunals, the magistrates ordered 35 hanged and 37 transported outside the United States. Twenty-three were acquitted, 2 more died while in custody, 3 were found not guilty and released but nonetheless whipped by the Workhouse warden on suspicion of involvement, and one free black was released on condition that he leave the state. (Four white men, including Jacob Danders, the alcoholic, German-born peddlar, received short prison sentences for showing excessive sympathy for those hanged.) In all, the two courts hanged more men than were executed in any other Southern slave conspiracy. (For a complete list of the 101 men put to trial, see appendix.)

As white fear and anger subsided, concern over lost property rose accordingly. The death or transportation of seventy-two men meant not merely the loss of skilled craftsmen and domestics, it represented nearly as many hundreds of dollars in irreclaimable capital investment. Because some of those who had lost slaves numbered among the most powerful politicians in the state, it was not difficult for indignant owners to obtain a hearing in the state Assembly. On December 16, a special Senate committee reported a bill to amend the Negro Act so that masters who had lost their bondmen to insurrection might receive compensation. But masters first had to assign "to the state, all right of property in said slaves," and they were to receive only "$122.86 for each slave," roughly one-fourth of the market price for a young, skilled bondman. The low sum was both a testimony to the state's sagging economy and a rebuke to those masters who had failed to properly control their bond-

56. Charleston *Mercury,* August 3, 5, 9, 10, 1822; Hamilton, *An Account,* 43; Hartford *Connecticut Courant,* August 13, 1822; Martha Proctor Richardson to James Screven, August 7, 1822, Arnold and Screven Papers, SHC, UNC.

men. A chagrinned Governor Bennett nonetheless requested his $367 for Rolla, Ned, and Batteau. The state paid out $2,326 for executed or transported slaves, together with a $200 reward for Peter Prioleau and another $1,000 for William Penceel, whose free, mixed-race status necessitated a higher amount.[57]

The process of transporting convicted bondmen out of the country went no more smoothly. Several rebels sailed for Liberia, the West African colony purchased by the American Colonization Society. Having been released under the promise that he leave the state, free black Quash Harleston, together "with his family and two or three other free persons of color," boarded the *Dolphin* just before it sailed for Cape Mesurado. Joining Harleston was Prince Graham, another free man, and perhaps also Saby Gaillard. But these men were already free, and for the slaves awaiting transportation, it would hardly do to reward them for their crimes by liberating them in their ancestral home. Instead, the penurious state required individual masters to arrange and pay the cost of transportation to another American slave society (which several impoverished widows could ill-afford to do). In 1826, a German visitor to the state prison discovered one rebel still chained to "an iron ring in the floor" of his cell. Four years after his sentence, the warden explained, the bondman yet remained in prison "till his master can find some opportunity to ship him to the West Indies and there sell him."[58]

As for Governor Bennett, the trials proved a burden on more than just his purse. The devout paternalist never came to grips with the hard fact that his beloved servants so wanted to be free that Rolla would allow one of his soldiers to slay him as he slept. Nor had the irregular proceedings in the dank Workhouse changed his view—which he publicly shared with his brother-in-law, Justice Johnson—that the Negro Act did not adequately protect black defendants. But when the governor formally called upon the legislature to amend the law, and thus implicitly condemn Kennedy's tri-

57. Charleston *Courier,* December 25, 1822; South Carolina Treasury Records, Journal C, 1814–1824, SCDAH.

58. Richmond *Enquirer,* September 6, 1822; Washington *National Intelligencer,* August 27, 1822; Bernhard, *Travels Through North America,* 2:9.

bunal, the furious Assembly overwhelmingly voted to table Bennett's message without printing it.[59]

The court stood vindicated, the governor humiliated. Public opinion regarded Thomas Bennett as a naive fool whose once-promising career had reached an inglorious end; he had lost control of both his household and the state legislature. White military domination having been adequately demonstrated by the noose, Charleston slowly began to return, as one gentlewoman observed, to "its wanted security."[60] But Anna Haynes Johnson was wrong; South Carolina was never the same after the summer of 1822. The execution of Denmark Vesey elevated an obscure carpenter into a national martyr and a symbol of struggle for the African-American and abolitionist communities. For the white citizenry, the close call with *their* Night of Fire wedded them to an increasingly militant political course that hastened them down the tortuous path to civil war.

59. Freehling, *Reintegration of American History,* 55.
60. Anna Haynes Johnson to Elizabeth Haywood, July 18, 1822, Haywood Papers, SHC, UNC.

Chapter Nine

The Temple Finished
1822–1865

DENMARK VESEY WAS DEAD, but few Carolinians believed that they had disposed of his cause as easily as the surgeons had his body. In the decades after 1822, Charleston authorities and Columbia legislators labored to abolish the conditions that had allowed for the conspiracy to exist, just as they tried to transform the countryside into a harsh, unforgiving rural penitentiary. "I am afraid this *very instance* will induce others to be harder with *them* than *they* were previous to it," lamented Mary Lamboll Beach. "Ah! *Slavery is a hard business.*"[1] But they failed. The Southern slave community, and increasingly, Northern abolitionist voices, kept Denmark Vesey's name alive until the day that Carolina bondmen could again rise for their freedom by donning blue uniforms.

Even as city and state lawmakers prepared to fasten the chains of bondage ever tighter, discerning Carolinians were painfully aware that no mere law, no scrap of paper, could effectively prevent another Vesey from rising out of the city streets or remote plantations.

---

1. Mary Lamboll Beach to Elizabeth Gilchrist, July 5, 1822, Beach Letters, SCHS.

Indeed, some whites feared that legislative efforts to eliminate the few meager privileges permitted to slaves might actually create, rather than inhibit, angry rebel leaders. Despondent voices predicted more bloodshed, and those depressing opinions remained constant over time. It was hardly surprising that Martha Proctor Richardson, writing only four days after Vesey's death, "fear[ed another] such an attempt will one day be made." Three years later, state legislator Whitemarsh Seabrook pronounced it a "melancholy truth" that the slave quarters would yet "raise up a Toussaint or a Spartacus against us." A single "educated slave or colored freeman," Seabrook worried, remained "capable of infusing the poison of insubordination into a whole body of the black population."[2]

The paradox, as nervous planters across the South repeatedly observed, was that "the most humanely treated negroes" in Charleston had listened to Vesey. For several decades, masters had increasingly discussed their bondpeople in the soothing tones of paternalistic responsibility (although their violent actions often gave the lie to their words). Now their happy slaves had paid them back by sharpening rusty sabers. It was "distinctly proved," observed a perplexed James Hamilton, "that without, scarcely an exception," Vesey's unwaged disciples "had no individual hardship to complain of." The Virginia editor of the *Petersburg Intelligencer* agreed: The "larger portion of the slaves concerned in this plot, were those who had been most indulged by their masters, and not a few of them were educated men," a fact "pregnant with wholesome instruction."[3]

Seabrook's pessimism notwithstanding, many white Carolinians concluded that slave rebelliousness might be rendered less common by putting an end to such "extreme indulgence." Although few slaves ever imagined themselves to be indulged by their owners, most masters now perceived themselves to have been too lenient to their servants. Many nodded approvingly as they read Edwin C. Holland's fiery 1822 rejoinder to those critical of the mass hangings.

2. Martha Proctor Richardson to James Screven, July 6, 1822, Arnold and Screven Papers, SHC, UNC; Hunt, *Haiti's Influence*, 114.

3. Hamilton, *An Account*, 29; *Petersburg Intelligencer* quoted in Washington *National Intelligencer*, September 16, 1822.

"Let it never be forgotten, that our Negroes are truly the *Jacobins* of our country," Holland wrote, "the barbarians who would, IF THEY COULD, become the DESTROYERS *of our race*." Both editor and citizen agreed upon the need to teach the black community a hard lesson. The executions were "an awful but a necessary" lesson, editorialized the Charleston *Courier,* while Martha Proctor Richardson prayed that "the examples . . . written in Blood" might "deter similar efforts for 20 or 30 years."[4]

Particularly in need of instruction were domestic servants, too many of whom had joined Vesey's ranks. "I have heard it remarked by several that all confidence in them now is forever at an end," reported one genteel lady, a sentiment repeated almost verbatim in the correspondence of Martha Proctor Richardson. "[A]ll confidence is lost in our [house] servants," she confided to James Screven, for "the condemned slaves belonged to the most humane & indulgent owners." Although Assistant Warden John S. Cogdell feared that the insurrection would depress the value of all slaves "very much," the price of young male "field negroes" quickly rebounded as cotton prices rose in 1825. But the selling price of domestic slaves—even women—remained low for years, owing, factor Frank Kinlock speculated, "to the bad conduct of great numbers of that description at the time of the projected revolt in Charleston."[5]

Kinlock's inability to secure ready buyers for domestic slaves was hardly surprising. Within months of Vesey's death, the concerns first expressed in private correspondence found their way into numerous pamphlets and published accounts of the affair, as South Carolina's intellectual leaders hurried to articulate the need to crack down on the black majority. The first extended commentary came from the pen of Edwin C. Holland, a native of the city and the

4. Holland, *A Refutation of the Calumnies,* 86; Charleston *Courier,* August 12, 1822; Martha Proctor Richardson to James Screven, September 16, 1822, Arnold and Screven Papers, SHC, UNC.

5. Mary Lamboll Beach to Elizabeth Gilchrist, July 5, 1822, Beach Letters, SCHS; Martha Proctor Richardson to James Screven, August 7, 1822, Arnold and Screven Papers, SHC, UNC; John S. Cogdell to Langdon Cheves, July 6, 1822, Cheves Papers, SCHS; F. Kinlock to Thomas Waties, April 29, [1825?], Waties Papers, Folder 12, SCL.

staunchly-proslavery editor of the *Charleston Times*. On October 29, 1822, Holland obtained a copyright for his treatise, *A Refutation of the Calumnies Circulated Against the Southern and Western States*. Although Holland was more concerned with defending the actions of Kennedy's court than he was with justifying slavery itself as a benevolent institution, he assailed the "general spirit of insubordination among our slaves and free negroes—springing from the relaxation of discipline on the part of whites." If the intelligentsia needed to explain "to the Legislature" the ruthless course that lowcountry whites had collectively, if perhaps unconsciously, decided upon, Holland was more than ready to take the lead.[6]

Nor was Holland alone in his quest to persuade the state Assembly to fall into line with popular sentiment, not that much persuasion was required. By late 1822, both James Hamilton and Kennedy and Parker published their narratives of the plot in pamphlet form. At nearly 200 pages, Kennedy's *An Official Report of the Trials of Sundry Negroes* was a far more complete compilation of documents than Hamilton's brief, forty-eight page *An Account of the Late Intended Insurrection Among a Portion of the Blacks of This City*. But both were designed to demonstrate to upcountry whites how dangerously "far" the rebels had gotten "before a disclosure" of their plans. Both pamphlets urged changes in how urban masters supervised their slaves, and both writers hoped to prove "to our brethren throughout the Union" the upstanding and fair-minded "character of our city." Hamilton's *Account* quickly went through numerous printings, as the influential Richmond *Enquirer* urged its subscribers to purchase copies and spread its "truth and nothing but the truth throughout the United States." Whether New England readers accepted Mayor Hamilton's self-serving description of his tenacity and courage in putting down the rebellion was doubtful, but Northern readers bought the pamphlets in numbers great enough to justify a late-1822 Boston republication of Hamilton's treatise under the title *Negro Plot*.[7]

6. Larry E. Tise, *Proslavery: A History of the Defense of Slavery in America, 1701–1840* (Athens, 1987), 59–60; Holland, *A Refutation of the Calumnies*, 82–83.

7. William Jones to S. P. Jones, January 22, 1823, Jane Bruce Jones Papers, USC; Charleston *City Gazette*, July 27, 1822; Richmond *Enquirer*, September 3, 1822.

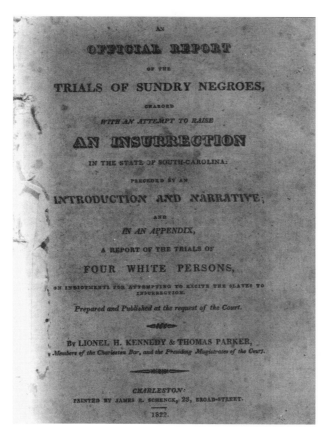

The title page of Kennedy and Parker's *An Official Report of the Trials of Sundry Negroes. Courtesy of The Charleston Museum, Charleston, S.C.*

For those who neither fell into line on the question of further restricting the alleged liberties currently enjoyed by Carolina bond-people nor regarded Kennedy's tribunal as a triumph of judicial decorum, there was little option but to fall silent or incur the public's wrath. The first to fall victim to what Thomas Bennett dubbed the "excite[d and] anxious" mood of the lowcountry was the governor himself. Already humiliated by the public knowledge that the conspiracy virtually had been hatched in his home, Bennett made matters worse by releasing a lengthy statement on August 10 designed to calm popular "passions." Although the address contained the requisite defense of slavery, Bennett heaped praise upon the "fidelity and attachment" of the city's free blacks. Because wealthy mulattoes identified with Charleston's business class, Bennett insisted, there would always "be the certainty of detection" of any "extensive conspiracy." The governor was quite correct in his assessment, but as the public now regarded Denmark Vesey (rather than George Wilson) as the quintessential freeman, they were in no mood to listen to reason. The "Governor by his circular published today makes as little of [the conspiracy] as possible," sneered one merchant. "I believe his wish is that it may soon pass into oblivion."[8]

Oblivion was not likely, as Bennett's brother-in-law discovered when he added his lonely voice to Bennett's censure of Kennedy's court. William Johnson's early doubts about the legality of Carolina's slave codes became the subject of vicious public rumor as the summer progressed, spiteful enough that—as his daughter explained—the Justice believed it necessary to take up his pen in hopes "of silencing all the impertinent rudeness which was let afloat to his disadvantage." As early as June 29, Justice Johnson placed a card in the Charleston *Courier,* notifying the public of his intention to answer "the most groundless and unprovoked attacks ever made upon the feelings of an individual."[9]

Although scholarly in presentation and rational in tone, Johnson's *To the Public of Charleston* was as much at odds with the public temper as was Bennett's defense of the brown elite. For weeks, elegant society discussed almost nothing besides Johnson's "foolish ill-timed publications." John Potter dismissed the pamphlet as "weak a piece" as "ever a man in his sober senses could write." Genteel ladies entered the fray as well. Martha Proctor Richardson criticized Johnson's "very unreasonable & unnecessary admonition" to

8. Thomas Bennett to Secretary of War John C. Calhoun, July 15, 1822, in Hemphill, ed., *Papers of Calhoun,* 7:210; Richmond *Enquirer,* August 30, 1822; Stephen Elliot to William Elliot, August 23, 1822, Elliot and Gonzales Papers, SHC, UNC.

9. Anna Haynes Johnson to Elizabeth Haywood, July 24, 1822, Haywood Papers, SHC, UNC; Charleston *Courier,* June 29, 1822.

the court as "very lame." Because several of Vesey's officers "belonged to his Brother in law Bennet[t]," Richardson huffed, "delicacy should have kept him silent." So great was the outcry against Johnson's implication that Kennedy's tribunal had committed legal "murder," that the editor of the *Courier* printed a public apology in which he insisted that he had run Johnson's card "after having been read over in a very hasty manner."[10]

As a Jefferson-appointee to the Supreme Court, William Johnson's sinecure, unlike his reputation, was beyond assault. (Johnson did confide to Jefferson, however, that if "such be the laws of this country, this shall not long be my country.")[11] But the popular clamor served as a warning that Carolina society would tolerate no disapproval by public servants too delicate to do what was required to dominate the black majority. Not surprisingly, terrorized planters were even less inclined to endure "the gibes and jeers" of Northern critics. Because several black defendants, including Vesey himself, named New York Senator Rufus King as a distant champion, diplomat Thomas Pinckney, in yet another conspiracy-inspired 1822 pamphlet, *Reflections Occasioned by the Late Disturbances in Charleston,* identified the "indiscreet zeal in favor of universal liberty, expressed by many of our fellow-citizens in the States north and east of Maryland" as "the most obvious" cause of the plot. Joel R. Poinsett also believed "the Missouri question at Washington, among other evils, produced this plot," but Edwin C. Holland's assessment was the harshest of all. "In many of the Northern and Eastern prints, there has been a great deal of whining, canting, sickly kind of humanity," he fumed, "which is as disgraceful to the character of those journals, as it is contemptible in the eyes of all intelligent and reflecting men."[12]

10. John Potter to Langdon Cheves, July 5, 1822, June 29, 1822, Cheves Papers, SCHS; Martha Proctor Richardson to James Screven, July 6, 1822, August 7, 1822, Arnold and Screven Papers, SHC, UNC; Charleston *Courier,* June 29, 1822.

11. William Johnson to Thomas Jefferson, December 10, 1822, Jefferson Papers, Library of Congress.

12. Vipperman, *Lowndes,* 263–64; [Thomas Pinckney], *Reflections Occasioned by the Late Disturbances in Charleston* (Charleston, 1822), 6; Joel R. Poinsett to James Monroe, Monroe Papers, Library of Congress; Holland, *A Refutation of the Calumnies,* 13.

The utterly inaccurate belief that Northern voters uniformly regarded "domestic slavery as an evil which the southern states" could
"easily get rid of," also attracted the ire of Henry William Desaussure,
who added his voice to the growing body of anti-Vesey literature.
Convinced that the reading public was eager to acquire innumerable
pamphlets on the matter, Desaussure poured his indignation into
*A Series of Numbers Addressed to the Public, on the Subject of the
Slaves and Free People of Colour.* Although in fact Desaussure had
little new to offer in the debate, his depiction of Northern reformers
as "bitter enemies" aptly captured the acrid tone found in most private missives. One sarcastic correspondent, for example, proposed
to ship "all these black free incendiaries" north to *"your kind,* and
tender hearted Philadelphians, as well as Quakers." Even in later
years, the fury of lowcountry whites who blamed their woes on outside agitators never abated. As late as 1835, an aged Thomas Napier
angrily denounced Vesey's conspiracy as "the fruits of Abolitionists."
Remembering that terrifying night in a long-ago June, Napier accused "anyone that would advocate their principles [of being] the
worst enemy of man and destitute of every Christian principle."[13]

Charleston journalists, as eager for sales as they were anxious
to challenge their Northern counterparts, promptly weighed in.
Isaac Harby, whose Jewish faith marked him as an anomaly in the
predominantly Protestant state, proved especially eager to defend
the Southern way of life. Like Pinckney, Harby's *Gazette* blamed
the conspiracy on the antislavery politicians who had advanced the
"Missouri poison." Harby was particularly incensed by comments
printed by Theodore Dwight, editor of the *New York Daily Advertiser*
and brother of the late theologian Timothy Dwight. In a September
editorial, Harby reminded his readers that in 1741, a New York court
had burned, hanged, or exiled 120 slaves charged with plotting to
torch the city, a comparison that pleased Kennedy so much that he
included it as an extract in his *Official Report.* Certainly the most

13. [Henry William Desaussure], *A Series of Numbers Addressed to the Public,
On the Subject of the Slaves and Free People of Colour* (Columbia, 1822); John Pot-
ter to Langdon Cheves, July 10, 1822, Cheves Papers, SCHS; Freehling, *Prelude to
Civil War,* 60–61.

defensive was the ardently-proslavery Charleston *Mercury.* "The people of this city are as humane, as pious, as obedient to the calls of charity and to the dictates of mercy and Christian forgiveness as are the citizens of New York," pronounced editor Henry Laurens Pinckney. "They want no newspaper lectures."[14]

Charleston editors took great solace in the way other Southern journalists rallied to their defense. The Charleston *Courier,* a nationalist journal ordinarily given to endorsing the candidacy of John Quincy Adams, was pleased to report "the tenderness and sympathy" with which the hangings were reported "by the journals in our sister states." The Richmond *Enquirer,* not wishing to engage in hypocrisy, blandly observed that South Carolina had only resorted "to the policy which was forced upon Virginia in 1800" by Gabriel's army. "Let humanity weep as much as it pleases over such scenes," Thomas Ritchie observed in an obvious swipe at Northern critics, but the entire South was determined "that our fair fields shall not be sprinkled with blood." Modern historians tend to regard antebellum South Carolina, the only state to then harbor a black majority, as atypically fanatical on matters involving slavery, but even the moderate Washington *National Intelligencer,* the mouthpiece of the neo-Federalist economic policies of President James Monroe, endorsed the "rigid but necessary punishment" meted out to Vesey's disciples. African Americans "are a lazy pampered race," it observed, "and if they meditate murder when thus indulged they must suffer for it."[15]

With Carolina's planter and intellectual elite firmly behind the policy of retribution and increased supervision, the next logical step was for city and state politicians to attempt to legislate servile rebellion out of existence. Although the lowcountry gentry, even during the rhetorical apogee of the Revolutionary era, had never exhibited much shame over the ownership of other humans, neither had they

14. Zola, *Isaac Harby,* 95–96; Charleston *City Gazette,* September 27, 1822; "Extracts," in Kennedy and Parker, eds., *Official Report,* no page; Charleston *Mercury,* August 15, 1822.

15. Charleston *Courier,* August 12, 1822; Richmond *Enquirer,* August 2, 1822; Washington *National Intelligencer,* July 20, 1822.

believed it necessary to defend their society and its peculiar organi-zation of labor. But after the summer of 1822, white Carolinians un-derstood themselves to be under siege from both within and without. To deal with external critics, lowcountry statesmen like White-marsh Seabrook determined to permit—or at least publish in the local press—no further national discussion of slavery that might "in-cidentally introduce [the] most malevolent and serious excitement." For internal enemies, rural Carolinians formed vigilante societies to patrol the countryside. Typical was the Pineville Police Association. Founded in 1823 for the purpose of "apprehending or dispersing" runaways and religious gatherings, the Association quickly took on the task of harassing "any individual [caught] trading with negroes without a written permission."[16]

Urban vigilantes were no less attentive. Painfully aware of the "deficiencies" in the way the old night watch failed adequately to patrol the city, the *Mercury* encouraged Kennedy's and Parker's court to examine "the police laws of the state and city" before disbanding and suggest changes in "the present system." But no formal recom-mendation was required to prod local mobs into attacking any black widow who dared appear on the streets in mourning clothes. One freeman who worked for Vesey at the time of the conspiracy later recalled watching as "several [mourners] were abused in the street, and some put in prison, for appearing in sackcloth," a coarse weave traditionally donned following the death of a spouse.[17]

Vigilante justice was but a temporary expedient. On Decem-ber 21, 1822, the City Council voted to create a permanent force of 150 guardsmen to patrol the streets around the clock. An imposing guard house was built on the southeastern corner of Broad and Meet-ing streets, from where officers employed mounted couriers to main-tain contact with guardsmen on the "beat." The enlarged force was far from inexpensive. For a largely agrarian region with a limited rev-enue base, its annual cost of $24,000 was a burden on the city. Few

16. Freehling, *Prelude to Civil War,* 109; McCurry, *Masters of Small Worlds,* 117–18.

17. Charleston *Mercury,* August 20, 1822; Higginson, *Black Rebellion,* 264–65.

whites complained. "With these means," crowed Robert Y. Hayne, "there cannot be a doubt that Charleston is placed in a condition of entire safety."[18]

The guardsmen, of course, grew especially vigilant at night and on Sundays, as rural slaves flocked toward the city to market their wares. The watch never forgot that a Sunday was to have been the moment of Vesey's assault. Promptly at nine o'clock every evening, the bells of St. Michael's rang out across the city, a signal for bond-people to return quickly to their masters' homes. Any slave found wandering the streets after that hour without a pass was taken to the guard house, "with strong probability," W. Hasell Wilson smirked, "of a whipping in the morning following." On Sunday mornings, as Charlestonians flocked to services, a detachment of guardsmen marched out of the station house armed with "loaded muskets with fixed bayonets." Two patrolmen remained at "sentry duty in front of [every city] church" for the duration of the service. In the past, such precautions adopted after an insurrection scare had decreased as time passed. But 1822 was different. Almost two decades later, visiting British actress Frances Anne Kemble marveled at the "most ominous tolling of bells and beating of drums, which, on the first evening of my arrival, made me almost fancy myself in one of the old fortified frontier towns of the Continent."[19]

Bondmen unlucky enough to be plucked off the streets as they made their way across the city to visit their wives often found themselves walking the new treadmill at the Workhouse. Constructed in 1823, the treadmill, which abolitionist Sarah Grimké described as "an instrument of torture," used two large wheels for grinding corn. As many as twelve slaves, each manacled to a rail above their heads, marched on each wheel as drivers hurried them along with a "cat o' nine tails." (Ever mindful of the high cost of surveillance, the Workhouse marketed the ground corn to help finance the operation.) But the most impressive symbol of racial control was the Citadel, built in 1825 to house the arsenal and the sixty-man state guard. Eighteen

18. Fraser, *Charleston*, 203–5; Wade, *Slavery in the Cities*, 99.
19. Pharo, ed., *Reminiscences of Wilson*, 7; Powers, *Black Charlestonians*, 33.

years later, the edifice became the home of the South Carolina Military Academy, although residents continued to call the school by its former name.[20]

As if heightened supervision and state-sanctioned brutality was not protection enough, terrified Charlestonians continued to suggest further modifications to their system of racial control. Perhaps the strangest was advanced by Thomas Pinckney, a former soldier, diplomat, and one-time Vice Presidential candidate. The elderly general suspected that neither Citadel nor treadmill could frighten truly determined rebels, and to that end he advocated turning Charleston into a wholly white city. House servants like Rolla Bennett might be sold into the countryside, and the practice of bond artisans hiring their time should be ruthlessly suppressed. Pinckney's unrealistic vision was just that, and no pamphleteer seconded his curious scheme. But several writers did endorse one of his proposals. Pinckney thought it dangerous that so many masters permitted their domestic slaves to ignore the clothing requirements of the Negro Act; when slaves dressed as gentlemen, Pinckney observed, they often forgot they were slaves. Alexander Garden, writing under the pseudonym "Rusticus" in the *Southern Patriot*, heartily agreed. The city guardsmen, he thought, could perform a far more useful service "by disrobing these modern fine gentry" than "by nabbing poor simple blacky after a bell ring." The City Council would not go so far as to strip slaves in the boulevards, but a Charleston grand jury did begin to indict bondpeople caught wearing clothing "subversive of that subordination which policy requires to be enforced."[21]

General Pinckney was less confident that an even greater danger to white hegemony, the ability of urban slaves to learn to read, could ever be eradicated. Laws against black literacy rarely penetrated Charleston's back alleys, and he feared this "evil will increase rather than diminish." But city authorities were determined to try.

20. Fraser, *Charleston*, 203; Bernhard, *Travels Through North America*, 2:10; Harlan Greene, *Charleston: City of Memory* (Greensboro, N.C., 1987), 32. The Citadel moved to its current campus in 1922.

21. Vipperman, *Lowndes*, 263; [Pinckney], *Reflections*, 14; Charleston *Southern Patriot*, September 12, 1822; Wade, *Slavery in the Cities*, 130.

Armed with the knowledge that Vesey and most of his key lieutenants could both read and write, the City Council announced it
would vigorously enforce existing ordinances against teaching enslaved African Americans to read. That it was all but impossible to
enforce such decrees in Charleston's mean streets could be seen by
the fact that in 1833 the indefatigable Whitemarsh Seabrook believed it necessary to introduce an amending act into the state Assembly. The new statute, which passed the following year, established heavy fines and "up to fifty lashes" for teaching even *free*
blacks to sign their own name.[22]

Nor were rhetorical attacks on the perceived rights of blacks the
province of planter-legislators alone. White artisans, in a transparent
effort to eliminate their chief competitors, eagerly seconded Pinckney's recommendation that the city crack down on the practice of
hiring out. The "recent serious occurrences in the City," lectured
one craftsmen, came at the hands "of this very class of our black
population." Too many politically-connected businessmen routinely
employed slave artisans for the state Assembly to legislate against
what the South Carolina Mechanics Association labeled the "great
evil" of skilled slaves working outside their masters' homes. Instead,
a Charleston grand jury took a swipe at middle-class shopkeepers by
imposing limits on the large "number of [liquor] Licenses which are
annually granted to Watchmen, or their Wives." With good reason,
the grand jury feared that guardsmen who "encourage Negroes" to
frequent their "Dram-shops" might be lenient when they caught
their best customers committing some nighttime infraction.[23]

When changes in state law worked to the benefit of the ruling
elite, however, the Assembly was swift to act. This was especially
true after Intendant Hamilton resumed his seat in the lower chamber of the state legislature. On December 8, 1822, Hamilton introduced a bill to grant "compensation [to] those persons whose slaves

---

22. Pinckney, *Reflections*, 9; Cornelius, *When I Can Read My Title Clear*, 39–41;
"An Act to Amend the Laws in Relation to Slaves and Free Persons of Color," in
Cooper and McCord, eds., *Statutes at Large*, 7:468.

23. Loren Schweninger, "Slave Independence and Enterprise in South Carolina," 115; Morgan, *Slave Counterpoint*, 308.

have been executed" or deported. Hamilton reasoned, despite past experience, that masters concerned with losing a valuable bondman might not report servile conspiracies to the proper authorities. In reality, too many influential gentlemen—including the governor—had lost too much money to be ignored. But a region reliant on agricultural exports had few means of raising revenue, and although the bill passed, the Assembly granted a paltry "$122.40 for each slave so executed" for a total of $4,162.06, a sum that covered merely a fraction of their individual worth. Hamilton, however, was not present in Columbia to hear the inevitable complaints. He parlayed his growing notoriety into a seat in Congress and arrived in Washington in time to take the oath of office on December 13. (Hamilton served until March 3, 1829, when he was elevated to the governor's chair as a nullifier.)[24]

If the state Assembly thought it too much an imposition on urban businessmen to prohibit their right to employ slave artisans, the legislature was willing to impose new penalties on slaves who hired their own time. Under a tough 1822 act, masters had to serve as employment agents for their bondpeople. Upon the conclusion of one task, urban slaveholders were required to immediately find their slave a new job or return him to their own home, a time-consuming ordeal that few masters cared to undertake. The law also limited the number of slaves any master might hire out at one time, and a clause flatly banned the hiring of "male slaves [to free] negroes."[25]

As the ban on hiring bondmen to freemen indicated, the Assembly was as determined to drive freemen out of the state as it was in tightening the fetters on those who remained in bondage. Although mulattoes like George Wilson, William Penceel, and Peter Prioleau had lived up to their reputation of siding with the white minority, in the eyes of most Carolinians, the term "free negroes" now conjured up images of Denmark Vesey. The result was a legislative tendency to see all people of color as enemies of order. In a

24. Charleston *Courier,* December 14, December 20, 1822; Charleston *Mercury,* December 19, December 31, 1822; South Carolina Treasury Rolls. Ledger B, p. 403, SCDAH.

25. Johnson and Roark, *Black Masters,* 176; Charleston *Mercury,* December 18, 1822.

further attempt to persuade freemen to emigrate the state, a statute required "free male negroes above the age of fifteen to have [white] guardians, and to give security for their good behavior." To ensure that no African American who fled South Carolina returned to visit family or friends, another law prohibited the reentry of freemen on pain of physical punishment or reenslavement (on second offense). Free blacks who chose to remain in Charleston were required to register twice a year with the intendant and pay an annual "tax of fifty dollars."[26]

Mindful that Vesey had once been a black mariner and that African seamen and Haitian sailors ferried word of Caribbean freedom struggles into Charleston harbor, the legislature next turned its attention to freemen who resided outside the state. On December 22, the Assembly passed the Negro Seamen Act, which placed a quarantine on any vessel from another "state or foreign port, having on board any free negroes or persons of color." In an attempt to halt any conversation between black sailors and enslaved dock workers, the legislators required all African-American seamen "confined in jail until the vessel departs." If the ship's master refused to pay the cost of incarceration, or tried to evade the law altogether, the foreign seamen were deemed "absolute slaves" and auctioned into bondage to defray expenses. The following summer, Justice William Johnson, while serving as judge of the United States circuit court in Charleston, struck the law down as unconstitutional. Defiant of federal authority, the Assembly renewed the act in late 1823.[27]

Carolina legislators, ironically, failed to perceive that the Negro Seamen Acts actually encouraged, rather than inhibited, communication between Atlantic mariners and enslaved Charlestonians. African sailors incarcerated in the city jail had ample opportunity to pass news to Charleston slaves who had been swept up by the night watch. In one instance, the frustrated jailor resorted to beating a

26. Cooper and McCord, eds., *Statutes at Large,* 7:461; Charleston *Mercury,* December 18, 1822.

27. George C. Rogers, Jr., *Charleston in the Age of the Pinckneys* (Norman, 1969), 145; Philip M. Hamer, "Great Britain, the United States, and the Negro Seamen Acts, 1822–1848," *JSH* I (1935): 3–4; Cooper and McCord, eds., *Statutes at Large,* 7:461; Charleston *Mercury,* December 18, 1822.

black mariner caught scolding "three or four" cellmates as "fools for doing what [he] ordered them." The level of subterranean discourse grew so bold that in 1843 the City Council petitioned the Assembly to incarcerate black sailors "in a prison or building by themselves."[28]

The Assembly's defiance of Johnson's circuit court ruling, however, pointed to an even greater danger for South Carolina—and for the federal union. As lowcountry legislators labored to protect themselves from future insurrections, it became increasingly clear that the state would defy any authority that seemed to threaten their security. Editor Edwin C. Holland warned that the "sovereign and independent" state of South Carolina had "an indisputable right to frame whatever laws [deemed] necessary to its prosperity and happiness," regardless of any constitutional scruples of the "people of the North and East." It would be no coincidence that many of those who nullified federal law in 1832—including Governor Hamilton, who resigned his office the following year to command troops in defense of his state's right to resist national tariffs—were veterans of the tribunal that blamed slave unrest on congressional interference in Missouri.[29]

Having shored up their defenses against slave hirelings and meddlesome Yankees, Carolina authorities next turned their attention to the thorny question of African-American religiosity. Kennedy's published account made it all too clear that the African church had been a hotbed of revolution. Many planters had long resisted the introduction of Christian doctrine into the quarters, and now they had evidence, as Martha Proctor Richardson observed, that "a little learning is a dangerous thing." Consequently, Vesey's conspiracy gave new life to the old debate about whether bondpeople should be introduced to the Bible. In a letter published in the Charleston press, "Many Citizens" urged an end to *all* religious in-

28. Bolster, *Black Jacks,* 202–3.
29. Holland, *A Refutation of the Calumnies,* 10–11. The classic explication of the connection between Vesey's conspiracy and the nullification crisis is Freehling, *Prelude to Civil War,* especially 150–51. Robert V. Remini's assertion that the nullification movement had little to do with slavery is less persuasive. See his *Andrew Jackson and the Course of American Democracy, 1833–1845* (New York, 1984), especially 535.

struction. Autonomous black churches served to "diminish the influence and authority of the master," and even when white supervision was imposed, "black class leaders" like Vesey remained "the real wire pullers." Editor Holland agreed that Africans could not be trusted to properly appreciate the word of God. "[P]hilanthrop[ic] and open-hearted" white clergy only "excited among our Negroes such a spirit of dissatisfaction and revolt," he maintained. If western traditions only served to "bewilder and deceive," Carolina society was wiser to leave Africans to their native religions.[30]

Other whites instead identified the city's two African Methodist Episcopal congregations as the nucleus of "religious Fanaticism." The Vesey conspiracy had "its origin among the Black class leaders of some of the different religious associations," worried one gentlewoman, while financial agent John Potter complained to Langdon Cheves, a South Carolina resident then living in Philadelphia, that the rebels "were aided by the black missionaries from your City." The thunderous outcry against further proselytization was loud enough, Mary Lamboll Beach sighed, "to make Satan triumph." But she prayed that "God can overrule it for good," and that the outcome instead would be the closure of the despised African Church.[31]

Beach's prayer, lonely though it was, had several influential supporters. Among those most determined to prove that the conversion of slaves was not incompatible with lowcountry security was the Reverend Richard Furman of Beaufort. Furman, the city's leading Baptist clergyman, complained to a sympathetic Thomas Bennett that recent events rendered "many Citizens, unfavorable to the Use of the Bible among the Negroes." Like many discerning observers, Furman understood that Vesey had turned to the Old Testament for religious sanction. The answer, as Whitemarsh Seabrook once recommended, was to emphasize the Christian teachings of St. Paul.

30. Martha Proctor Richardson to James Screven, August 7, 1822, Arnold and Screven Papers, SHC, UNC; Wade, *Slavery in the Cities,* 83; Holland, *A Refutation of the Calumnies,* 11–12.

31. Martha Proctor Richardson to James Screven, July 6, 1822, Arnold and Screven Papers, SHC, UNC; John Potter to Langdon Cheves, June 29, 1822, Cheves Papers, SCHS; Mary Lamboll Beach to Elizabeth Gilchrist, July 5, 1822, Beach Letters, SCHS.

The theory that "Holy Writ [was] unfavorable to the holding of Slaves" was quite "without just Foundation. Its lawfulness," Furman lectured the governor, "is clearly recognized in the New." Not content with preaching to the state's chief officer, in 1823 Furman added to the growing number of Vesey-inspired pamphlets with his proslavery *Exposition of the Views of the Baptists, Relative to the Coloured Population of the United States.*[32]

Sharing Furman's conviction that the Bible, if properly abridged, could produce both docile Christian servants and a stable slave society was Frederick Dalcho, the English-born son of a Prussian soldier. Like Mary Lamboll Beach, who insisted that "not one Episcopalian is among the guilty,"[33] Dalcho's 1823 treatise, *Practical Considerations Founded on the Scriptures, Relative to the Slave Population of South Carolina,* sought to exonerate white clergymen who preached on nearby plantations. "None of the Negroes belonging to the Protestant Episcopal Church were concerned in the late conspiracy," he wrote. Instead, the fault lay with those who allowed "preachers of their own colour" to fuse the violent tales of the Hebrew Bible with the sacred teachings of Africa. "Much animal excitement may be, and oftentimes is, produced, where but little real devotion is felt in the heart."[34]

Armed with impeccable proslavery credentials, Furman and Dalcho carried the day; the pace of conversions on the countryside slowed for a time after 1822, but baptisms did not stop. Rather, as Mary Lamboll Beach hoped, city authorities focused their ire on the African church alone. Although Intendant Hamilton was careful to publicly observe that "no evidence" of complicity in the plot had "been discovered against" the AME leadership, the African congregations could not long survive the vengeful mood of the city. Kennedy and Parker privately encouraged the Reverend Morris Brown to

32. Richard Furman to Thomas Bennett, no date, Richard Furman Papers, USC (Although undated, the letter was written shortly after "the late projected Insurrection."); Tise, *Proslavery,* 61; Snay, *Gospel of Disunion,* 26, 55.

33. Mary Lamboll Beach to Elizabeth Gilchrist, July 25, 1822, Beach Letters, SCHS.

34. Tise, *Proslavery,* 61–62; [Dalcho], *Practical Considerations Founded on the Scriptures,* 33–36.

leave the state because of the "strong suspicions" against them, but one magistrate, John D. White, went considerably farther. White ruled that by traveling to Philadelphia, the ministers violated the act of 1820 that prohibited freemen from returning to the state, and he gave them fifteen days to pack their households. With Brown and Henry Drayton forced to relocate North, the congregations—according to James Hamilton—"voluntarily dissolved." City authorities razed the Hampstead church sometime during the fall of 1822, but by then Brown was in Philadelphia. In 1828 he was ordained a bishop in the AME church, and three years after that he succeeded Richard Allen as superintendent of the parent organization.[35]

The demolition of the African church and the forced exile of its ministry was a devastating blow to Charleston's black community. Following the failure to implement class-leader Vesey's Old Testament brand of revolutionary theology, enslaved Charlestonians instead began to selectively apply Christianity in response to their increasingly brutal situation. Although mass escape had proven impossible, bondpeople continued to resist their bondage, not by picking up the sword, but by forging a strong, religious collective that kept them from giving in to hopelessness. For their part, white ministers at length resumed their conversion efforts on the countryside and grudgingly shouldered the burdens that came with preaching in a slave society. "I hear that Bishop Bowen after all his poor health had to *ride* Patrole all Saturday night," fretted one genteel congregant, "though he had to preach the next day."[36]

Despite all of the laws the Assembly could devise, despite all of the proslavery sermons poor, unwell Bishop Bowen could muster, the saga of Denmark Vesey lived on, especially through those who had known him well yet survived the summer of 1822. Among his companions, those who profited most from his death were the three men who helped white authorities to take his life. Living amidst a black majority, the planter elite had long ago, as one

35. Hamilton, *An Account,* 30; Narrative, in Kennedy and Parker, eds., *Official Report,* 44; Ripley, ed., *Black Abolitionist Papers,* 3:196–97 note 14; Alton Hornsby, *Chronology of African-American History* (Detroit, 1991), 16.

36. Washington, *A Peculiar People,* 24; Mary Lamboll Beach to Elizabeth Gilchrist, July 25, 1822, Beach Letters, SCHS.

Southern editor gloated, perfected the art of rewarding those "servants of principle and integrity who will discover and frustrate such guilty projects." On December 11, lowcountry legislators introduced an act to purchase and liberate Peter Prioleau and George Wilson, and to reward William Penceel. The bill included a curious, proslavery clause designed to pay $100 each year to Peter should he "refuse to accept his freedom." The bill sailed through the state Senate ten days later, and the "Slave Peter [was] Emancipated [for] $1200."[37]

The curious clause, which Peter wisely declined to accede to, pointed to an obvious flaw in the Assembly's proslavery mentality. Carolina legislators assured themselves that their childlike African wards were best protected when guided by their intellectually superior white masters, yet they rewarded black informants by turning them out into the dangerous world of freedom. As English visitor Harriet Martineau mocked when told that loyal bondmen were granted their liberty as a compensation: "A reward! What! When the Slaves are convinced that their true happiness lies in slavery?" But Peter evidently saw no contradiction in buying his freedom with the lives of fellow bondmen, and so the mulatto cook finished out his days as a moderately-prosperous drayman. In addition to his freedom, Peter Prioleau, as he now called himself, enjoyed the unique privilege of being the only man of property in the state exempted from all taxes by special statute.[38]

Because William Penceel was already free and even a member of the Brown Fellowship Society, the Assembly thanked him for his advice to Peter by awarding him a sum of $1,000 and exempting him from the Free Negro Tax. To further demonstrate his fealty to the master class, Penceel used part of his reward to purchase Africans. Within one month, Penceel bought Sukey and her two children—but not Sukey's husband—for $700. By the spring of 1825, Penceel's

37. Richmond *Enquirer,* September 3, 1822; Charleston *Courier,* December 20, 1822; Charleston *Mercury,* December 19, 31, 1822; South Carolina Treasury Rolls, Ledger B, p. 405, SCDAH.

38. Martineau, *Retrospect of Western Travel,* 2:93; Higginson, *Black Rebellion,* 273–74.

net worth was $3,234, nearly one-third of which had been gained for urging Peter to betray William Paul.[39]

The last of those rewarded for their role in Vesey's death, George Wilson, fared less well in later years. Although the same legislation that liberated Peter promised freedom to George as well, Major John Wilson chose to delay George's liberation until "after matters settled down." Finally, on Christmas Day, 1825, the state compensated the Wilson family $1,150 for "Slave George." But unlike Peter and Penceel, the pious George was deeply troubled at causing the death of his old friend Rolla Bennett. In an attempt to disassociate himself from his troubled past, George began to call himself George Watkin. A new surname, however, could not extricate George from the slave society he inadvertently had helped preserve. Because his family was owned by L. S. Campbell, his wife and children remained human property. After saving for some years, George was able to purchase his wife and children, but because newly-freed bondpeople had to leave the state, George remained his family's owner of record. In 1835, he petitioned the Assembly for a special deed of manumission, but despite his earlier service, the legislature denied his request, and so he continued to own his family, and ultimately, his grandchildren as well. In March 1848, George found he could no longer live with his past; he lost his reason and died shortly thereafter.[40]

Following the execution of her husband, Susan Vesey was evicted from their rented Bull Street home. She moved first to Coming Street, a predominantly black area on the Charleston Neck, and then in 1823 to Alexander Street. As a married woman she had taken in laundry, and presumably she continued to live an impoverished existence as a domestic. In 1830 she lived on the Neck in a household of thirteen people; a common survival technique of freedpeople was to pool their meager resources. After that date she disappeared from the public record. At the age of thirty-five, she had reached the

39. Koger, *Black Slaveholders*, 180.

40. Charleston *Courier*, December 14, 1822; W. Hasell Wilson to Robert Wilson, no date, CLS; Pharo, ed., *Reminiscences of Wilson*, 6; South Carolina Treasury Rolls, Ledger B, p. 406, SCDAH; Koger, *Black Slaveholders*, 178–79.

average life expectancy for African Americans in the young republic. Perhaps she merely found the surname of Vesey too burdensome in post-conspiracy Charleston, and so like George Wilson, adopted a new identity in vain hopes of forgetting a painful past.[41]

The rest of Vesey's families also disappeared or fled the state. Although all of Denmark's children were slaves at the time of the conspiracy, Robert Vesey, at least, evidently found his way to freedom prior to the end of the Civil War. Polydore Vesey never appeared again in the public record. But a clue to Sandy Vesey's ultimate fate appeared in 1825. Sandy had been spared the gallows in exchange for transportation beyond the United States, and although city authorities never revealed where the convicts went, some, and perhaps all, became slaves in Spanish Cuba. In that year, three slaves expatriated from Charleston for their role in the "intended insurrection" were arrested for plotting a revolt in the Guamacaro province. Perhaps Sandy escaped the noose in Charleston only to find it in Cuba.[42]

The last to go was Captain Joseph Vesey, who, in a strange, circuitous fashion, had precipitated the events of 1822 by plucking Telemaque from the waters of Charlotte Amalie harbor in 1781. On May 20, 1835, the old captain died from natural causes at the age of eighty-eight, one of only a handful of octogenarians in the entire nation during the 1830s.[43]

The death of the last participant in the affair, however, hardly meant that Denmark Vesey faded from collective memory. In fact, long before the old captain passed into the shades, the once-obscure carpenter had became a national legend and antislavery martyr. Within weeks of his execution, Northern papers began to debate the justness of his cause. Although several border state journals echoed their Southern editor brethren—the Philadelphia *National Gazette* spoke of Vesey's "abominable cruelties and crimes" while the New Jersey *Camden Star* warned that emancipation could never

41. State Free Negro Capitation Tax Books, Charleston, 1822, p. 29, 1823, p. 28, SCDAH; Carter G. Woodson, ed., *Free Negro Heads of Families in the United States in 1830* (Washington, 1925), 157.

42. Escoto Collection, Box 10, Houghton Library, Harvard University. I am grateful to Robert L. Paquette of Hamilton College for this citation.

43. [No editor], "The Shirmer Diary," *SCHM* 69 (January 1968): 60.

be won "by the sword, bloodshed, and rapine"—most Northern newspapers defended Vesey's behavior. The *Boston Evening Gazette* placed the rebels in the young republic's often-violent revolutionary tradition by insisting that "nobody can blame the servile part of the population for attempting to escape from bondage," a sentiment repeated by Theodore Dwight's *New York Daily Advertiser.* Dwight, the grandson of Puritan divine Jonathan Edwards, lectured that Africans "kidnapped by white men and dragged into endless slavery, cannot be expected to be contented with their situation." Even Baltimore's moderate *Niles' Register* editorialized that the "just man cannot blame the slave for seeking his freedom."[44]

At least one pamphleteer did more than just editorialize in Vesey's behalf. Among the free blacks who fled north following the demolition of the African church was young David Walker, who may have travelled as far as Philadelphia with Brown and Drayton. In 1829, Walker, who had at length settled in Boston, published his incendiary *Appeal to the Coloured Citizens of the World.* By invoking the sanction of "our Creator" in his battle with proslavery forces, and by asking Southern bondmen whether they "had not rather be killed" in a revolt "than to be a slave to a tyrant," Walker showed that he had listened carefully to the nocturnal sermons at the Hampstead church. Through David Walker's prose, Vesey's teachings returned to Charleston in March 1830, when authorities arrested Edward Smith, a white mariner, for distributing copies of the *Appeal* to black longshoremen. According to Smith, he had been approached in Boston "by a decent looking black man" who urged him to deliver the pamphlet "secretly to the Black people" of Southern ports.[45]

Walker never specifically mentioned Vesey in his treatise, but other black activists routinely invoked his name in their lectures and essays. In a speech of August 16, 1843, Henry Highland Garnet, gave his audience a detailed account of Vesey's "plan for the liberation of his fellow men." Historians, Garnet shouted, "will transcribe

44. Philadelphia *National Gazette,* New Jersey *Camden Star, Boston Evening Globe,* all in Charleston *Mercury,* August 26, 1822; *New York Daily Advertiser,* July 31, 1822; *Niles' Register,* September 14, 1822.

45. James O. Horton and Lois E. Horton, *In Hope of Liberty: Culture, Community and Protest Among Northern Free Blacks, 1700–1860* (New York, 1997), 172–73; Hinks, *To Awaken My Afflicted Brethren,* 145.

his name on the same monument with Moses, [Scottish warriors] Bruce and Wallace, Toussaint L'Ouverture, Lafayette and Washington." By then, as the Texas issue made antislavery ever more popular with Northern voters, Vesey's tale had reached almost mythical proportions. Attorney Robert Morris, the grandson of an African slave and one of the first blacks to be admitted to the Massachusetts state bar, took the lead in the battle to integrate Boston's public schools. His "heroes," Morris liked to say, were Denmark Vesey and Nat Turner, "whose very names were a terror to oppressors." Three years later in 1850, Henry Bibb, the first black writer to undertake an account of Vesey's revolt, published *The Late Contemplated Insurrection in Charleston, S.C.*[46]

By the 1850s, antislavery activists increasingly tried their hand at literature in an attempt to show refined Northern readers the human face of slavery. Frederick Douglass's fiery novel, *The Heroic Slave,* a fictionalized account of the mutiny aboard the slave ship *Creole* appeared in 1852, but far and away the greatest impact was had by Harriet Beecher Stowe. In 1855, the celebrated author of *Uncle Tom's Cabin* penned the introduction to William C. Nell's *The Colored Patriots of the American Revolution,* which included essays on Turner, Vesey, and David Walker. Inspired by Nell's research and Bibb's narrative, Stowe published *Dred: A Tale of the Great Dismal Swamp* the following year. As talk of civil conflict grew louder, Stowe replaced the saintly, Christian Tom with Dred, the fictional son of Denmark Vesey. Instead of running for Canada after 1822, Dred retreated to a Virginia maroon colony to plan his "day of vengeance." Using the "much-thumbed copy of the Bible" once owned by his father, Dred relied on the militant invocations of the Old Testament prophets to encourage his followers to "raise up for oppressed people."[47]

46. Speech of Henry Highland Garnet, August 16, 1843, in Ripley, ed., *Black Abolitionist Papers,* 3:409; Albert J. Von Frank, *The Trials of Anthony Burns: Freedom and Slavery in Emerson's Boston* (Cambridge, Mass., 1998), 42–43.

47. Robert S. Levine, *Martin Delany, Frederick Douglass, and the Politics of Representative Identity* (Chapel Hill, 1997), 161–69; Joan D. Hedrick, *Harriet Beecher Stowe: A Life* (New York, 1994), 258; Harriet Beecher Stowe, *Dred: A Tale of the Great Dismal Swamp* (New York, 1968 reprint of 1856 ed.), 2:214.

In 1862, Martin R. Delany made a case for black citizenship in *Blake: Or, the Huts of America.* In his novel, Delany, born of a free mother and a slave father in Charlestown, western Virginia, told the story of Henrico Blacus, a Caribbean freeman kidnapped into slavery in Louisiana. After escaping from his Red River plantation, Blake, as he had come to be known, traveled the South encouraging bondmen to join his planned region-wide rebellion. He too wandered into the Great Dismal Swamp, where he stumbled upon "old confederates" of Nat Turner. The aged runaways tell Blake that they "hold the names of Nat Turner, Denmark Veezie, and General Gabriel in sacred reverence."[48]

Several months later, the Union victory at Antietam Creek and the resulting Emancipation Proclamation transformed the war from a conflict over reunion into a campaign against slavery. Delany exchanged his pen for a blue uniform and began to recruit black soldiers. By the end of the war he was commissioned the first African-American major in the United States Army. Marching beside his recruits, it often seemed, was the ghost of the old conspirator. Black journalist George Lawrence, Jr., the editor of the New York *Weekly Anglo-African,* urged Southern bondmen to take advantage of the war's chaos and rise for their freedom. "We want Nat Turner—not speeches," he wrote. "Denmark Vesey—not resolutions; John Brown—not meetings."[49]

Frederick Douglass also put Vesey's memory to good use as he encouraged young men to do their part in the war against servitude. Recruiting in Rochester, New York, on March 2, 1863, in behalf of the Fifty-fourth Massachusetts Volunteers—a black regiment that would include Sergeant Major Lewis Henry Douglass and Private Charles Remond Douglass—Douglass told his audience of the opportunity now given them "to end in a day the bondage of centuries" in the Old South. "Remember Denmark Vesey of Charleston," he shouted as the audience roared, "remember Nathaniel Turner of

---

48. Levine, *Martin Delany,* 198; Martin R. Delany, *Blake: Or, The Huts of America* (Boston, 1970 reprint of 1862 ed.), 113.

49. New York *Weekly Anglo-African,* April 13, 1861, in Ripley, ed., *Black Abolitionist Papers,* 5:110–11.

Southampton." The War Department, unhappily, insisted upon white men as commissioned officers in the black regiments, but among their number was James Beecher, the brother of the novelist. Before the war's end, Beecher led his brigade against Charleston, carrying a banner designed by Harriet. Above a rising sun was printed the word LIBERTY in bold crimson letters, and below the words: "The Lord is Our Sun & Shield." When Harriet imagined her brother and his black troops planting the banner in Charleston harbor, she was sure that "the spirit of Denmark Vesey strengthened their arms."[50]

Confederate soldiers evacuated Charleston during the night of February 17, 1865. As roughly 10,000 weary veterans retreated northward up the peninsula, thousands more black Carolinians quit the plantations and poured into the city to celebrate their new-found freedom. War hero Robert Smalls, who marched into the city with Union forces, gleefully bought the house of his old master, Henry McKee, at a tax sale. Returning also to the place of his birth after a forty-three-year exile, was the aged former slave Robert Vesey. Presumably, Vesey arrived in the city in time to witness the procession of March 29, in which Beecher's 21st Regiment United States Colored Troops paraded about the city, trailed by 4,000 black artisans waving their tools and nearly 2,000 school children bearing placards reading: "We know no caste or color." Sixteen days later, dressed in his finest suit, Robert Vesey boarded the *Planter*, as he and Robert Smalls and Major Martin Delany prepared to watch Major General Robert Anderson raise the flag over Fort Sumter, high above his father's city.[51]

50. Frederick Douglass, *Life and Times of Frederick Douglass* (New York, 1962 reprint of 1892 ed.), 341; Hedrick, *Harriet Beecher Stowe,* 305. Despite the regiment's name, many of its soldiers came from outside Massachusetts; Douglass recruited more than 100 young men—including his sons—from upstate New York. See William S. McFeely, *Frederick Douglass* (New York, 1991), 224.

51. Fraser, *Charleston,* 272; Philadelphia *Christian Recorder,* October 14, 1865.

Appendix: The Charleston Hanged

Slaves and Free Blacks
Accused of Insurrection, 1822

Accused/owner	Occupation	Church	Sentence
William Paul/John Paul			Transported
Peter Poyas/James Poyas	Ship wright	AME	Hanged July 2
Mungo Poyas/James Poyas			Acquitted
Ned Bennett/Thomas Bennett	Domestic		Hanged July 2
Batteau Bennett/Thomas Bennett	Domestic		Hanged July 2
Rolla Bennett/Thomas Bennett	Domestic	AME	Hanged July 2
Matthias Bennett/Thomas Bennett			Acquitted
Denmark Vesey/free black	Carpenter	AME	Hanged July 2
Jesse Blackwood/ Thomas Blackwood			Hanged July 2
Amherst Lining/Mrs. Lining		AME	Acquitted
Stephen Smith/Thomas R. Smith			Acquitted
Jeffrey Grant/free black			Acquitted
John Horry/Elias Horry	Coachman		Hanged July 12
Jack Pritchard/Paul Pritchard	Ship Caulker	AME	Hanged July 12
Monday Gell/John Gell	Harness Maker	AME	Transported
Charles Drayton/John Drayton	Cook		Transported
Bram Lucas/Jonathan Lucas			Acquitted
Richard Lucas/Jonathan Lucas			Acquitted
Robert Hadden/free black			Whipped
Samuel Guifford/free black			Whipped
Pompey Bryan/John Bryan			Acquitted
Harry Harleston/Mr. Harlston			Acquitted

Accused/owner	Occupation	Church	Sentence
Harry Haig/David Haig	Carpenter		Died in prison
Pompey Haig/David Haig	Cooper	AME	Acquitted
Nero Haig/David Haig	Cooper		Transported
Mingo Harth/William Harth	Cook	AME	Hanged July 26
Lot Forrester/Mr. Forrester		AME	Hanged July 26
Joe Jore/P. L. Jore	Cook		Hanged July 26
Julius Forrest/Thomas Forrest			Hanged July 26
Tom Russell/Mrs. Russell	Blacksmith		Hanged July 26
Smart Anderson/Robert Anderson	Drayman	AME	Hanged July 26
John Robertson/John Robertson	Ropemaker	AME	Hanged July 26
Robert Robertson/John Robertson	Ropemaker	AME	Hanged July 26
Adam Robertson/John Robertson	Ropemaker	AME	Hanged July 26
Polydore Faber/Catherine Faber	Sawyer	AME	Hanged July 26
Bacchus Hammet/ Benjamin Hammet			Hanged July 26
Dick Simms/William Simms	Wheelwright		Hanged July 26
Pharaoh Thompson/Jane Thompson			Hanged July 26
Jemmy Clement/Sarah Clement		AME	Hanged July 26
Jerry Cohen/Mordecai Cohen			Hanged July 26
Dean Mitchell/James Mitchell	Cooper		Hanged July 26
Jack Purcell/Mrs. Purcell			Hanged July 26
Bellisle Yates/Joseph Yates		AME	Hanged July 26
Naphur Yates/Joseph Yates		AME	Hanged July 26
Adam Yates/Joseph Yates		AME	Hanged July 26
Jacob Glen/John S. Glen	Carpenter	AME	Hanged July 26
Charles Billings/John Billings	Coachmaker		Hanged July 26
Jack McNeill/Neil McNeill		AME	Hanged July 30
Caesar Smith/Naomi Smith	Drayman	AME	Hanged July 30
Jacob Stagg/Jacob Lankester	Painter		Hanged July 30
Tom Scott/William M. Scott		AME	Hanged July 30
Peter Ward/Mrs. Ward		AME	Acquitted
Sandy Curtis/Francis Curtis			Acquitted
Isaac Trapier/Paul Trapier			Acquitted
Charles Shrubrick/Mrs. Shubrick		AME	Acquitted
Cuffy Graves/Charles Graves			Acquitted
Pierre Louis/Mr. Chapeau			Acquitted

Accused/owner	Occupation	Church	Sentence
Caesar Parker/Mrs. Parker			Acquitted
William Colcock/Mrs. Colcock	Painter		Acquitted
William Garner/Martha Garner	Drayman		Hanged Aug 9
Louis Cromwell/Samuel Cromwell			Transported
Seymour Kunhardt/William Kunhardt			Transported
Saby Gaillard/free black			Transported
Isaac Harth/William Harth	Coachman		Transported
Paris Ball/Ann Ball	Stevedore	AME	Transported
Peter Cooper/Mrs. Cooper			Whipped
Dublin Morris/C.G. Morris	Porter	AME	Transported
George Bamfield/Thomas Bamfield		AME	Transported
Sandy Vesey/Jacob Schnell		AME	Transported
William Palmer/Job Palmer			Transported
John Vincent/D. Cruckshanks		AME	Transported
Billy Robinson/Paul Robinson	Porter		Transported
Edwin Paul/John Paul			Transported
Frank Ferguson/Ann Ferguson			Transported
Adam Ferguson/Ann Ferguson			Acquitted
George Theus/Mr. Theus			Transported
Perault Strohecker/J. Strohecker	Blacksmith		Transported
Billy Bulkley/Stephen Bulkley	Ropemaker		Transported
John Enslow/Joseph Enslow	Cooper		Died Workhouse
Scipio Simms/William Simms	Carpenter	AME	Transported
Agrippa Perry/Mr. Perry	Wheelwright		Transported
Samuel Bainstill/Henry Bainstill			Transported
Denbo Martin/John Martin		AME	Transported
Adam Bellamy/J.H. Merritt	Carter	AME	Transported
Jack Cattell/William Catell			Transported
George Evans/James Evans	Stone Mason	AME	Transported
Harry Butler/William Butler			Transported
George Parker/Samuel Parker			Transported
Pompey Lord/Richard Lord			Transported
Prince Graham/free black	Drayman	AME	Exiled Liberia
Buonaparte Mulligan/ Francis Mulligan			Transported
Abraham Poyas/Dr. John E. Poyas			Transported

Accused/owner	Occupation	Church	Sentence
Butcher Gibbs/James L. Gibbs		AME	Transported
John Taylor/Mrs. Taylor			Transported
Prince Righton/ Elizabeth Righton	Painter		Transported
Quash Harleston/free black			Emigrated
Harry Purse/William Purse			Transported
Panza Mitchell/Dean Mitchell			Transported
Liverpool Hunt/Mrs. Hunt			Transported
Friday Rout/Catherine Rout			Acquitted
Philander Michau/free black			Acquitted
Stephen Walker/Mr. Walker			Acquitted
James Walker/Mr. Walker			Acquitted
Harry Nell/J. Nell	Ropemaker		Acquitted

Suggested Reading

THERE IS AN ENORMOUS BODY of scholarship on slavery in the Caribbean, but little on the tiny island of St. Thomas. The late Neville A. T. Hall, *Slave Society in the Danish West Indies: St. Thomas, St. John, and St. Croix* (Baltimore, 1992), is scholarly and thorough, but one should also consult the memoirs of C. G. A. Oldendorp, who arrived on St. Thomas in 1766, most likely the year of Vesey's birth. See his *History of the Mission of the Evangelical Brethren on the Caribbean Islands of St. Thomas, St. Croix, and St. John,* Johann Bossard, ed. (Ann Arbor, 1987). C. L. R. James, *The Black Jacobins: Toussaint Louverture and the Saint Domingue Revolution* (New York, 1963 edition) remains the classic account of the slave revolt that shook the Americas, but two recent monographs also provide a great deal of information on the French colony where Vesey briefly labored as a boy: Thomas O. Ott, *The Haitian Revolution, 1789–1804* (Knoxville, 1973), and Carolyn E. Fick, *The Making of Haiti: The Saint Domingue Revolution from Below* (Knoxville, 1990). Martin Ros, *Night of Fire: The Black Napoleon and the Battle for Haiti* (New York, 1994), is a lively, popular study.

James Hamilton, *An Account of the Late Intended Insurrection* (Charleston, 1822), contains detailed biographical material about the purchase and early years of Denmark Vesey. This information could only have been supplied by then-seventy-five-year-old Captain Joseph Vesey, who lived in Charleston until his death in 1835. Former slave Archibald H. Grimké, however, included material not

233

available in Mayor Hamilton's *Account*; presumably he obtained some of this information from the oral traditions of black Charlestonians as well as from his white aunt, abolitionist Angelina Grimké, who was seventeen-years-old at the time of Vesey's execution. See his *Right on the Scaffold, or, The Martyrs of 1822* (Washington, 1901). Both pamphlets are readily available on microfiche.

Although I argue that young Telemaque's tenure as a cabin boy aboard Joseph Vesey's *Prospect* was shorter than previously supposed, his brief career as an enslaved mariner clearly shaped his early life as well as his understandably harsh opinions of Euro-Americans. W. Jeffrey Bolster, *Black Jacks: African American Seamen in the Age of Sail* (Cambridge, Mass., 1997), details both the dangerous life within wooden walls and the empowering ability of African Americans to ferry information about the Atlantic world. Marcus Rediker, *Between the Devil and the Deep Blue Sea: Merchant Seamen, Pirates, and the Anglo-American Maritime World, 1700–1750* (Cambridge, England, 1987), also emphasizes the egalitarian nature of old salts. On the ghastly commerce in humans, Philip D. Curtin, *The Atlantic Slave Trade: A Census* (Madison, 1969), is the most scholarly, while Hugh Thomas, *The Slave Trade: The Story of the Atlantic Slave Trade, 1440–1870* (New York, 1997), is the most readable.

Charleston slavery was hardly characteristic of African-American bondage in the early republic. Richard C. Wade, *Slavery in the Cities: The South, 1820–1860* (New York, 1964), is still the best survey of urban bondage, although virtually all historians dissent from his theory that no plot existed in 1822 (see below). Walter J. Fraser, Jr., *Charleston! Charleston! The History of a Southern City* (Columbia, 1989), is a superb local study. Bernard E. Powers, *Black Charlestonians: A Social History, 1822–1885* (Fayetteville, 1994), begins his detailed account with the aftermath of the conspiracy, although his early chapters contain valuable insights on Vesey's city.

The investigation of the thriving internal economy, in which slaves bought and bartered goods of their own making, is perhaps the most important recent development in slave historiography. My chapter on Charleston's underground trade owes a debt to Betty Wood, *Women's Work, Men's Work: The Informal Slave Economies of Lowcountry Georgia* (Athens, 1995) and Larry E. Hudson, Jr., *To*

Have and To Hold: Slave Work and Family Life in Antebellum South Carolina (Athens, 1997). Philip D. Morgan has written numerous influential essays on the topic, but see especially his monumental *Slave Counterpoint: Black Culture in the Eighteenth-Century Chesapeake and Lowcountry* (Chapel Hill, 1998). Two leading scholars, however, warn against ignoring the power relationships inherent in Southern society. Gary B. Nash, "Slavery, Black Resistance, and the American Revolution," and Peter Coclanis, "Slavery, African-American Agency, and the World We Have Lost," both in *Georgia Historical Quarterly* (1993 and 1995) suggest that an overemphasis on the underground economy neglects the obvious fact that slaves were unpaid, dependent agricultural laborers.

Several excellent surveys contain useful insights into Vesey's world. The seven editions of John Hope Franklin's pioneering *From Slavery to Freedom: A History of Negro Americans* (New York, 1947 to 1998), offer concise summaries of Vesey's plot, as does Vincent Harding, *There Is a River: The Black Struggle for Freedom in America* (New York, 1981). Peter Kolchin, *American Slavery, 1619–1877* (New York, 1993), and Donald R. Wright, *African Americans in the Early Republic, 1789–1831* (Arlington Heights, Ill., 1993), both provide perceptive comment on the conspiracy. Eugene D. Genovese, *From Rebellion to Revolution: Afro-American Slave Revolts in the Making of the Modern World* (Baton Rouge, 1979), examines Vesey's plans and goals within a hemispheric perspective.

On Vesey's precarious life as a dark-skinned freeman in a slave society, see Ira Berlin, *Slaves Without Masters: The Free Negro in the Antebellum South* (New York, 1974), which remains the definitive account on the difficult existence of emancipated bondpeople. My interpretation of Charleston's atypical (at least for English North America) three-caste system, however, relies heavily on Marina Wikramanayake, *A World In Shadow: The Free Black in Antebellum South Carolina* (Columbia, 1973), Larry Koger, *Black Slavemasters: Free Black Slave Masters in South Carolina, 1790–1860* (Columbia, 1985), and especially Michael P. Johnson and James L. Roark, *Black Masters: A Free Family of Color in the Old South* (New York, 1984).

Sorting out Denmark Vesey's various families proved particularly difficult. The classic study on slave families is Herbert S. Gutman,

The Black Family in Slavery and Freedom, 1750–1925 (New York, 1976). Two newer works, however, pay far greater attention to the strains inherent in fragile, extralegal slave relationships. Brenda E. Stevenson, *Life in Black and White: Family and Community in the Slave South* (New York, 1996), informed much of my discussion of polygamy, while Wilma King, *Stolen Childhood: Slave Youth in Nineteenth-Century America* (Bloomington, 1995), explores the pressures placed upon slave children to obey the commands of the white master as well as a demanding black parent—which Denmark Vesey clearly was. Insights on the naming of sons provided by Cheryll Ann Cody, "Naming, Kinship, and Estate Dispersal: Notes on Slave Family Life on a South Carolina Plantation, 1786–1833," *William and Mary Quarterly* (1982), supplied a clue in tracking down Dolly, whom I believe to be Vesey's second wife.

Vesey's profound religious faith and the troubled history of the Charleston AME Church laid the basis for his conspiracy. Had the African church not existed, neither, most likely, would have his dream of a modern-day exodus. The essential study for the history of black religion in South Carolina is Margaret Washington, *"A Peculiar People": Slave Religion and Community-Culture Among the Gullahs* (New York, 1988), but one should also consult Alan Gallay, *The Formation of a Planter Elite: Jonathan Bryan and the Southern Colonial Frontier* (Athens, 1989), on early attempts to Christianize Africans—and the resistance to conversion efforts on the part of both concerned planters and indifferent slaves. The best general study remains Albert J. Raboteau, *Slave Religion: The "Invisible Institution" in the Antebellum South* (New York, 1978), although my discussion of Vesey and revolutionary theology is at odds with Raboteau's explication of the connection between Christianity and slave unrest.

The eighty-six pages of trial transcripts, plus letters to and from Governor Thomas Bennett, supply the main source for Vesey's plot. Despite Richard C. Wade's curious suggestion that "the few surviving original documents have been carefully edited," the rough, extensive, original transcripts may be found in the South Carolina Department of Archives and History, Columbia; all of the documents are now on microfilm as well. The long depositions also provide a great deal of biographical material on the leading rebels. Some scholars refrain from using jailhouse testimony as hopelessly tainted documents, and admittedly they must be used with great care. But testimony obtained from bond defendants under emotional duress—sometimes even under torture—is not by definition spurious; it is merely coerced. Workhouse inquisitors typically sought to obtain corroborating testimony, and few examples of what today might be regarded as leading the witness exist in these documents. Moreover, pathetic attempts on the part of incarcerated slaves to tell their jailers what they believed they wanted to hear often ring as false as do the jailers' frequent editorial comments. Certainly any historian who writes about slave rebellions wishes they had access to less subjective documents. Yet few historical documents are objective, and the fact remains that without such trial depositions and testimony, scholars could not recover the life of a Denmark Vesey or a Nat Turner.

The raw transcripts in the Columbia archives also contain information omitted from the two accounts of the proceedings published in 1822, notably the reference to the planned poisoning of Charleston wells. But the magistrates' published record also includes a wealth of material absent from the raw data, such as Rolla Bennett's jailhouse confession and the judges' narrative of events. It is also readily available—if not easily readable—on microfiche, a resource clearly invented by someone who hates scholars. See Lionel Kennedy and Thomas Parker, eds., *An Official Report of the Trials of Sundry Negroes, Charged With an Attempt to Raise an Insurrection in the State of South Carolina* (Charleston, 1822).

Two older documentary collections relating to Vesey's conspiracy, Robert S. Starobin, *Denmark Vesey: The Slave Conspiracy of 1822* (New York, 1970) and John O. Killens, *The Trial Record of Denmark Vesey* (Boston, 1970), have been superseded by Edward Pearson's definitive edition, *Designs Against Charleston: The Denmark Vesey Conspiracy of 1822* (Chapel Hill, 1998). Whereas both Starobin and Killens relied on Kennedy and Parker's published record, Pearson's collection ingeniously folds together material from the original trial records with data from Kennedy's polished pamphlet. Pearson's thoughtful introduction, which reads more like a short monograph than a traditional preface, places Vesey in the context of Atlantic radicalism without slighting the importance of religion in his life.

For secondary accounts of the plot, journalist John Lofton's pioneering study, *Insurrection in South Carolina: The Turbulent World of Denmark Vesey* (Yellow Springs, Ohio, 1964), is now rather dated in conception. Scholars, of course, can only write what the current historiography allows them to write, and at the time that Lofton began his research, much thinking on antebellum slavery was still informed by U. B. Phillips' racist *American Negro Slavery: A Survey of the Supply, Employment, and Control of Negro Labor as Determined by the Plantation Regime* (New York, 1918). With little published scholarship on slave culture, the black church, or African religiosity to guide him, Lofton paid little attention to the African church, and consequently Vesey was portrayed as an oddly peripheral figure in his account of the plot. Still, Lofton rescued Vesey from obscurity at a time when only black historians remembered the great abolitionist; few white scholars even granted Vesey the dignity of a cameo in their monographs or textbooks. As late as 1944, biographer Charles M. Wiltse could produce the first of three exhaustive volumes on *John C. Calhoun, Nationalist: 1782–1828* (New York, 1944) without once mentioning the name of the man whose intrigues so occupied the attentions of the Secretary of War. (Wiltse only alluded to unnamed "half-literate Negroes [who] had concluded that their servitude was in defiance of the [Missouri] law.")

In the same year that Lofton published his account of the plot, Richard C. Wade, in both "The Vesey Plot: A Reconsideration," *Journal of Southern History* (1964), and in *Slavery and the Cities: The South, 1820–1860* (New York, 1964), insisted that the conspiracy was little more than idle talk among disgruntled slaves. Having demonstrated that slave controls were largely incompatible with cramped urban conditions, Wade backed away from his findings that cities provided ample opportunity to plan insurrections. Instead, he suggested that urban bondmen were too pragmatic to risk losing their quasi-freedom by engaging in potentially suicidal rebellions. Wade's theory never gained wide acceptance, but William W. Freehling challenged Wade's hypothesis in *Prelude to Civil War: The Nullification Controversy in South Carolina, 1816–1836* (New York, 1965) and effectively dismantled Wade's use of evidence in a 1986 essay republished in *The Reintegration of American History: Slavery and the Civil War* (New York, 1994).

On slave law and court procedure in South Carolina, see Norrece T. Jones, Jr., *Born a Child of Freedom, Yet a Slave: Mechanisms of Control and Strategies of Resistance in Antebellum South Carolina* (Hanover, 1990), and Thomas Morris, *Southern Slavery and the Law* (Chapel Hill, 1996). Two important articles are Daniel J. Flanigan, "Criminal Procedure in Slave Trials in the Antebellum South," *Journal of Southern History* (1974) and Donald J. Senese, "The Free Negro and the South Carolina Courts, 1790–1860," *South Carolina Historical Magazine* (1967). Although Philip J. Schwarz's splendid *Twice Condemned: Slaves and the Criminal Law of Virginia, 1705–1860* (Baton Rouge, 1988) examines the evolving slave codes of a state in the upper South, his analysis has important implications for the study of law in any slave society.

Many of the men involved in the tribunals that took Vesey's life have been the subject of biographies. For the Secretary of War, Charles Wiltse's magisterial *John C. Calhoun,* 3 vols. (New York, 1944–1951) is overly sympathetic and should be supplemented with Irving H. Bartlett's balanced *John C. Calhoun* (New York, 1993). Donald Morgan, *Justice William Johnson: The First Dissenter* (Columbia, 1954), is a solid account of the tribunal's most vocal critic. Both Theodore D. Jervey, *Robert Y. Hayne and His Times* (New York, 1909), and J. Fred Rippy, *Joel R. Poinsett, Versatile American* (Durham, 1935), show their age. Astonishingly, the contentious political career of James Hamilton, who drowned in 1857 trying to save a mother and child, has never been chronicled; William Freehling correctly calls this omission "a scandal of South Carolina historiography." Perhaps it is less surprising that the short, unhappy political life of Thomas Bennett has attracted no biographers.

The execution of thirty-five slaves and freemen inspired an unusually-large outpouring of pamphlets and essays, all of which are currently available on microfiche or microfilm. In addition to the official accounts published by Hamilton, and Kennedy and Parker (cited above), Thomas Pinckney, *Reflections Occasioned by the Late Disturbances in Charleston* (Charleston, 1822), and Henry William Desaussure, *A Series of Numbers Addressed to the Public, on the Subject of the Slaves and Free People of Colour* (Charleston, 1822), are the most defiantly proslavery. Henry Bibb, *The Late Contemplated Insurrection in Charleston, S.C.* (New York, 1850), provided the earliest rebuttal by a black abolitionist. Supreme Court Justice William Johnson defended his unpopular censure of Kennedy's and Parker's tribunal in *To the Public of Charleston* (Charleston, 1822), while Richard Furman, *Exposition of the Views of the Baptists, Relative to the Coloured Population of the United States* (Charleston, 1823), and Frederick Dalcho, *Practical Considerations Founded on the Scriptures Relative to the Slave Population of South Carolina* (Charleston, 1823), addressed the religious dimensions of the plot. Many of these writings are discussed at length in Larry E. Tise, *Proslavery: A History of the Defense of Slavery in America, 1701–1840* (Athens, 1987) and Mitchell Snay, *Gospel of Disunion: Religion and Separatism in the Antebellum South* (New York, 1993).

Following his execution, Denmark Vesey lived on in antislavery lectures and novels. Regrettably, even those with a taste for overly-long nineteenth-century fiction may find Harriet Beecher Stowe, *Dred: A Tale of the Great Dismal Swamp* (1856), ponderous reading. Vesey is not as important a character in Martin R, Delany, *Blake: Or, The Huts of America* (1862), but Virginia-born Delany had a better sense of Southern language and culture. (Although Stowe's Dred is portrayed as being the son of Vesey, he frequently sounds more like a New England minister than a Carolina runaway.) The speeches and documents collected by C. Peter Ripley, ed., *The Black Abolitionist Papers,* 5 vols. (Chapel Hill, 1992), contain numerous references to the martyred activist—a warning to those who persist in excluding Southern rebels from the pantheon of abolitionist leaders. John O. Killens' modern novella, *Great Gittin' Up Morning* (Boston, 1972), disappoints as both literature and history. One hopes that Walter Robinson's "folk opera," *Look What Jesus Has Done,* and Vincent Plush's oratorio, *Denmark Vesey Takes The Stand,* will one day be commercially available.

Index